SPEAKING FOR THE CHIEF

African Systems of Thought

General Editors
Charles S. Bird
Ivan Karp

Contributing Editors
James W. Fernandez
Luc de Heusch
John Middleton
Roy Willis

SPEAKING FOR THE CHIEF

Ọkyeame and the Politics of
Akan Royal Oratory

KWESI YANKAH

INDIANA UNIVERSITY PRESS
Bloomington & Indianapolis

Library of Congress Cataloging-in-Publication Data

Yankah, Kwesi.
    Speaking for the chief : ȯkyeame and the politics of Akan royal
oratory / Kwesi Yankah.
        p.   cm.—(African systems of thought)
    Includes bibliographical references and index.
    ISBN 0-253-36801-4 (alk. paper).—ISBN 0-253-20946-3 (pbk. : alk. paper)
    1. Akan (African people)—Politics and government.   2. Speeches,
addresses, etc., Akan.   3. Akan (African people)—Rites and
ceremonies.   4. Negotiation—Social aspects—Ghana.   5. Oral
tradition—Ghana.   6. Ghana—Social life and customs.   I. Title.
II. Series.
DT510.43.A53Y35   1995
808.5'1'089963385—dc20   94-27094

1   2   3   4   5   00   99   98   97   96   95

Contents

Acknowledgments

This book has benefited tremendously from a good number of individuals, to whom I would like to extend my gratitude. I highly appreciate the critical comments of Kofi Anyidoho, Richard Bauman, Alessandro Duranti, John McDowell, Elliott Oring, and Beverly Stoeltje during the preparation of this manuscript in the United States.

It is to my informants and indigenous instructors, however, that I owe a still greater debt of gratitude. Koo Nimo, the world-renowned Ghanaian folk musician, was the first to ignite my interest in a project of this dimension, which would bring to the fore the wealth of knowledge possessed by the akyeame, or royal orators of Ghana. He made particular reference to the most experienced among the akyeame of Ashanti, Ȯkyeame Baafuor Akoto. True to Koo Nimo's observation, Baafuor Akoto proved to be not only a very eloquent orator but also a human library on Akan oral traditions, and to him I express my deep appreciation. To the Asantehene, Nana Otumfuor Opoku Ware II, I owe a debt of gratitude for granting me permission to observe and document the legal proceedings of the Kumasi Traditional Council. Several other chiefs and orators of Agona, Kwahu, Bono, and Ekumfi were very helpful in this project; these include two female chiefs, Nana Baah Okoampa III of Ekumfi Atwia and Nana Agyemfra Nyama I of the Agona Nsaba traditional area. Ȯkyeame Kofi Amoakwa of Nsaba and all his professional colleagues educated me a great deal on the art of the royal orators.

One of the greatest assets in this project has been Bosie Amponsah, a former student of mine, working for the Ghana Broadcasting Corporation. His insights on Akan oral traditions, along with those of James Agyeman Fokuo, formerly of Cape Coast University, assisted me greatly. Other research assistants include David Adu Amankwah, Enoch Akyeampong, Kofi Agyekum, Joe Bernard Appiah, and Edward Intsiful.

Finally, I am thankful to the Humanities Center of Stanford University, which granted me a Ford Foundation Fellowship to do further library work in Stanford and write up the manuscript there. I also appreciate the cooperation of the African Studies Center of the University of California, Los Angeles, where the manuscript was revised.

This work, however, is entirely mine, and I am solely responsible for its shortcomings.

Prologue

Venue: Palace of the King of Ashanti
Occasion: A scene prior to a judicial hearing

Elders are seated, wearing traditional wrap-around cloths. Also seated are various divisional chiefs of Kumasi, the seat of the Ashanti state. The mood is solemn. The occasion is a judicial hearing by the traditional council, chaired by the king.

The royal courtyard is filled to capacity by members of the public, courtiers, elders, relatives of litigants, and so forth. It is a typical Thursday.

Soon the court crier, a hunchback, shouts a formula signaling the king's approach. All murmuring ceases. The king's long entourage starts emerging from the palace. The state hornblowers come first, followed by praise singers, porters of royal paraphernalia, stool carriers, subchiefs, courtiers, all richly clad. The king walks majestically among the throng, distinguished by a large umbrella. He is flanked by his *akyeame,* royal counsellors gifted in public speaking. Each *òkyeame* holds a staff of authority with a proverbial symbol atop. As the king walks to his seat, the congregation rises in deference, while the herald in a shrill voice proclaims his arrival and runs a commentary on his gait and comportment, in verse:

Slowly! gently!
Slowly! gently!
You are climbing!
Let the front proceed!
Let the front proceed!
Slowly! gently!
The sole of your sandals!
Softly!
You are taking your seat!
You are taking your seat!
You are sitting gently!
You have sat in style!
Your elegance today surpasses past times.

The king takes his seat. To his immediate right are seated his akyeame, all placed in order of rank, with the most senior *òkyeame* closest to the king.

Before the judicial hearing begins, visitors present themselves to the king.

One party arrives to greet the king and present drinks, as custom demands. As they approach the king's seat, the courtiers are all alert for any possible infringement of the norms of formal communication. The spokesperson for the party must be well versed in formal communication, for he bares his shoulders and slips his feet out of his sandals. He then makes a courteous bow. In accordance with the norms, he does not address the king directly. He turns to face one of the akyeame, and channels his message through him so it might reach the king; for nobody, except an ökyeame, has direct communicative access to the king in formal settings.

The king's ökyeame listens attentively to the message and relays it to his lord, who responds through the ökyeame, who then transmits the reply to the party.

As the ökyeame relays the message, he embellishes it with proverbs, idioms, and witticisms, transforming the chief's brief statement into a longer poetic discourse, to the admiration of the audience.

Royal oratory in several parts of Africa is in this way a composite of the chief's words and a spokesperson's verbal embroidery. The two go hand in hand. But the mode of oratory here is better understood in the context of allied customary practices that knit the two functionaries in a ritual bond and facilitate their mutual access to each other's world.

As one of the orators has put it, "It is the cockroach that best understands the language of the night beast."

SPEAKING FOR THE CHIEF

1 / INTRODUCTION

IN MOST PARTS of Ghana the word *ȯkyeame,* or its cognates, connotes rhetorical competence *par excellence,* the reason being that it designates the most crucial diplomatic and communicative position within traditional Ghanaian political hierarchies.[1] The ȯkyeame (pl. *akyeame*) is, among other things, the chief's diplomat and orator. In such areas as West Africa, where there is a great passion for persuasive public speech, any functionary whose discourse is regarded as the quintessence of rhetoric must be held in high esteem indeed. In the words of a nineteenth-century explorer,

> The art of oratory is in West Africa carried to a remarkable pitch of perfection. At the public palavers, each linguist stands up in turn and pours forth a flood of speech the readiness and exuberance of which strikes the stranger with amazement, and accompanies his words with gestures so various, graceful and appropriate it is a pleasure to look on, though the matter of oration cannot be understood. These oratorical displays appear to afford great pleasure to the audience, for every African native is a born orator and connoisseur of oratory, a fact that becomes manifest in the Courts of Justice in the protectorate, where witnesses address the juries in the most able and unembarrassed manner; I have seen little boys of eight and ten hold forth to the court with complete self-possession and with an ease of diction that would have struck envy unto the heart of an English member of parliament. (Freeman 1958:13, also quoted by Finnegan 1970:444)

Granted that this explorer's impressions may have been tinged with a measure of romance, the basic significance of oratory in traditional West Africa and many other non-literate communities is very well known but little explored (Finnegan 1970; Bloch 1975). In the words of Finnegan, "For all the passing references to the significance of oratory, there seems to be little detailed documentation on the actual practice of public speaking as a skill in its own right" (1970:445).

My own interest in oratory arose partly from its pervasiveness in my own environment as a native Akan speaker. From a scholarly perspective, however, my interest was kindled during the extensive research I did on the ethnography of proverb communication among the Akan during the greater part of the eighties (Yankah 1989a). In that project, which required the documentation of real-life discourse interactions in various settings, I found the institution of ȯkyeame of critical importance. Even so, I realized the topic could not at that point be given the attention it deserved, since it constituted a major subject of investigation in itself.

In 1987, after the proverb project, I retraced my steps to the earlier akyeame I

---

1. *Ȯkyeame* has been used as the name of a literary magazine in Ghana and is currently the name of a weekly newspaper published in London by Ghanaians.

had worked with and extended my scope of investigation to other Akan-speaking areas. My original ambition had been to study the geographical distribution of the institution throughout Ghana, possibly making a comparative study. However, this soon appeared too grandiose a scheme, and was not pursued. Instead, I thought it expedient to begin with the Akan, the culture I know best, and work my way later toward other cultures. The reasons went beyond mere practicality; the institution of ɔkyeame was started by the Akan and then borrowed by other ethnic groups in Ghana over the past two or three centuries (see chapter 3).

In past ethnographies and historical accounts, the term *ɔkyeame* has been mistranslated as "linguist," in apparent reference to an ɔkyeame's skills in public speaking. For lack of a precise English rendition I shall stick to the use of the indigenous term in this book, partly to distinguish the ɔkyeame from the academic philologist or linguist. Even so, the widespread application of the term "linguist" to ɔkyeame in books and throughout Ghana has worked somehow in favor of this project; for the present writer is both a scholar in verbal art and a linguist teaching in the linguistics department of the University of Ghana. To several Ghanaians who did not know what linguistics is about and got to know of a scholar in the linguistics department working on the Ghanaian "linguist," the issue appeared to resolve itself. In certain parts of Ghana, I was sometimes introduced to chiefs and elders as belonging to the department that studies the affairs of akyeame. Indeed, some elders have lamented the negligence of my department in ignoring, until now, a topic that is its *raison d'être*.

Leaving aside the obvious problem posed in the mistaken application of the label "linguist" to ɔkyeame, the issues raised by the informants above should not be dismissed lightly. They comment unwittingly on the linguist's initial preoccupation with the abstract concerns of ideal grammar, without reference to the social relevance of speech. If the ethnography of speaking, rather than comparative philology, had marked the genesis of linguistics as an academic discipline, the oratorical art of the ɔkyeame would, perhaps, have attracted the interest of the linguist much earlier. In studying the sociocultural norms of speaking in West Africa, the scholar would have inevitably stumbled upon triadic communication—the art of communicating with another through a third party—as a remarkable phenomenon in formal discourse.

The topic itself need not be the monopoly of sociolinguists, political anthropologists, and ethnographers of speaking. In embarking on this study I have benefited from work in academic frontiers other than the above. Recent studies in speech acts, the philosophy of language, discourse analysis, pragmatics, and verbal art performance have introduced perspectives that have shaped aspects of this work. *Nyansa wɔmmfa no faako* (wisdom is not acquired from one source), say the Akan. The greatest sources of my wisdom, however, have been my informants, akyeame and chiefs spread across the Akan-speaking areas of Ghana—Ashanti, Adansi, Bono, Kwahu, Agona, Fante.

But for these, who led me into their personal and official lives and whose discourses in real-life interactions I documented and studied, fieldwork-based studies in the ethnography of speaking and political anthropology would still be dominated by observations that dismiss creativity in the oratory of traditional societies. Discussing the pervasiveness of formalization in traditional society, Maurice Bloch, for example, states:

> The formalization of speech [therefore] dramatically restricts what can be said so that the speech acts are either all alike, or all of a kind, and thus, if this mode of communication is adopted, there is hardly any choice of what can be said. Although the restrictions are seen usually as restrictions of form rather than of content, they are a far more effective way of restricting content than would be possible if content were attacked directly. Formalization goes right through the linguistic range. It leads to a specially stylized form of communication: polite, respectful, holy, but from the point of view of the creativity potential of language, impoverished. (Bloch 1975:17)

More recently, Bloch's stated position on the fixity of traditional oratory has been dismissed by Robert Paine:

> The principal difficulty arises over the way Bloch associates formalization with an absence of negotiation between speaker and audience. Bloch sees coercion where we see persuasion; whereas he sees formalization as given, which constrains the speaker, we see it as an outcome of rhetorical artistry and political acumen by which an audience is constrained; that is to say, the politician strives to have his audience see the world through his interpretation of speeches. Formalization of language is an instrument to this end in the general sense of introducing restrictions of form, but there need not be implications of language impoverishment. (Paine 1981:3)

It takes only a cursory look at the art of the ɔkyeame to demonstrate creativity in formal oratory. Being counsellor and intermediary to the chief, he is responsible, among other things, for enhancing the rhetoric of the words the chief has spoken. In the absence of an ɔkyeame's editorial art, the royal speech act is considered functionally and artistically incomplete. The public art of the ɔkyeame thus turns on creativity. But his mode of accomplishing his duties also overlaps with the public enactment of power within the royal domain, for nobody speaks to the chief *in situ* except through the ɔkyeame.

Formal oratory within the royal domain is thus mediated in a way that enhances the aura surrounding royalty:

> At the political center of any complexly organized society, there is both a governing elite and a set of symbolic forms expressing the fact that it is in truth governing. No matter how democratically the members of the elite are chosen or how deeply divided among themselves they may be, they justify their existence and order their actions in terms of a collection of stories, ceremonies, insignia, formalities, and appurtenances that they have either inherited, or in more revolutionary situations, invented. It is these that mark the center and give what goes on there its aura of being not merely important but in some odd fashion connected with the way the world is built. (Geertz 1983:124)

Besides the symbolic clout it lends to the royal domain, the art of routing royal messages (and royal-bound ones) through a third party should not be seen in isolation. It is the political dimension of a pervasive system of rhetorical indirection that characterizes the aesthetics of communication in West Africa, expressing itself in circumlocution and in metaphorical and proverbial speech. Social and verbal mediation are two sides of the same process: in both cases, opportunities are created for artistic transformation. In the public art of ȯkyeame, the two converge.

Hence in constructing this study, I have found the general ethnography of Akan oratory indispensable to a thorough understanding of the politics and rhetoric of royal speech. Similarly, I have avoided separating the ȯkyeame's mode of speaking from the wider political system of which he is part. Thus both the ȯkyeame and his patron, the chief, as well as other political and communication functionaries, were subjects of field investigation.

The study unfolds in nine chapters. Chapter 2 explains the significance of triadic communication and highlights an allied phenomenon which appears to have more universal relevance: what I call *surrogate performance,* engagement in the art of public display or performance for or on behalf of another. The two allied modes of discourse converge in the public art of the ȯkyeame. I discuss the artistically and geographically diverse manifestations of triadic discourse in several parts of the world, particularly Africa, the Americas, and the Pacific, arguing the artistic and political value of this form of speech in social interaction.

Chapter 3 discusses the evolution of diplomacy in the history of West Africa. The aim is to put into historical perspective the sociocommunicative art of mediation and its multimedia realizations in oral and visual codes. The latter part of the chapter narrows the discussion down to the significance of visual icons (carved staffs) in Akan political diplomacy, as well as their strategic uses in oratory.

Chapter 4 begins the ethnography of oratory among the Akan. I discuss the sociopolitical significance of formal speaking and explain the various linguistic and stylistic devices that distinguish it from everyday speech. Highlighted is the element of politeness, which is expounded in various stylistic and rhetorical modes. This chapter also puts the position of the akyeame in a wider ethnographic perspective, relating them to other communication functionaries in the Akan political and religious system. Chapter 5 is a close follow-up to the previous chapter. Noting the cultural significance of gender in political functions and artistic expression, I focus on women in Akan rhetoric and examine the emergence of female akyeame in parts of the Akan world.

Chapter 6 considers the ethnographic factors that undergird the ȯkyeame-chief interaction in discourse. Subtitled "the politics of immunity," the chapter examines the roles of the two functionaries, as well as the ritual and cultural bonds that knit them and permit their mutual rhetorical alliance. The linguistic and ritualistic manifestations of royal avoidance are discussed and linked to the practice of triadic communication in royal discourse. This chapter leads naturally to a discussion of the circuit of formal talk in chapter 7. I examine here the extent to which the existing power relations between the two functionaries are brought to play in formal discourse. I dwell on the structural constituents as well as the pragmatic circuit of the royal speech act, pointing out its explicit metalinguistic refraction in formal discourse. Triadic communication is not just practiced; it is linguistically mapped out and executed. I illustrate with field data.

In chapter 8, I take a closer look at the various strategies by which orators animate royal discourse. Juxtaposing source and interpretive deliveries, I discuss the analytic and poetic embellishment of royal speech as well as verbatim relay, bringing into focus also the dynamics of deictic (e.g., personal pronouns) and semantic shifts in direct and indirect modes of presentation.

In chapter 9, I portray the ɔkyeame in autonomous discourse, without metaphrastic reference to his patron. Here the ɔkyeame becomes directly responsible for the source discourse, itself animated by a subordinate. Since the political stakes are higher, such 'solo' orations are the greatest test of the rhetorical and cultural ingenuity of royal orators.

Interactions cited in this work are all taken from real-life situations enacted in the past six or seven years. Their spontaneity appears to have been little influenced by the ongoing research, since matters discussed were of grave social and political concern. In a few especially sensitive cases, I have found it expedient to leave out the geographical source of the interaction to protect participants' identities. In almost all others, I have substituted initials and dashes for specific names. Most of the interactions were recorded during formal meetings, ceremonial observances, and legal proceedings in Akan areas.

The designation "Akan" refers to a wide variety of ethnic groups occupying a large part of southern Ghana. The groups are culturally and linguistically homogenous, and may be subgrouped as Ashanti (Asante), Fante, Akwapem, Kwahu, Akim, Bono, Wassa, Agona, Adansi, Denkyira, and others. Even though each of these groups speaks a separate dialect and may have subtle divergences in cultural practice, the mutual intelligibility of their dialects and the uniformity of their cultural norms, including the use of akyeame, are beyond doubt.

From the sixteenth century onwards, the ethnic groups constituting the Akan were independent traditional states fighting each other for dominance. The most powerful, the Ashanti state, reached its peak of prominence during the reign of Osei Tutu, who died in the eighteenth century. An Ashanti confederacy established in 1701 was finally broken by the British in 1900; the British colonized Ashanti in 1901. The next biggest Akan group is the Fanti, whose state was annexed by the British in 1874 to the Gold Coast colony. Data used in this book are mainly from formal events among the Ashanti, Fanti, Bono, Agona, and Kwahu.

Texts used here have been arranged in poetic format to distinguish them from informal speech, and also to make provision for the responses—typical of some forms of formal talk—that appear at clause boundaries and between breath groups in the speeches.

2 / ÒKYEAME
A Theoretical Framework

Introduction

RECENT RESPONSES by linguists, anthropologists, and folklorists to Dell Hymes' call (1962, 1972) for the study of communication as a process governed by culture-specific rules have brought to light several inadequacies in the text-oriented view of language. Indeed, the more language is viewed as a text, the deeper the impression that it is a frozen, disembodied unit, organized outside a dynamic ecology. A significant dimension that ethnographers of communication have come to emphasize in the study of language (after Malinowski 1926, 1935) is the notion of context in all its ramifications (Bauman 1983).

In addition to recognizing the influence of socio-cultural context in the framing of communication (Bateson 1955, Goffman 1974, Bauman 1977) and the associated expansion of communication beyond referential uses of language, a close study of the scope of possible interactants in any given communication points up the primitivity of the Jakobsonian and Saussurian (1977:13) models of communication. Culture-specific studies of communication patterns have alerted us to the simplicity of the notions of sender/receiver and addresser/addressee as the primary actors in communication and to the existence of more complex communicative structures (Hymes 1972).

In the study of speech genres, the above dichotomies are seen to transmute in the case of interactions where the two roles, at various stages of performance, are conflated. Indeed, such situated transformations of basic roles urge a closer look at the theory of artistic performance, with a view to placing greater emphasis on the notion of *emergence,* i.e., the absence of permanence in role structures (Bauman 1977:37-48; Bakhtin 1986:67-73).

The sensitivity to social context which contemporary studies in ethnolinguistics enjoin brings the scholar face to face with the issue of the role played by intent and power in the conduct and shaping of communication (Bloch 1975). Closely associated with this are questions about specific cultures' attitudes toward the spoken word, as well as the ways in which political power combines with the potency of the spoken word in cultural mores governing communication (Brenneis and Myers 1984). To what extent do these factors key and shape communication? What are the cultural mechanisms whereby communication is socially managed in order to "step down" the power of the spoken word and its face-threatening potential? In short, of what significance is mediation in a theory of face-to-face communication?

Essential to distinguish in this respect are the *social* and the *semiotic* aspects of mediation. The former deals with the coordination of discourse interaction by discourse intermediaries or socially constituted role participants, while the latter influences communication through direct manipulation of code or channel, translating into verbal indirection.

The interplay between the social and semiotic systems is hinted at in Richard Bauman's theory of verbal art. He refers to what Hymes (1975) has called *metaphrasis* in performance—situations where a performance is reinterpreted by another: "a reframing of what is conventionally a performance genre into another mode" (Bauman 1977:34). He laments, "This is a poorly documented aspect of performance systems, but one richly deserving of study, as a key to the creative vitality and flexibility of performance in a community" (p. 35).

If this aspect of performance is poorly documented, the same cannot be said of its manifestations in everyday use of language, as seen in the scholarship on pragmatics, philosophy of language, and *metalinguistics*—the study of speech about speech. While the ethnography of speech about speech has not been rigorously pursued (see William Hanks 1989), scholars in the philosophy of language (e.g., M. M. Bakhtin 1981, Volosinov 1973, Ervin Goffman 1974) have pointed out the permeation of everyday speech with other people's talk:

> That one of the main subjects of human speech is discourse itself has not up to now been sufficiently taken into consideration, nor has its crucial importance been appreciated. There has been no comprehensive philosophical grasp of all the ramifications of this fact. The specific nature of discourse as a topic of speech, one that requires the transmission and reprocessing of another's word, has not been understood. (Bakhtin 1988:355)

Reported Speech

Reported speech is, perhaps, the commonest example of this (Volosinov 1973:115). Since human speech is generally filled with other people's words, which are transmitted with various degrees of accuracy, one could investigate the dynamic interrelationship of talk about talk, the extent to which social context and norms condition the dynamics of reported speech. Does the speech under consideration fall within the mode of what Bakhtin calls "authoritative discourse" (Bakhtin 1981:343)? Is the imputed principal an individual, or the collective wisdom of a people (Goffman 1974:522)? Does it enjoin unconditional allegiance, allowing of little or no semantic change? Or does the speech fall within the domain of internally persuasive discourse, with an open semantic structure and free stylistic variation?

From yet another perspective, one could consider the nature of framing rules at work on the basis of the motive behind the replay. Is it to faithfully protect the original speaker's image and words, or is it with the intent of parodic distortion, for the sake of mockery and slander? As we will see, in situations and cultural contexts where political power and authority are closely intertwined with speech, and where

norms governing the exercise of formal speech require gravity in artistic representation or faithful reporting, parodying and mockery have little place.

It is in this context that the ὸkyeame should be viewed. The ὸkyeame is many
things—royal confidant, diplomat, personal assistant—but above all he is the royal
spokesperson, and in performing the latter role, the ὸkyeame can be said to be a
master of reported speech. Indeed, the ὸkyeame's performance/speaking roles
belong entirely to the domain of metalinguistics. For in formal situations, a Ghanaian chief or king does not speak directly to an audience in his presence; he speaks
only through his ὸkyeame, who relays or repeats his words to the audience present,
whose words to the chief must also pass through the ὸkyeame.

Communication within the royal domain is thus a triadic phenomenon in the
areas with which we are concerned. In situations where there is more than one
speech intermediary, and where cultural norms demand that the message be channelled through all of them in turn, the phenomenon becomes even more
meandering. One such case is reported among the Mossi of Burkina Faso:

> The message to be communicated originates with the source. He whispers it up to his
> friend, who in turn whispers it to a lesser chief, who in turn whispers it to the big
> chief's main spokesman, who then finally brings the message in an audible voice to
> the chief's hearing. (Tarr 1979:204)

Such chains of mediated speech, as we shall see, can also be found among the
Akan, although they are not the most common case.

Surrogation

The àkyeame, then, are social mediators of speech, or rather specialists in the
artistic reporting or representation of speech. The speech they report is often ornamented with witticisms and poetic embellishments not part of the original message.
But the àkyeame are also agents of a sort, for they speak on another's *behalf.* Even
where they only relay words the chief has spoken, their part in a royal speech act is
more indispensable than the chief's. Without their voice, a royal communicative act
is incomplete (see chapter 7).

The element of acting on another's behalf is indeed an integral part of the
àkyeame's metacommunicative duties: the two go hand in hand. For lack of a more
precise label, I refer to the category to which their orations belong as *surrogate
performance* (in this case surrogate oratory), the exercise of performance through
an agent, instrument or intermediary. From a broader perspective, one could enlarge
the scope of surrogate performance or interaction to encompass the audience constituent, addressing as a corollary the exercise of *listening* through a proxy.

The concept of surrogation here is roughly parallel to such phenomena as "surrogate motherhood" (motherhood on behalf of another), voting by proxy (the exercise of voting rights on another's behalf), ventriloquy, puppetry, and other
phenomena that imply the delegation of performance responsibilities to an agent. In

this work, however, the term "surrogate" does not necessarily imply unquestioning pliability; the functionary here is imbued with intellection, and may exercise discretion. The orator's duties range from strict reporting to discretionary interpretation. At certain other levels, the relationship between the surrogate and his principal is more of mutual reliance than dependency.

The phenomenon of delegating speaking responsibilities is universal. In the Anglo-American world, for example, it ranges from client-attorney relationship in the courtroom to the appointment of press secretaries—presidential or executive spokespersons who pass on and interpret executive policies and statements to the public. To analyze the significance of surrogate discourse, however, one needs to distinguish various positional settings in which speech participants may be brought into play and the extent to which this may affect the structure and content of discourse. Does the surrogate performance involve the co-presence of agent and principal, or is the client not visible on the scene of interaction? If both are present, what is the mode of performance: single-voice delivery, multiple voices, or overlapping ones? If one voice reports the other, what is the nature of the mediation? Is it that of interpretation, translation, amplification, editing, or repetition?

In a communicative situation of such complexity, a model of communication merely depicting speaker and addressee (e.g., Roman Jakobson 1960) proves inadequate. The constituents of communication become much more complex, and finer distinctions have to be made between source of message and sender, and target of message and receiver. In recent times, ethnographers of speaking (Hymes 1975), language philosophers (Goffman 1974), and students of pragmatics (Levinson 1983, Hank 1989) have widened the constituents of communication to encompass this complexity. Such a pragmatic framework would note that "the speaker or spokesman can be distinct from the source of an utterance, the recipient distinct from target, and hearers or bystanders distinct from addressees or targets" (Levinson 1983:68). Goffman, on the basis of framings within theatrical productions, makes a comprehensive statement on this, distinguishing *principal* or *originator* of discourse (the one held responsible for the utterance), from the *animator*—the actual sound box, the emitter whose voice is heard.

An individual engaging in ordinary talk ordinarily combines the two roles; he originates as well as animates the discourse (Goffman 1974:516-523). But where the two roles are separated, the question of responsibility for the display becomes significant. Who takes responsibility for performance flaws, and who takes credit? Goffman explains the situation in theatrical performance:

> Appreciation is not simply for the performer, but somehow has a diffuse target involving, in addition to the performer, the character he stages, the producer, the director, the playwright, and the entire dramatic effect (there is reason after the curtain falls for the whole circus to come back on to take a bow collectively). (p. 540)

Issues that are raised by the use of surrogates in performance go beyond those concerning the constituents of communication. The phenomenon invites a look at culture-specific rationales for rituals of avoidance, deference, and mediation, and, more generally, at the nature of face-to-face interaction. Whereas all the above are relevant to human communities in general, there is a case for putting greater emphasis on their manifestations in predominantly nonliterate cultures, partly because it is within such cultures that speech intermediaries (of the sort explained in this work) have mostly been noted, and also due to the overwhelming reliance on face-to-face behavior and the spoken word in nonliterate societies.

The Spoken Word

In cultures where writing is only a recent development—often called pre-literate, residually oral, or cultures with pristine orality (Ong 1982:11, 1987:6-15)—the practice of using speech intermediaries attains an added significance. This is partly due to the sociopolitical significance of oratory in such cultures, but also because of the potency they often attach to the spoken word (Weiner 1984).

Being the embodiment of acoustic energy (Ong 1982, Anyidoho 1983) and ordinarily enjoining co-presence of all participants in the communicative enterprise, the spoken word has an immediate impact; a capacity to make or break, a potential for instantly enhancing the sociopolitical status of its practitioner, as well as the capacity to undermine his or her social and artistic standing (Yankah 1985a). According to the Yoruba, "Speech is an egg, when dropped it shatters" (Owomoyela 1981:11). It is the potency of the spoken word that compensates for its evanescence. The spoken word dissipates as soon as uttered; it lives only for as long as it is activated in sound. Yet being bound up with its ecology, or rather with the sum total of the social and cultural environment within which it is framed, it is a powerful instrument of communication. In certain societies, the spoken word in such religious contexts as divination may have a performative (Austin 1962) or magical potency—the power to alter reality—so long as certain "felicity conditions" are satisfied in its negotiation (e.g., the use of the right formulas, the membership of the practitioner in an esoteric group, and adherence to prescribed ritual-specific rules of communication). According to Judeo-Christian tradition, for example, the world was created by the spoken word.

Besides its performative power in such restorative contexts, the spoken word may be held as potentially destructive, for which reason cultures may take certain steps to contain it. In many societies there are beliefs that anticipated events may not be mentioned for fear that they may be jinxed. In others, one does not tell a bad dream or nightmare experienced the previous night to another immediately on waking up the next morning. For fear of the dream's fulfillment, a ritualistic act must be performed to preface the telling. Certain societies consider the appropriate place for the initial narration to be the dunghill, which steps down the dream's potential as a destabilizing force and renders it safe as a subject of communication (Anyidoho 1983).

A reflection of the power attributed to speech may be found in the general avoidance of taboo words and the compensatory strategy of deploying euphemisms (Peter Farb 1977:73-92). The Ibo custom of referring to a snake as a "thread" is one example. Others include the early European "brown one" or "honey-eater" for a bear, the ancient Hebrew "the Almighty" or the tetragrammaton JHWH for God, and even the modern Anglophone stage term "the Scottish play" for *Macbeth*. One could argue that reacting to words rather than to what they stand for is one mark of human irrationality, since the sign is arbitrary; yet it is a natural human tendency to disregard the arbitrariness of language in our attitudes (Hayakawa 1978:20-28). On one level this tendency is reinforced by culture-specific notions and beliefs about the power of the spoken word. On another level, it is reinforced by the realization that language should not just be studied as propositional—i.e., making a statement about something—, but also as constituting social *behavior.*

Face-to-Face Behavior

An important corollary of the power of speech, as against that of the written word, is the basic risk involved in all face-to-face communication. The spatial and temporal link between the speaker and his audience puts discourse participants at considerable risk since, by contrast with writing where evaluation is delayed, there is here an instant evaluation of each other's communicative competence (Yankah 1985a), as well as a test of the ability of discourse participants to deal spontaneously with emergent or unforeseen structures.

Thus the stakes in oral communication are high; and they become higher in public speaking, where discourse participants have a wider audience to contend with. The situation here compels culture-specific strategies for overcoming or minimizing the inherent menace in face-to-face interactions, whether the interaction be storytelling, praise singing, conversation, or speechmaking. The elaborate thesis on language and politeness offered by Brown and Levinson provides a useful framework for understanding the nature of "face":

> Face is emotionally invested, and can be lost, maintained or enhanced, and must be constantly attended to in interaction. In general, people cooperate in maintaining face in interaction, such cooperation being based on the mutual vulnerability of face. (1978:66)

To ward off face-threatening acts, therefore, redressive strategies have to be adopted by both speaker and addressee. *Facework* is the relevant term used by Erving Goffman. It designates "actions taken by a person to make whatever he is doing consistent with face. Facework serves to counteract incidents—that is, events whose symbolic implications threaten face" (Goffman 1967:12).

Besides the use of verbal interactional strategies such as indirection, politeness and deferential formulae, reference honorifics, and so forth (Brown and Levinson 1978) to soften face-threatening acts, societies consciously or unconsciously appear to deploy preinteractional strategies to minimize the hazards of face-to-face behavior. These may include long periods of training and apprenticeship prior to an event, use of immunity formulas to forestall the hazards of performance (Ferry 1976), ingestion of herbs (Babalola 1966:44), and ritual prayer.

In certain genres and cultures, the strategies adopted to mitigate the hazards of face-to-face behavior may include engaging a surrogate, animate or non-animate, to execute the interaction—a category we briefly touched on earlier. By inanimate agencies, I refer to puppetry—the manipulation of inanimate figures by human hands—a remarkably wide field in the semiotic study of surrogation. In the words of Frank Proschan,

> Puppets are not the only objects we invest with the powers to speak or to move. Dancers who wear masks, bards who use scroll paintings or dolls to illustrate their narratives, children who create dramatic scenes in dollplay, worshippers who bear icons in a religious procession, and storytellers who trace images in snow or sand all manifest the urge to give life to nonliving things, as they animate objects in dramatic performances and use material images as surrogates for human actors. (1983:3)

Likewise, in real-life situations outside the sphere of dramatic performances, many cultures provide for the artful negotiation of meaning by verbal or non-verbal means. Among Trobrianders, as Weiner reports, though anger may not be directly expressed, it may find expression in the exchange of yams (1984). This way, one's thoughts are stated without the danger of exposure or confrontation. In the verbal realm, often the surrogate or mediating entity utilized in place of a principal is human and capable of intelligent thought. Indeed, such a person is often a highly sophisticated specialist in face-to-face behavior. In the realm of formal oratory, the surrogate is the master of the spoken word.

In this case, the inherent risks in public display are transferred to the professional surrogate, who is considered better equipped to minimize, overcome, or control the hazards of face-to-face behavior. It is assumed that the proxy has the fullest knowledge of the communicative resources the community offers for effective persuasion and negotiation. The human surrogate, in other words, has control over *strategic interaction* (Goffman 1969) at key moments in community life.

There are other reasons for the use of surrogates. Communicative and physical distancing between prospective interactants may be consciously maintained in recognition of an entity's higher social status (Marcus 1984, Duranti 1988), sacredness, or membership in a metaphysical realm. Under such circumstances elaborate taboos against personal contact by the uninitiated may prevail, and the need for specialized performance intermediaries may arise to preserve the "ideal sphere" that lies around a revered participant. The deployment of such strategies of deference may be subsumed under the general rubric of *avoidance ritual*—"those forms of deference which lead the actor to keep a distance from the recipient" (Goffman 1967:62). This is in addition to the deployment of an appropriate *power semantic,* i.e., a particular word choice or turn of grammar used to mark the interactants' uneven status (Brown and Gilman 1972; Scollon and Scollon 1981).

At the farthest extreme, it is within such a scheme that one can locate the discourse of fetish priests, diviners, prophets, and related religious mediums. These are ritual personages or intermediaries sitting at the confluence of the human and metaphysical worlds and mediating speech and social interaction between these two asymetrical realms. The two spheres, natural and supernatural, may each have different sets of communicative norms of their own; yet they need to interact to maintain and promote social stability. Communication between the two worlds therefore has to be mediated by specialists who are on familiar terms with both worlds. In the absence of such intermediaries, a mutual violation of the two spheres may result, making a social crisis inevitable.

The phenomenon of oration through intermediaries has been widely reported in several parts of Africa and its cultural extensions in the new world, in Oceania, and in other isolated places, even though few in-depth, culture-specific studies have been done. Wherever it exists, mediated oratory appears to be closely associated with monarchies, formal speech, and ritual ceremony.

Reflexes and Scope

The term 'surrogate oratory' is only a convenient analytical label, inadequate to fully encapsulate the cultural nuances of the phenomenon to which the local term òkyeame does greater justice. The various ways in which the phenomenon may find expression are described below. These are not hypothetical; they are reflexes of an òkyeame's real public duties, which have also been documented in a number of other cultures.

(1) Principal speaks, mediator transmits the message in embellished form, either through artistic elaboration or paraphrasing.

(2) Principal speaks, mediator literally repeats words spoken or a part thereof.

(3) Principal speaks, mediator ratifies by affirmative formulae, confirming the truth in the principal's word.

(4) Principal is present but does not speak; his message is spoken by an orator.

(5) Principal is absent from the scene of discourse; his orator speaks on his behalf.

All five modes of transmission have one thing in common; they all involve the use of an agent (instead of the principal) as the main focus of communication. Whether the principal is visible or unseen, the speaking agent is the main focus of the interaction. Yet his role in the discourse is purely metalinguistic—his discourse feeds on or is directed at a principal's discourse. Depending on the mode of speaking he adopts in specific situations, he may or may not use reporting verbs. But whether he reports his principal's word or not, the speech act is incomplete without him.

In Africa, the òkyeame's style of transmitting his principal's word varies from analytic transmission (comment, modification, elaboration, paraphrase as in mode 1), to linear repetition (mode 2), to token affirmation (mode 3). In modes 4 and 5, where the principal does not speak, the "intermediary" transmitting his master's

word may even indulge in *quasi-direct discourse,* omitting reporting verbs and dis-
solving into the character of his principal (Volosinov 1973:150). Here the element
of reporting may not necessarily be overt.

It is, perhaps, the fourth and fifth modes of surrogate oration that are better
known the world over—an attorney speaking on a client's behalf, in the latter's
presence; or a spokesperson speaking on behalf of a functionary or government
leader in the latter's absence. It is indeed in these modes that the element of surrogation is most visible. The orator here does not compete for attention on the stage,
holding a virtual speaking monopoly.

In the first three modes of co-speaking, which are less common, the element of
surrogation is not clearly defined, since the performance role is shared and prominence in speaking roles may shift. In fact, in the third mode, the gravitational center
of the display is reversed, since the "orator" becomes a mere respondent or
answerer who passes on the message with a ratifying formula without actually
repeating it. The common denominator here, however, is the dialogic nature of the
message delivered—the fact that the performance is carried out by a speaking duet,
with one party calling and the other responding.

The phenomenon of "answering" in certain speech genres in Africa and black
America may be argued to constitute a refraction of the mediated oratory explained
here. Quite beside the fact that an ôkyeame's public performance may be nothing
more than answering his principal's word, supporting the truth in it (mode 3), all
five performance modes explained above imply a search for consensus or affirmation. For the practice of employing a surrogate, or respondent, is in part a strategy
for emphasizing the objectivity of the speaker's word. Using an ôkyeame to repeat,
confirm, or elaborate a principal's word implies that the principal's viewpoint is not
subjective, but arises from shared experience. In the words of Roger Abraham,
"Each experience is interesting only insofar as it is able to enlist participation; that
is, if the planning produces some sense of discovery, some appearance of sponta-
neous exchange of energies with others" (1986:89).

With its several extremely useful functions in mind, we need hardly be surprised
to find this form of oratory in many parts of the world. Besides Africa and Oceania,
surrogate oratory and its reflexes have been found in parts of Asia and in North and
South America.

Dell Hymes, for example, reports that among the Wishram Chinook natives of
the state of Washington in the northwestern United States, "recitations of myths are
formal communicative events; and the speaker, who is a spokesman, repeats the
source words" (Hymes 1972:61). Among the Cuna Indians of South America,
whose ways of speaking have been extensively studied by Joel Sherzer, one type of
formal speech event—the *sakla namakke,* or congress—is distinguished by the role
of the *arkar,* the chief's spokesman who "interprets," edits, or paraphrases the
chief's words. The interpretation may be of the chief's chant, which is often dense
with metaphor, or it may be in clarification of his general advice, "which is interpreted and elaborated on by the *arkars.* Interpretation often involves the creative
and flexible adaptation of metaphors" (Sherzer 1974:266).

Ritual language among the Rotinese of Eastern Indonesia is a formal speech code based on 'binate semantics.' It requires that phrases and verses be coupled or reproduced by another (Fox 1974). This pattern of what has been called "ceremonial dialogue" is also common among the indigenous peoples of South America. Greg Urban refers to it as "pragmatic turn taking" and explains that among the Shokleng, "one speaker utters a stretch of speech—a syllable, word, line, or sentence—and this constitutes his pragmatic turn at speaking. The respondent replies with another stretch of speech—a syllable, word, line or sentence—and this constitutes his turn" (1986:373). It is, however, unclear whether this mode of oratory in South America belongs generally to the royal domain. Nor is it clear whether, in all cases, the respondents are specially appointed, as they are in Africa.

It is in Oceania that the institution of royal orator, or "talking chief," has been most widely studied. Instances have been reported in the Maori, Samoan, Fijian, Tikopian, Tongan, and Balinese communities, all in the Pacific (cf. Bloch 1975, Brenneis and Myers 1984).

In her study of oratory among the Ilongot of Northern Philippines, Rosaldo makes reference to speech situations where someone may agree to "lend his tongue" to another to speak on his behalf (1973). And in a good part of Polynesia or Oceania, high-ranked individuals avoid risking their integrity in face-to-face behavior by hiring orators to speak on their behalf. Among the Samoans, it is done so that "the source of authority and wisdom represented by the chief is protected by having the lower ranking orator expose himself to potential retaliation and loss of face" (Duranti 1988:22). Among Tongan nobles, Marcus states that ad hoc speaking is avoided. Rather, oratory is the task of ceremonial attendants, *matapule*, who are employed to sit at their sides. "Any failure of avoidance or mediation to protect a noble from unexpected public interactions leads to visible mutual discomfort and embarrassment among those interacting" (Marcus 1984:253). In Tikopia, as Raymond Firth states, "Chiefs do not orate or address public assemblies; they give instruction to their *maru* to speak for them. They 'hand over the speech' to their orator, and commonly are not present at a *fono* where their orders are promulgated" (Firth 1975:35). Among the Balinese, orators are designated as *juru raos*, and they comprise an informal elite (Hobart 1975:77). Similarly, various factions among the Maori of New Zealand and the Lau of Fiji may also be represented by orators (Salmond 1975).

Surrogate Speech in Africa

In Africa, very little by way of formal studies has been done on the institution of surrogate oratory and its reflexes. In some parts of Africa, hints of the existence of the phenomenon can only be gleaned from historical accounts by scholars and missionaries prior to the 20th century. In Ghana, for instance, passing references to *ȯkyeame* (often mistranslated as "linguist," as mentioned earlier) among the Akan, can be gleaned from historical and a few ethnographic accounts (cf. Rattray 1923:276, Ward 1958:52, Caseley Hayford 1903:68). Caseley Hayford at the beginning of this century gives a vivid picture of the Akan royal orator:

When the linguist rises to speak in public, he leans upon the king's gold cane, or a subordinate holds it in front of him. He is going to make a speech now, and it is sure to be a happy effort. It will sparkle with wit and humor. He will make free use of parables to illustrate points in speech. He will indulge in epigrams, and all the while he will seem not to possess any nerves—so cool, so collected, so self-complacent! He comes of a stock used to public speaking and public function. (1903:68; cited by Finnegan 1970:447)

The concept of *òkyeame* in Ghana does not exist among the Akan only. Even though it probably started with the Akan, it also exists among the Ga, Adanme, and Ewe, and evidence suggests that it has parallels among some ethnic groups in the northern and upper regions of Ghana, as well as in certain other parts of West Africa.

W. H. Whiteley in his work on African prose refers to the Ga and Ashanti (Akan) royal orators, and cautions that their oratory merits study before the art is lost, "or at least undermined by the written word" (1964:166). Significantly, the Ga and Ewe designations for spokesperson, *tsiame,* are borrowings from Akan, whence they borrowed the whole institution of chieftaincy. Michael Verdon refers to the Ewe *tsiame* who interprets between villagers and the chief when the latter is addressed in his capacity as the *dufia.* "A village chief cannot be greeted or addressed directly, nor does he converse directly with interlocutors. Linguist repeats requests and replies between chief and audience" (1983:94).

In certain parts of Northern and Upper Ghana, particularly among the Mamprusi, Dagomba, and Gonja, there are clues to the existence of royal orators—a position possibly borrowed from the Ashanti, who extended their suzerainty to the north from the seventeenth century onwards (Wilks 1975:243–309). It is significant, though, that designations given to the institution up north are not cognates of the Akan or Ashanti term, even though other military and royal terms in their lexicon are clearly borrowed from Ashanti. The royal orator among the Dagomba is called *mbadugu,* Ya-Na's "official linguist conducting all the audiences of *Ya-Na,*" according to Staniland (1975:28). On the other hand, Rattray also refers to a related functionary among the Dagomba known as *Dambale* or *Na-nol-lana,* literally meaning "Owner of the chief's mouth," who at assemblies of chiefs passes on the chief's salutation (Rattray 1932:573). Among the Mamprusi, they have the *Talana,* who is the most important official of the *Na's* court. He acts as the spokesperson before the *Na* (Rattray 1932:555).

Outside Ghana, parallels of the *òkyeame* may be found in certain groups along the west coast of Africa, for example in Benin and parts of Nigeria. Among the Ijo of Nigeria, the *ogulasowei* is the spokesman (Alagoa 1976). Of the Alafin of Oyo, Talbot remarks that, "He made a speech in a low tone which was repeated aloud by the head eunuch" (1926:569). Of the people of Edo a historian remarked, "Whatever any person would say to the king, must first be told to the three great lords who would then report it to him and bring his answer" (Talbot 1926:580). Royal communication among the Fon of Dahomey (present-day Benin) appears similar. Two types of spokesmen are reported: the *meu,* who speaks from the king to the people, and the *migan,* who speaks from the people to the king. Richard Burton noted in the nineteenth century that "it is not customary to address the royalty, even though the presentee be acquainted with the language" (1966:150). And as we have already seen, surrogate oratory is also found in a highly developed form among the Mossi of Burkina Faso.

Ruth Finnegan, who refers to the Akan "linguist" (referring to the òkyeame) in her major book exploring different varieties of oral literature (1970:444–80), significantly alludes to forms of oratory among the Limba of Sierra Leone that parallel the pattern discussed in this book:

> The most elaborate and lengthy of all speeches are the long funeral harangues given on the occasion of memorial rites for some important man several years after his death. . . . One of the highlights is the speeches made by the leading men; they speak in turn, often going on for several hours, and their words are relayed, half intoned sentence by sentence, by a herald who is specially engaged for the occasion. (Finnegan 1970:454)

It is not clear from Finnegan's survey, however, the extent to which this form of oratory is institutionalized among the Limba and in other parts of Africa. Ethel Albert's excellent study of speech behavior and oratory in Burundi cites no instances of speech intermediaries (Albert 1964). In Madagascar, though, ceremonial speech such as in wedding or marriage solicitation calls for the use of *mpikabary* ("speech makers") who speak on behalf of the two parties, winding their words with analogies, proverbs, and extended metaphors (Keenan 1974).

It is significant that royal speech intermediaries in Africa often utilize both verbal and visual arts in the negotiation of public oratory. The royal orators speak wittily, but also enhance their rhetoric by holding a staff of office that depicts a proverbial statement. Indeed, the use of the staff is a mode of mediation in itself, as we shall see in more detail later.

While the institution of speech intermediary in Africa may have originated within the royal domain, it has spread to all communicative settings where social status and verbal wit can be asserted for social or political advantage. Any formal, traditional proceedings in Ghana involving communication between two or more parties require the use of akyeame. The institution has been adopted within *abusua,* lineage groups, who all have *abusua akyeame* (lineage spokespersons). Similarly, deities and fetish priests have *abosom kyeame,* who interpret the words of the priests to their clients. The institution was adapted from traditional to modern politics in 1962 by Kwame Nkrumah, who appointed an òkyeame for the state and modified his original functions (Yankah 1985b). Here, instead of the òkyeame speaking after the principal, he spoke before him. Indeed, the indispensability of a speech intermediary in several parts of Africa and the overwhelmingly triadic nature of formal discourse therein has compelled one scholar, Michael Appiah, to propose the *òkyeame* concept as a model for communication within the "Afrocentric" world (Appiah 1979). Understanding the reasons for the popularity of triadic communication in the royal domain will help us better understand the different forms this phenomenon assumes in practice.

Royal Distance

The practice of using speech intermediaries in royal discourse may be rationalized by the opportunities this creates for the flowering of language in the relay process. Yet it is a fact that the very sacredness of kingship the world over encourages royal seclusion from the world's dangers, including its judgments. At a minimum, certain chiefs in Africa, such as those in the traditional Dahomey and Akan states, are considered in close relation to spirits of the ancestors, even though they are not vehicles of spirits themselves. At a further extreme are the Yoruba kings, for example, whose bodies on installation are imbued with powers of the dynastic ancestors or gods. Ibo kings are also said to be semidivine (Talbot 1926:592). Among the Edo, the King "was practically deified during his lifetime" (Talbot:576).

Because the king is sacred, care is taken to preserve his person and maintain his sanctity. In the Dahomey kingdom, for instance, there is a special assistant who precedes the royal footsteps, to remove any sticks or stones likely to offend (Argyle 1966:66). These conditions naturally rule out direct communication with the king. But the manner of the king's public outfit and demeanor often makes this even more impracticable. Late in the nineteenth century, for instance, a historian described the sultan of Salaga, in northern Ghana, as wearing "a beautiful Hausa robe, and the beautiful red woolen king's mantle on top. He had pulled the hood over his head, a tassel hanging from its point over his black face" (cf. Johnson n.d.:7).

It is reported that among the Ijebu of southern Nigeria in the last century, the king was never seen, and any communication was made to him through a screen until recently (Talbot 1926:574). Even now his face is mostly concealed by masses of beads hanging from his crown. Indeed, among the Yoruba in general, rulers of the ancient provinces claim descent from the god-man Oduduwa, father of the Yoruba, and are honored as seconds of the gods. They therefore wear sacred crowns that suggest divine linkage. The most honored crown (*ade*) is beaded with a frontal veil, such that the wearer's face is unseen. While the king wears this on ceremonial occasions he incarnates divine powers, and it is considered dangerous to stare at his naked face. In the words of art historian Robert Thompson:

> The vaguely perceived outlines of the face of the ruler match, in a sense, the generalized qualities of the frontal faces on the crown. Veiling diminishes the wearer's individuality, so that he, too, becomes a generalized entity. Balance between the present and the past emerges. No longer an individual, the king becomes the dynasty. . . . The use of the veil extends a tradition in force since the sixteenth century, when Joaõ Barros reported that ambassadors were only allowed to view curtains of silk, behind which sat the king of Ile-Ife, for the king is regarded as sacred (1972:232).

Not only must others not look on the king's face while he is so adorned, but also the gaze of the king himself must not fall upon the inside of his fringed crown, for there are supposed to be magical forces within the crown that have the potency to blind the careless wearer (Thompson 1972:232). According to the cultural rules, then, even communication by eye contact is restricted by a sacred presence.

Another remarkable example of distancing within the royal domain was that prevailing in the environment of the King of Benin (in present-day Nigeria). In the middle of the sixteenth century, his noblemen were not expected to have eye contact with him:

> When his noblemen are in his presence, they never look him in the face, but sit cowering upon their buttocks with their elbows upon their knees, and their hands before their faces not looking up until the king commands them. When they depart from him, they turn not their backs towards him, but go creeping backwards with reverence. (see Talbot 1926:580)

The adoption of various distancing strategies in royal presence is partly meant to preserve the sanctity of royal space. It insures the royalty against the perils of face-to-face interaction where his person could be defiled and where speech directed at him may be spiritually potent.

The royal surrogate then becomes not only a mouthpiece, but also the buffer on which all dangerous words are deflected. Through him, the potency of the incoming spoken word is stepped down and rendered safe for royal consumption.

But from yet another perspective, the issue of speech mediation may be seen to benefit both parties of royal discourse. The concept of kingship in Africa carries with it associated beliefs in a king's spiritual potency, which could be used for destructive ends and which has to be contained in the interest of order. Among certain groups, including the Akan, a chief's slap or curse is believed capable of causing madness. In moments of royal wrath, an agent is needed to contain the destabilizing forces capable of being activated. Thus boisterous or undignified remarks indiscreetly made by the chief are instantly softened and passed on without retroactive damage; for, since the royal speech act is not complete until relayed by the chief's ọkyeame, it does not take effect until that point either.

Indeed, formal discourse within the royal domain scarcely qualifies as communication without an intermediary who smooths out the rough edges of talk. These roughnesses need not involve malicious words; they may be stylistic, structural, lexical, or thematic; for the ọkyeame is in many cases both a master of occult science and lord of diplomacy. In the ọkyeame's care, royal words, whether whispered or spoken, may be paraphrased, elaborated, punctuated with history, ornamented with metaphor, enlivened with proverbs and allegories, or even dramatized outright. Through the art of the surrogate orator, royal words are refined, poeticized, and made palatable for public consumption.

"Answering" in Performance

The pattern of formal speech interaction involving surrogation and verbal mediation partly underscores the search for consensus in the art of persuasion—the aim of the interactant to engage the support of his audience. As was mentioned earlier, deploying a surrogate or auxiliary to repeat or confirm words or arguments lends a measure of objectivity to the opinion expressed, implying that the speaker's viewpoint is not a subjective one, but one based on shared experience.

A significant example of this mediative consensus-building may be found in the phenomenon of "answering" in performance—a refraction of the wider rhetorical strategy explained above. In parts of Africa and the African diaspora it constitutes an integral part of performance in oratory and other verbal genres, including storytelling, libation prayer, epic performance, folk preaching, and black American blues singing.

Indeed, one tradition of storytelling in Africa has the institution of intermediary as a required component in the structure of performance. Prior to a performance, an intermediary is chosen by the narrator. The performer then directs the narration first to the intermediary, who "passes it on" to the wider audience. This pattern of performance has been reported mainly in West Africa, where the institution of royal spokesperson is also widespread. In fact, in some parts, this functionary is called an "ôkyeame" or its equivalent local term. This reflects the fact that the storytelling answerer is the medium through whom the principal performer narrates. Like the surrogate orator, the answerer receives the narration in bits as it is told, and either literally repeats it or adjoins a phrase of assent.

Institutionalized mediation in narrative performance is found among the Agni-Bona of Ivory Coast, the Mossi of Burkina Faso (Giray-Saul, personal communication), the Limba of Sierra Leone, and the Nzema and Dagaare, both of Ghana. It is Finnegan who refers to the intermediary in Limba storytelling as the "answerer" (Finnegan 1967). Agovi describes the same functionary among the Nzema of Ghana as "story linguist" (1973) in reference to the similarity of this role to that of the "linguist" or spokesperson, while Galli refers to this functionary among the Agni as the "epicenter" (1983). Significantly, Galli traces its source to the institution of royal spokesperson, *kiame* (cognate of the Akan word) among the Agni, who are Akan.

Galli's description of the phenomenon as it exists in folktale performance among the Agni-Bona of Ivory Coast deserves an extended quotation:

> A public word needs someone to receive and transmit it. That is the reason why the epicenter always follows the storyteller like a shadow. The spoken word manifests itself in a ternary circuit: emitted by the narrator, received by the epicenter, retransmitted to the audience.
>
> The emitted word is composed of two elements; it has a binary structure. The first element is the word emitted by the storyteller. This word has full semantic content: here is concentrated the essential part of the message.
>
> The second element of the segment is the epicenter's answer, semantically poorer than the first part. It is usually composed of the mono-syllables "hem," "eh," "ah," the adverbs "really," "sure," the pronoun "nobody," and sometimes by short sentences: "it is exactly as you say," "all, really all," "I too was there," "we have to go," and so on. The comment in the epicenter's answer, sometimes a comment on the tale, is ordinarily a sign that the word is received, but this answer is as important as

the narrator's word. If it is true that the most important part of the message is condensed in the first part of the binary unit, it is also true that the second part, semantically weak, forms, with the first one, a complete unit: one cannot exist without the other. (Galli 1983:33)

Epic performances in parts of Africa also involve supportive responses from an auxiliary, who interpolates the griot's words with affirmative interjections. Among the Mandinka of Mali, the relevant functionary is called *Namu Namu,* the very words of affirmation he typically utters (Johnson 1986:25). In Ghana, a close parallel of this are the supportive remarks (*wiè, ampa*—"truly,") made by an appointed auxiliary during a libation prayer (see chapter 9). Among the Akan and Ewe the responses are made by a single appointed assistant, while supportive responses in a Ga libation are given by a chorus of voices timed to coincide with the end of clause groups.

Pentecostal sermons and certain traditions of storytelling among black Americans constitute one widely studied example of antiphonal responses in performance, evidently carried over from the practice of "answering" in African narrative art. In fact, in a recent study of oral literary practice among the Gullah of the sea islands in South Carolina and among the Geechee in Georgia—free descendants of slaves from Barbados and West Africa—Jones-Jackson notes a widespread practice of not addressing a narration directly at an audience, but rather through an intermediary.

[A narrator] may single out a person whom he knows, or one he may not know well, and seem to speak directly to this person, ignoring all the others. He has eye contact with this one hearer alone and may even turn his back to the other members of the audience sitting next to him. (Jones-Jackson 1987:44)

The writer here is referring to the interaction between the performer and his appointed answerer or respondent. But she notes also of audiences that "they respond as a chorus by repeating some of the speaker's words or phrases in unison or singularly," just as they do among the Igbo, Yoruba, and Ibibio of Nigeria, where the Gullah are believed to have originated (Jones-Jackson 1987:43). An excerpt from a tale narration among the Creole-speaking Gullah goes like this:

Once upon a time, way back in the olden day—some part of Alabama—way down South. *Yeah!* Black man had done a crime. *Um huh!* And they put em in prison. *Um huh!* And those days they was punish you the way they feel like. *Yeah! Uh huh! That's right!*

So they put this man in a rice field, which was very low in time a summer time. *Uh huh! Summer time* And mosquito was very bad. *Um hum. Very bad.* (p. 101)

Compare the above performance pattern to the following extract from a narration among the Agni-Bona of Ivory Coast, who have institutionalized the art of answering:

One day a king   *hem*
A king like those who lived in the ancient times   *hem*
Who had supreme power   *all really all*
Has done a thing which should not have been done   *what thing?*
He took the python   *hem*
And he started to raise it   *really*
Besides nobody could speak to this king   *sure*
If you went to talk to him   *hem*
He cut off your head   *It is exactly as you say.* (Galli 1983:27)

The practice of commenting on speech, or of narration through phrasal injec-
tions, finds its utmost fulfillment in religious settings, whether in black Pentecostal
churches in the United States or in libation prayers among several ethnic groups in
Ghana. In black American churches, even though there are no specially appointed
answerers that stand between the performer and the audience, both prayers and
sermons receive interjective approval responses from the congregation, with the
rhythm and intensity of response increasing with the preacher's level of eloquence.
An example from the Gullah of South Carolina follows: (Jones-Jackson 1987:91)

God is the Bread of Life
God will feed you when you get hungry   *Oh yes! I know he will.*
All right! Yeah! Amen! Yes sir!
Look on the mountain
Beside the hill of Galilee   *My Lord*
Watch his disciple
Riding on the sea   *Yeah! Uh huh!*
Tossing by the wind and rain   *Yeah. Come up*
Going over the sea of temptation   *Uh hum*
Brother I don't know
But I begin to think
In this Christian life   *Yes!*
Sometime you gone be toss   *Yes, yeah!*
By the wind of life   *Yes, my lord!*
The wind gonna blow you
From one side to the other *Yes!*
On this Christian journey
The way ain't gone be easy on us children   *No!*

The rhythm and pattern of responses here may be compared to those of libation
prayers in parts of Ghana. Among the Akan, the prayer is incomplete unless an
assistant has been appointed to stand beside the officiant and support the officiant's
words. The supportive phrases, *wiė, ampa, siȯ,* are injected at the discretion of the
answerer, but they are timed to coincide with the end of breath groups, and sometimes act as fillers while the performer is groping for fitting words. The situation
among the Ga offers an even closer parallel to a black American sermon. Ga libation prayer involves co-participation by the entire audience, who interject responses
in unison and may clap their hands throughout the performance to sustain the

rhythm and tempo of the prayer. Compare Jones-Jackson's descriptions of sermons among the Gullah of South Carolina:

> Once the rhythm is established, it is maintained through various means, most important of which is the reply from the listeners. Some truly impressive prayer-givers excite an audience to maximal response through their energetic diction and explosive tone alone. Others may intensify the rhythmic effect by drumming with a chair, tapping a cane against the floor, just swaying back and forth in time to some inaudible sound. (p. 78)

In referring above to response patterns in storytelling, epic, and sacred genres, it has been my intention to draw attention to the coincidence of the rhetoric of respondents with certain modes of akyeame's public performance. It is true that the semantic burden in the above-named performances belongs more within the talk of the principal performers, rather than their auxiliaries'; and there is a sense in which the respondent, where one has been appointed, plays only a peripheral role as far as delivery is concerned. Yet the phenomenon belongs generally within the scope of our framework, since in certain manifestations, the performances, as in royal oratory, are not addressed to an audience, directly but through intermediaries, who have the discretion to repeat, pass on by a token formula, or fully reinterpret the message of their principals. Certainly supportive responses are expected of akyeame as their patrons direct public speech at them, and the options at their disposal range from being near-silent on the scene of interaction to completely taking over speaking roles on behalf of their principals. In verbal art performance, it is only natural that the roles of principal performer, animator, and audience are occasionally merged or transposed—a phenomenon which, from the observer's perspective, serves to underscore the impermanence of participant roles.

Supportive responses in verbal art, like the ȯkyeame's full transmission of his or her principal's message, generally belong within the realm of *metacommunication*. Here, an ȯkyeame, whether as answerer, interpreter, or intermediary, builds an interpretive frame within which the message communicated is to be understood. Whether executed by a single voice or in unison, supportive responses tend to sharpen the rhythm and tempo of performance, promote greater synergism between performer and audience, and enhance the credibility of the speaker, since the testimony the speaker presents is depicted as having eyewitnesses. Verbal genres in which speech mediation is a built-in device, whether oratory, storytelling, epic performance, or Pentecostal preaching, tend to diffuse the hazards of performance, since the interaction is intrinsically conditioned to achieve token concord. This is in keeping with the very aim of verbal art performance in general:

> It is part of the essence of performance that it offers to the participants a special enhancement of experience, bringing with it a heightened intensity of communicative interaction which binds the audience to the performer in a way that is specific to the performance as a mode of communication. Through his performance, the performer elicits the participative attention and energy of his audience, and to the extent that

they value his performance, they will allow themselves to be caught up in it. (Bauman 1977:43)

In performance mediation through an ȯkyeame's supportive responses the process of eliciting audience approval is enhanced, since the answerer's metacommunicative interjections are themselves a rhetorical ploy implying the oration's credibility and worthiness of consensual support. Even so, it still remains with the principal performer to demonstrate that he or she is capable of enlisting voluntary approval beyond the built-in nominal affirmation of the verbal display; for, by and large, the degree of enthusiasm in response rests on the potency of the stimulus. In the practice of diplomacy the responsibilities placed on the intermediary's shoulders are far heavier and more complex, as we shall see in the next chapter.

3 / MEDIATION
The Evolution of Royal Diplomacy

THIS CHAPTER takes a look at the evolution of the politics of royal representation in West Africa during colonial and precolonial times with a view to putting into historical perspective the use of royal spokespersons in discourse, as well as the dynamics of their strategies of surrogation. It is seen in the final analysis that the system of discourse mediation which the spokesperson represents has yet another dimension to it. Besides presenting himself as a royal surrogate, his oratory or the official policy he interprets may be embodied in another form of surrogation he holds, a royal staff, *akyeamepoma,* which often encapsulates a pithy policy statement. Thus two interlocking forms of mediation are at play here: the social, represented by the royal spokesperson, and the symbolic, via an iconic reinforcement of his surrogation. Before these are discussed, the interpretive role of the royal spokesperson needs to be distinguished from that of another mediating functionary, the bilingual interpreter of the colonial era.

Bilingual Interpreter

The bilingual interpreter was crucial in communication between colonial representatives and the local states. The interpreter and the ȯkyeame, both masters over language and both agents of verbal mediation, could be mistaken for each other, as indeed they have been in the literature on akyeame. The mistaken application of the word "linguist" to the royal spokesperson in West Africa could be traced to this crisis of identity.

The word "linguist" itself has a host of meanings. According to the Shorter Oxford English Dictionary, "linguist" could mean any of the following: 1) one skilled in other languages besides his own; 2) an interpreter or bilingual translator; 3) an eloquent person, and 4) a student of language. The first two meanings are irrelevant to the ȯkyeame, since they concern knowledge of more than one language. The third is very relevant, but could apply as well to any eloquent person in the community. The fourth meaning, referring to the scholar of language, is not relevant either, since the ȯkyeame is a language analyst only in a very remote sense, and does not belong to the discipline of linguistics, a twentieth-century discipline which was known as philology in the nineteenth century.

Indeed, it is Caseley Hayford, a historian, who suggests that the royal spokesperson was first erroneously called "linguist" "by a half-educated native tasked to explain his position to the whiteman" (Caseley Hayford 1903:68). Cole and Ross also suggest that the term was applied to the spokesperson after the latter started using the European cane used by the bilingual messengers in the seventeenth century (Cole and Ross 1977:161). The confusion, of course, would not have arisen if the cultural uniqueness of òkyeame's role had been acknowledged, and no attempt made to find his equivalent in the Western tradition. The word òkyeame simply resists a precise translation and should have been left intact.

Missionaries, slave traders, or representatives of foreign governments interacting with local chiefs always employed the services of local bilingual interpreters, who were proficient in both the colonial and local languages. In the sixteenth and seventeenth centuries, for example, the language used between Africans and Europeans was often Portuguese. From the eighteenth century onward, trading contacts spread the use of English, German, and French in both speech and writing, and colonial officers relied on bilingual interpreters (Smith 1976:25–26). G. E. Ferguson, for instance, reports that on his arrival in Salaga, northern Ghana, he was accompanied by a friend and by two local interpreters, one of whom spoke jargon German and the other English (M. Johnson, n.d.:2).

The presence of bilingual interpreters implies that the complexity of the triadic pattern of communication already prevailing in the royal domain was further compounded by the addition of another mediating functionary. The following statement by Richard Burton on his visit to the king of Dahomey supports this: "The sovereign's words are spoken to the Meu (spokesman), who informs the interpreter, who passes it on to the visitor, and the answer must trickle back through the same channels" (Burton 1966:150).

That a bilingual interpreter must have wrongly translated the Akan term òkyeame as "linguist" need not surprise us. There is evidence that some of those interpreters were mediocrities, often lacking diplomatic courtesy and translation skills. M. J. Bonnant, a French explorer to Salaga, reports one incident illustrating the problem. On being received by the king, he began speaking English to be translated by the interpreter; "but seeing that my interpreter did not correctly translate my thoughts, I began to use Ashanti myself," he writes (cf. Johnson n.d., sal 2, and also Adjayi 1984:106–107).

In an era where interstate diplomacy was crucial for the maintenance of peace, errors in mediation, whether in translation or in intralingual interpreting, could be costly to a ruler. It is not surprising that the king of Dahomey acknowledged and reacted to this by law. Faulty translation in his court attracted the death penalty (Argyle 1966:2). As will be seen later (chapter 6), flawed representation of an Akan chief's word by the òkyeame likewise constitutes a serious breach of the law.

Genesis of Diplomacy

Prior to the emergence of modern states on the Guinea coast of West Africa, the office of the royal spokesperson in some states fell under the king's diplomatic or foreign affairs portfolio, the office responsible for good-neighborliness between kingdoms, negotiations for peace, reception of royal visitors, etc. It is not surprising, then, that this functionary among the Ashanti-Akan has been described not only as spokesperson but also as confidant, ambassador, foreign minister, etc., positions that require knowledge of diplomacy as well as skills in the management of face-to-face interactions. As Robert Smith, a historian of West African political diplomacy, has stated:

> Diplomacy, which is the fundamental means by which foreign relations are conducted and a foreign policy implemented, far from being an invention of capitalism or of the modern national state, or of classical antiquity either, is found in some of the most primitive communities and seems to have been evolved independently by peoples in all parts of the world. (1976:11)

Functionaries responsible for the conduct of foreign affairs in the colonial and precolonial life of West Africa have been variously described as "ambassadors," "messengers," and "linguists." The latter word was, and still remains, used for ambassadors of the Gold Coast (now Ghana). The status of such envoys, however, varied from state to state. Some served ad hoc and had other substantive duties; others were full-time ambassadors. Members of royal families have been sent on diplomatic errands, as among the Ashanti in the nineteenth century (see Owusu-Mensah 1974) and in Congo in the sixteenth century. In the seventeenth century, Ashantis and Denkyiras sometimes sent traders and royal wives as ambassadors, while the Igbos sometimes sent priests. Even slaves and men of humble birth could be made ambassadors, as happened in Abuja (Smith 1976:19). The significant fact here is that such functionaries must have had considerable mastery over words, diplomacy, and traditional lore. The earliest historical reference to diplomatic relations in West Africa is said to be al-Sagri's account of the sending of an ambassador by a ninth-century imam in North Africa to a Sudanese state. Since then, numerous references have been made to diplomatic activity on the West African coast either between nation states or between coastal states and representatives of the colonial government.

The delicate nature of diplomacy during war times, the absence of vehicles capable of giving rapid mobility, and the overriding necessity to safeguard state secrets, demonstrate the delicate nature of the work of diplomats and confidants and the crucial role they played within the political setup. Prior to 1903, when the first locomotive arrived, Ashanti diplomats and messengers in Kumasi were part of a whole category of human resources serving the ends of communication within and across states. The rest were *akwansrafo,* scouts or highway police (Fynn 1971:33); *akwanmufo,* responsible for road maintenance; and merchants. Diplomats, messengers, and merchants sent on the king's behalf would swear upon the pain of death not to reveal any state secrets, but on return from missions to give all information learned and events observed (Wilks 1975:135). Besides this, information carried on behalf of the king was expected to be judiciously and accurately transmitted. Where necessary the message was committed to memory. In the kingdom of Dahomey, there was a relay system of communication:

Messengers travelled in pairs, so that one might act as a check on the other to ensure accurate repetition of the message. On the road from Abomey, there were various stations, where the messengers were relieved by relays of others, so the message was conveyed by running speed all the way. (Argyle 1966:68)

But diplomats were not mere parrots; they sometimes exercised personal discretion in negotiation, based on previous experience and knowledge of foreign policy and history, as well as of traditional logic and oratory. In Ashanti, where royal spokesmen were (and still are) prosecutors in court, mastery over the forensic arts was of even greater necessity. The learning of traditional lore and diplomacy at an early age, and the general penchant for diplomatic talk in Africa at the time, was observed by Reade:

> It is a mistake to suppose that the Africans are a stupid people because they have no books, and do not wear many clothes. The children do not go to school, but they sit around fire at night or beneath the town tree in the day, and listen to the elders, who discuss politics, and matters relating to law and religion. Every man in a tribe, and every slave belonging to a tribe, has learnt at an early age the constitution by which he is governed, and the policy pursued towards foreign tribes. In such a land as Ashanti the king and chiefs are skilled in the arts of diplomacy. (Reade 1874:288)

In the nineteenth century the preeminence of diplomacy, or verbal negotiations, was such that the operative maxim in Ashanti and other states was to "make diplomacy do the work of arms," or "never to appeal to the sword while a path lay open for negotiation" (Wilks 1974: 324).

Though interstate negotiation was crucial to a state's survival, its conduct was often hazardous. But diplomats, or spokespersons, and others acting on the chief's behalf were so dear to a ruler that special laws were made for their protection in the course of their duties. Their murder or maltreatment in a foreign mission was taken as a challenge to their states. In Ashanti, they were considered sacred and inviolate both inside and outside the state:

> No heathen can be perfectly secure in his person or property beyond the precincts of his sovereign's jurisdiction, excepting, however, the character of his ambassador, whose person should be held inviolate; that of the king's merchant or trader which is equally sacred; hunters of elephants in the king's name, and on his account; and lastly, men of rank, or others whose influence or interest at court is powerful enough to gain for them travelling protection by the use of the king's name or recommendation to other sovereigns and princes. These, and only such characters, are passports for the subjects of Ashanti, by which they may travel in security (Wilks 1974:17).

Cultural Source and Diffusion

The institution of ɔkyeame in Akan Society is believed to have been established by Awurade Basa, a sixteenth-century chief of Adansi, the earliest Akan state. This is confirmed by Adansi oral traditions (see also Ward 1958:52). The Adansi were not just the founders of the ȯkyeame institution; they were also the pioneers in other crafts such as *asėsėdwa* (stools), and Akan architecture. In the royal arts, they are also believed to be progenitors of *ntahera* (state horns). Yet it is for pioneering the ȯkyeame institution that they have been most noted. Being a powerful chief, Awurade Basa appointed one Mfrane (sometimes appearing as Mfenfrane) as his confidant and as one through whom the public could speak to the chief and vice versa. To this day, the Akan have a proverb attesting to this, *Worekasa akyerė Mfrane no, na wode Awurade* (As you speak to Mfrane, it's Awurade you address)—a proverb which clearly distinguishes the participant roles of *recipient* and *addressee*.

While the pioneering role of the Adansi chief in establishing the institution is not in doubt, the derivation of the word *ȯkyeame* is problematic, since its morphemic constitution, unlike that of many multisyllabic words in Akan, is not easy to decipher. According to one informant, the word is in reference to a statement made by the Adansi chief about his confidant's trustworthiness: *Ȯkye ma me a mentase mu* (When he roasts for me, I don't pick from it). In other words, the spokesman was so reliable he couldn't be suspected of poisoning; in metaphorical terms, the chief trusts his spokesman to accurately represent his views. In this etymology, the relevant verb is *kye,* to fry/roast.

According to another informant, however, the chief in commenting on his confidant refers rather to his way of walking, *N'akyea ma me mee* (His gait satisfies me). The *kye* in *ȯkyeame* is here related to the word, *akyea,* gait.

Yet another etiological narrative claims that *ȯkyeame* is derived from the name *Akyea* and the word *mene,* "to swallow," and that an Akan chief once organized a contest for the selection of his confidant. The test lay in the ability to swallow a ball of medicine prepared by a priest. All other contestants failed except one Akyea, who thus became the chief's spokesman. This version, which is unlikely, makes no reference to the Adansi chief.

According to yet another source, the word "is derived from the Akan expression, *ȯkyem ma me,* that is 'he makes perfect for me' " (Appiah 1979:xi). This, however, is not likely, since the verb indicated here, *kyem,* does not appear in the Akan lexicon in the sense of "make perfect".

A possible root source is the verb, *kyea,* to become oblique, distorted, crooked, in which case the full form could be, *ȯkyea ma me,* "he bends (my message) for me." The verb would then refer to the spokesman's art of twisting a message, making it more oblique.

The word *ȯkyeame* (or its cognates) is not only used by all Akan ethnic groups in reference to the royal spokesperson; it is also used by such non-Akan groups as Ga, Adanme, Ewe, Guan, and all the language groups belonging to the Volta-Comoe group, including the Agni and Baulé of the Ivory Coast, who are Akan. Unquestionably the non-Akan groups borrowed the institution, alongside other royal institutions, from the Akan-Ashanti, who extended their suzerainty over several southern and northern states in the Gold Coast, and "Akanized" some of the latter's institutions, from the seventeenth century onward. Indeed, there is evidence that Ashanti art and royal paraphenalia were often sent as rewards and honors to various subordinate chiefs as part of a strategy of integration. This happened, for instance, in Gonja, Dagomba, and Mamprusi, as well as in Western Bono, where the Ashanti met a highly mixed cultural situation combining Mande-speaking peoples such as the Dyula and the Ligbi with speakers of the Gur language family, such as the Kulango, the Mo, and the Nafana (Bravmann 1972:156).

The Gonja and Dagomba have talking drums that speak Akan, as well as Ashanti regalia such as state umbrellas and swords, which are brought out on important festival occasions such as Damba. Items displayed often include gold-handled state swords and the Ashanti-Akan royal spokesman's staff (Bravmann, p. 159). Among the Nafana of Western Bono, not only were Ashanti regalia like stools and state swords paramount, but the Ashanti language itself spread rapidly and became the second language of the Banda people. It was the language used in rituals employing Ashanti regalia. Nafana chiefs dress like Ashanti chiefs and often have spokespersons attending them.

There is no doubt that the Dagomba, the Mamprusi, and the Gonja retained Akan-Ashanti institutions from their conquest by Ashanti, such as talking drums, royal stools, military institutions and titles, etc. (Rattray 1932:565–566). Of the Dagomba Staniland states, "There emerged bodies of appointed officials chosen by and responsible to the monarch. Many of the various offices of elder and councillor to the Ya-Na seem to have been created at the time of the conquest" (1975:27).

Besides this, the Ashanti left a substantial heritage of loan words, including personal names. Indeed, Tait and Strevens state that out of about forty-five principal titles the Dagomba have, about thirty appear to be Ashanti words (1955:195). It is significant, though, that the indigenous names for "royal orator" in some of these cultures are not cognates of the Akan word, òkyeame. The Mamprusi word, talana, and Dagomba mbadugu sound different, and it is not very clear whether the institution itself is a full or partial borrowing. It is evident, though, that like the òkyeame, the mbadugu performs other functions besides acting as speech intermediary. He is also controller of state treasury, supervises cooking in the royal household, and announces births (Staniland 1975:29).

Among the Akan, the òkyeame is not just a speech intermediary. He is envoy, counsellor, consultant, protocol officer, as well as ritual officiant responsible for libation prayers. These functions are replicated among the Adanme. The Ga have their tsiame performing similar functions, except that libation prayers are conducted on the chief's behalf only by the wulomo, or fetish priest. But whether Akan or not, it is clear that the royal spokesperson, wherever he has been found in Ghana, is a close confidant and the most reliable among the chief's council of elders.

Among the Agni-Bona (Akan) of Ivory Coast, the institution of kyeame, royal spokesperson, is so significant that its genesis is explained by a well-known folktale whose opening we have already seen:

One day a powerful king did one thing he shouldn't have done. He raised a python which was as cruel as the king. Nobody could go to the king and speak to him: he would cut off your head. But the python was terrible too. It ate all the chickens, goats and sheep in the village. It nearly devoured all the children too. Left with no alternative, the people deserted the village. But before then, a pregnant woman gave birth to a child and left it in a pumpkin, leaving also the knife with which the child's umbilical cord was cut. At noontime, python began singing in the village, and heard the child's reply. Python went to lie near the pumpkin, and the child took the knife and killed python. Those who escaped to the forest heard a loud noise and came home. They went to the king and reported the death of python. That is the reason why today, the king does not raise python, and that is why today you find by a king a good spokesman. When there is a question to be dealt with or a palaver to judge, the king always listens to the advice of his spokesman. (Galli 1983:27)

It is clear from this story that absolute power and tyranny, in the absence of a good diplomat and intermediary for the king, eventually gave way to reason, represented by the child. Thus the people do not only have partial access to their king now; they also have a king who takes advice from a royal confidant who has their interest at heart.

Visual Icons of Diplomacy

So important were royal spokespersons to a state that their image home and abroad were of special concern. Among the Ashanti, akyeame on royal mission had access to a public wardrobe from which they dressed in a manner befitting royal emissaries. Furthermore, like ambassadors in other states, they needed to carry symbols of authority and comport themselves as men of dignity. Generally, akyeame in West Africa carried credentials or badges of office in such forms as cane, baton, sword, or special clothing like caps or ties (as the Fante had), to ensure free passage everywhere. In Ashanti and Dahomey, as prevails to this day, it was a staff covered in gold or silver leaf, often bearing a proverbial design or depicting a symbol of authority. In the Dahomey kingdom, carved batons of this nature often had a design depicting the bearer's appellations or the chief's name (Smith 1976:21–22).

But such visual symbolic forms also varied in substance from one culture to another. Poro ambassadors conducting negotiations among the Mende chiefs put on devils' masks, to impersonate their guardian spirits. Among the Dan of Ivory Coast and modern Liberia, negotiators put on "large masks with animal-like features and movable jaw." Among the Igbo, spokesmen or peace negotiators had bells tied on their left hands, and their faces masked with chalk. The Alafin of Oyo, on the other hand, had messengers whose credentials were in the form of fans, which they held.

An intercultural semiotic thus existed at the diplomatic level, and was known by all spokespersons and envoys. Beyond this each society had its own code of indirect communication, often used among spokespersons, which helped to keep their political dealings and interactions secret. Occasionally,

Diplomatic communication took the form of symbolic messages conveyed by objects such as horses' tails sent to the French emissary by the Egba in 1884 as a sign of alliance or by cowries and other miscellanea arranged in a significant pattern, as in the congratulatory message sent by the Awujale of Ijebu to Oba Akitoye of Lagos after the latter's restoration in 1857. (Smith 1976:27)

In essence, it is hard to separate the verbal and visual arts in discussing the royal orator or diplomat; for these are mutually complementary and inseparable in the communicative and rhetorical art. The power of the ȯkyeame's oratory is expected to be consistent with his nonverbal rhetoric. Where the two contradict, a diplomatic crisis may begin. This is exemplified below with a discussion of the Akan royal staff, the *akyeamepoma,* used by royal orators on diplomatic missions.

It is contended by Cole and Ross, in an elaborate examination of historical sources, that the ambassadorial practice of using a royal staff of authority among the Akan was borrowed entirely from European bilingual messengers near the middle of the seventeenth century (Cole and Ross 1977:161). While this cannot be ruled out, there is evidence also that from time immemorial, chiefs and titled men in Africa have had one type of royal symbol or another, including staffs. Examples of such carved staffs were found in the eighteenth century in the palace of the king of Dahomey, each staff belonging to each of the eleven previous kings (Argyle 1966:2). Among the Kuba of Central Congo, each king-designate selects his emblem upon installation, and the Kuba have as many such emblems as they have had kings (Vansina 1972:45). Among the Igbo, men with Ozo titles have emblems, among which is a staff or spear (Cole 1972:85). In Ivory Coast, an assistant of a Baulé notable (the Baulé are Akan) may hold, on behalf of his patron, a spear, sword, or gold-plated flywhisk made of a horsetail; designs on these may depict proverbs (Himmelheber 1972:187).

The widespread use of the staff in other parts of Africa demonstrates its link with rank and authority. It was similarly used in parts of Europe. In England, for instance, royal assent to a bill in the middle ages was signified by the king's touching it with his scepter. The closest example of a similar relationship between the staff and authoritative oratory can be found in the Homeric period in classical Greek civilization, where classical scholars indicate that the scepter was used in connection with certain classes of Homeric society such as kings, heralds, priests, and judges (Combellack 1947). The scepter was what keyed the performance of a public speech, signalling that the speaker had the floor. It was held by heralds and taken by speakers who wanted to make a solemn statement at a public assembly. In this case the staff, as among the Akan, represented a combination of related entities: royalty, power, oratory, and authoritative performance.

Among the Ashanti-Akan, the spokesperson's staff has been traced as far back as the seventeenth century, and may have been employed by earlier Ashanti diplomats. According to oral traditions, the first Ashanti ȯkyeame to use a staff was an old woman who was so weak she needed a stick to support her. Spokespersons, *mbadugu,* among the Dagomba also held staffs covered in leopard skins.

Akan Staff Rhetoric

A further observation appearing to contradict the Cole-Ross thesis is that staffs used by the Ashanti (and the Akan in general) are much longer and heavier than maces and scepters used by European bilinguals; besides this, they were not just symbols of authority, but also keys to indigenous systems of indirect communication, often selected to suit the errand the bearer was running. Indeed, the proverbs communicated by their symbols are often an iconic capsule of official policy respecting a given situation.

There is thus, as indicated earlier, a sense in which the rhetoric of the Akan royal staff is another form of surrogation (a sign within a sign) presenting a message in lieu of the spoken word. Indeed, where the orator does not make a speech, he *can* rely entirely on the rhetoric of his visual icon to state, in very general terms, the official policy he represents. In this case, the mediation process is reinforced through a combination between animate and inanimate surrogates—the intermediary constituting the social agent of mediation, and the staff indicating the strategic shift in communication channel. In such a double-layered strategy of mediation, the likelihood of face-to-face chaos is almost completely averted.

Even so, conflict or confrontation is not altogether forestalled by such reinforced strategies of mediation. As will be seen in the following discussion, inherent ambiguities in the diplomatic icons are sometimes exploited to make subtle political comments, which when successfully deciphered by the intended target may lead to a diplomatic crisis. To avert such crises, Akan royal spokesmen strive to steer clear of ambiguity where no malice is intended. They strive to comply with norms of propriety ensuring harmony between the staff's message and the occasion of its use.

The position taken here regarding the strategic importance of the ɔkyeame's staff is not the same as that of scholars like Cole and Ross, who downplay the communicative dynamics of present-day Akan staffs: "Rather than being in active use as instruments to make specific social statements, linguist staffs are more important in simply announcing the presence of the chief's principal counsellor and in setting the mood for serious business" (1977:162). While this statement may be valid in reference to predictable social scenarios, it does not take into consideration the potential for misunderstandings in sensitive situations, possibly leading to diplomatic crises. At formal meetings involving chiefs of varied ranks, care is taken by akyeame not to remotely suggest innuendoes through the use of staffs. Oftentimes, akyeame make a special effort to be sure that they are in complete command over all possible ranges of proverbial meaning the staff they carry may represent.

Every Akan chief or king has two or more staffs. The higher a chief's status the wider the range of staffs, since an important chief deals with a greater variety of social and political situations and has to match various situations with relevant messages. A chief may add to the existing stock of staffs upon his or her installation. In some cases, an ɔkyeame may initiate a move to increase the stock by proposing a motif or message to the chief for consideration as a possible staff. If the chief agrees, the construction of a new staff is ordered and added to the existing repertoire.[1] There are also instances where government officials or paramount chiefs have given a new staff to a chief as a present.[2]

Akan *akyeamepoma* are many and varied (see also Cole and Ross 1977:158–164; Ross 1982; Opoku 1975), and their uses have been extended to domains outside the realm of chiefship. They are used currently to represent lineages and voluntary associations as well. Storytelling associations, for instance, have ɔ̀kyeame's staffs held by the narrator to signal control of the floor. Unlike those used in the royal domain, the symbols embossed on such pseudo-*akyeamepoma* are not rhetorical; they are often emblems of identity, based on myths of origins. Storytelling groups may have the spider designed as their staff emblem (see below), and lineages may have images of their totem animals (kite, snake, crow, leopard, dog, etc.) embossed on their staffs. Moreover, such imitation *akyeamepoma* are painted black and other colors; not covered with precious metal. Staffs used on behalf of chiefs are generally covered in gold or silver leaf, except for one particular staff, which is often singled out and covered with the dark skin of a monitor lizard (the *omanpam*). This unique staff is often short and unlike the others has no finial. It is called *asèmpa yè tia* (A good case is presented in brief).

A staff may be held by an ɔ̀kyeame sitting beside the chief; it is always held in the left hand of the ɔ̀kyeame whenever he or she makes a formal speech. It may also be used by the ɔ̀kyeame on a royal mission, as a symbol of authority and surrogation.

Like proverbial symbols on Akan gold weights and royal umbrellas (see Cole and Ross 1977:166–167; Rattray 1927), motifs on *akyeamepoma* are often direct visual representations of social and proverbial messages. The messages depicted on the staffs have public meanings, which occasionally change from one locality to another. The proverbial statements are not unique to the staffs; they are invariably maxims or proverbs already in oral circulation and subsequently represented in design. In the set of examples discussed below, I indicate instances where I have documented the oral use of the staff proverbs.

Messages embedded often convey political or social statements. They either define power relations between royalty and the rest of society or else are purely preceptive, advocating general principles of behavior, cooperation, initiative, etc. Either way, they are used to convey messages appropriate to given occasions.

Classifying them by situations of use, I distinguish two main uses, *judicial* and *political.*

Judicial Uses

By judicial uses I refer to the use of staffs in royal courts to convey appropriate messages relating to justice, peace, arbitration, and related issues. The following staffs are thus used accordingly:

---

1. This is true of the staffs of the king of Ashanti, according to Ȯkyeame Amoateng, one of the senior akyeame.

2. The chief of Atwia in the Central region of Ghana, for instance, says her staff depicting the proverb, "When two mouths meet, conflict is averted," was presented to her by a government official.

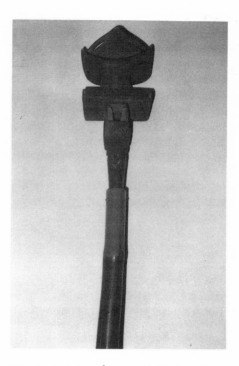

3.1. An imitation ȯkyeame staff, used by a
professional storytelling group, depicting the
spider trickster in Akan folktales. Assasan,
1988.

• Black staff covered in the skin of the monitor lizard, ȯmanpam (literally, "one
who sews states together in the search for peace,"), and carrying no finial. This is
called asėmpa yė tia, ("A good casė is argued in brief," see fig. 3.2).

This staff represents the very diplomatic essence of the ȯkyeame, since like the
monitor lizard, he stands for peace and order in society. It is used for funerals and
in the settlement of cases, or appeal hearings. Reminiscent of the communicative
principle of eighteenth-century Quakers (Bauman 1983), it advocates brevity in
speech, since truth in argument need not be belabored.

• Two birds with their beaks touching: Ano na ano hyia a ntoto mma (When two
mouths meet, conflict is averted). This is used at the court of the chief of Ekumfi
Atwia in settling disputes. It advocates the use of diplomacy, rather than physical
confrontation in the solution of problems. Mutual talk dissipates conflict, it says.
Like the preceding, this proverb is metacommunicative; it underscores the power of
the spoken word as a potential source of peace and stability.

• Two men seated opposite each other with a bowl of food between them, one
eating, the other observing (see fig. 3.3): Nea adeė wȯ no na ȯdie, na nyė nea ȯkȯm
de no (It's the rightful heir who inherits property, not the hungry man). This is taken

3.2. A short ȯkyeame staff with no
finial depicting the proverb, "A good
case is argued in brief." Asuom, 1984.

to arbitration courts, particularly where the issue contested involves inheritance or
succession. The proverb argues that in judging cases of succession, prevailing norms
and customs (should) take precedence over the material needs of the contestants.
Rules of succession are not based on need; they are based on rightful access.

• Two men seated on a long bench: *Ahennwa nyė babayėnten na yėatena so
mmienu mmienu* (The royal stool is no log long enough to seat two at a time). This
is also taken to cases dealing with inheritance. It implies that rules of succession do
not permit joint occupancy; heirs succeed one at a time, and there cannot possibly
be two occupants of a stool.[3]

• A man pointing to his eye with the index finger: *Merebėpeė mu* (I am here to
investigate). The ȯkyeame implies that the issue at stake bears thorough investigation, and that is exactly the royal mission.

Political

Political uses of the staff imply an assertion of royal power or authority.

• Significantly, there is one staff in this class whose message conveys surroga-

---

3. The oral use of this proverb has been documented by this writer (in Yankah 1989a:239).

3.3. Ọkyeame staff with one man eating and another staring: "It's the rightful heir who inherits property, not the hungry man." Kumasi, 1988.

tion. It depicts a hawk sitting on its eggs with a kite beside it: *Ọsansa kọ abu a ọde n'akyi gya akoròma* (When the hawk broods, the kite acts on its behalf).[4] This staff may be used in the company of an elder acting on the chief's behalf at a formal meeting.

• A blossoming palm tree standing upright (see fig. 3.4): *Nnua nyinaa bèwu agya abè* (All trees will wither but the palm tree). Used at formal meetings where the chief is the biggest political power, it depicts his supreme power and resilience over all entities present. "My power, unlike that of my subordinates, is evergreen and does not diminish with time and circumstances," it is implied.

• Thumb pointing upwards: *Wònkwati kokuroboti mmò pò* (One does not dispense with the thumb in tying a knot). It is used at meetings where the chief is the biggest authority. It demonstrates his indispensability in the solution of problems. He is the ultimate repository of wisdom. I have documented the oral use of this proverb elsewhere in this book (see chapter 4).

---

4. I have noted elsewhere the oral use of this proverb (Yankah 1989a:95).

3.4. Okyeame staff depicting a blossoming palm
tree, with a wilted tree beside it: "All trees will
wither but the palm tree." Kumasi, 1988.

• An elephant standing within a rainbow: *Okontokurowi a ȯda amansan kȯn mu*
(The halo encircling humanity). This is not a proverb; it is an appellation portraying
the chief's might and the pervasiveness of his presence. His power extends
throughout the territorial boundaries of his state; and he is so mighty, he virtually
sprawls on the shoulders of the strong (represented here by the elephant).

Akyeame are quick to emphasize that the above staffs depicting power imagery
may not be used by a subordinate chief who is visiting, or in the presence of a
superior one, since that would constitute a challenge to the latter's supremacy. Subordinate chiefs, however, may convey their submission to bigger royals by using
appropriate staffs such as the following:

• A smaller armadillo recoiled beside a bigger one: *Aprȇwa kuma hu aprȇwa kȇse
a ȯbobȯ* (The small armadillo recoils when it sees its bigger counterpart). This is
used for a subordinate chief meeting a superior one. It implies humility and submission to a greater power.

• A hedgehog lying beside a log (see fig. 3.5): *Apȇsȇ yȇ kȇse a ȯyȇ ma dufȯkye*

3.5. Ọkyeame staff with a hedgehog lying beside a log, its normal sleeping place: "When the hedgehog fattens, it fattens for the wet log." Asuom, 1984.

(When the hedgehog fattens, it fattens for the wet log). The hedgehog completely relies on the log for habitation and source of livelihood. It is therefore entirely at the service of the log. "When I prosper the log is welcome to my wealth," the animal implies. Similarly, subordinate chiefs derive their power from their superiors, and therefore need to show gratitude to them.

• It is important to stress that the power wielded by chiefs is not absolute, nor is it expected to lead to tyranny. A chief is expected to exercise the power he wields cautiously, or else he incurs the wrath of his subjects. One of the spokesman's staffs conveying the need for a judicious exercise of power depicts an egg cautiously held by the hand: *Tumi te sè kosua* (Power is like an egg). This is an abbreviation of the statement, "Power is like an egg; if carelessly held it breaks." This counsel is from the viewpoint of the chief's subjects, who are watchdogs of possible abuses of royal power.

• In implementing his authority, the chief is expected to assume the image of a tender mother, carefully tending his young ones. Thus integral to the power he wields is, paradoxically, the tender hand of a caring mother. This notion is invariably represented by the hen in related proverbs. Here, it is embodied in the image of a hen with its chickens surrounding it: *Ọbaatan pa a ne mma atwa ne ho ahyia*

3.6. Ọkyeame staff depicting the frog, symbol of fertility. Kumasi, 1988.

(The good mother surrounded by its young ones). What is expected of a chief is, after all, religious and political protection over his subjects.

• A related image advocates the constructive application of sanctions, where the need arises: A hen stepping on one of its chickens. *Akokò nan tia òba na ènkum no* (The hen steps on its young one not to kill it; see fig. 5.1, chapter 5). When sanctions are applied, it is implied, the rationale should be more corrective than penal. We shall encounter this proverb as spoken by a chief elsewhere in this book (see chapter 8).

Other staffs may not necessarily convey political or judicial messages, but may give general advice on the need for co-operation, initiative, etc. One such depicts three heads: *Ti koro nkò agyina* (One head does not consult). This is used at formal meetings between the chief and his elders to express the need for collaboration and consultation. A related one has a man attempting to scrape medicine from a tree (see fig. 3.7): *Obaako werè aduro a ègu* (When one man scrapes medicine alone, it spills). These proverbs advocate collaboration in social enterprise.

Ambiguity

To present the public meanings of staff proverbs is not to suggest that their use is completely predictable. The representation of proverbs by symbols occasionally leaves room for ambiguity, which is sometimes exploited to strategic advantage. The meaning of some of the symbols slightly changes from place to place, while

3.7. Okyeame staff with a man scraping medicine
from a tree: "If one man scrapes medicine alone, it
spills." Kumasi, 1988.

some symbols represent more than one proverb in the same locality. In several
Akan states, for example, the staff symbol of a thumb pointing upwards may
mean, "One does not dispense with the thumb in tying a knot," in reference to the
chief's indispensability; but it may also refer to the omnipotence of God via the
truncated saying *Gye Nyame* (Except God). Similarly, a porcupine symbol may
stand for the proverb *Obi ne kòtòkò nni nkònhyia* (One does not confront the porcupine in war), in reference to the animal's rich armory of spines. But it may also
stand for a synonymous proverb, *Kòtòkò renko a hwè n'amiade* (If the porcupine
will not fight, check its armor), which also alludes to the natural armor of spines on
which the porcupine relies. There is yet a third meaning that may be assigned to the
porcupine symbol, *Kòtòkò rekò kòtòkò a òmfa adididie* (When the porcupine is
going to its place of origin, it carries no food) (cited by Adi 1988). This latter
meaning may be implied if a chief visits another belonging to the same lineage. The
implication is that the visiting chief is actually no stranger, and expects the best of
hospitality.

Occasionally, the possible meanings conveyed may be contrastive. The symbol of an index finger pointed beneath the eye (earlier cited under judiciary symbols), meaning *Merebèpeè mu* (I am here to investigate) and used to denote the chief's or òkyeame's investigative role in court sittings, may also be a sarcasm, *Sè woahu* (You see?), implying that the case would not have assumed such serious proportions, if the litigants had listened to earlier advice.

Sometimes the ambiguity is based on different meanings assigned in different localities. A symbol of two cola leaves means the same as the three heads earlier explained, *Ti koro nkò agyina* (One head does not consult) among the Akwapim-Akan. However, among the people of Nsaba, who are Agona-Akan, the same two-leaved symbol stands for the proverb. *Esua bese na besepa ahaban, wòtase no òba nyansafo* (The genuine and the false cola leaves are discerned by the wise child). While the former proverb points to the need for cooperation, the latter refers to the hazy boundaries in ethics and social life which need critical judgment and experience to discern. The leaves of the two cola species are, in fact, look-alikes and can be easily mistaken for each other by the unsophisticated. Similarly, chiefship requires wisdom and sophistication in distinguishing good and evil in judicial matters.

Diplomatic Incidents

Besides the ambiguity inherent in the motifs, the very semantic indefiniteness of proverbs in their metaphorical application makes the staffs of tremendous significance as rhetorical assets. It also, however, compels the exercise of caution in their application in various contexts. For this reason, certain staffs may not be sent on errands if one dimension of meaning they carry may arouse controversy.

One example of such a staff is the one bearing the motif of an elephant with an antelope beside it. According to the akyeame of Agona Nsaba, even though that is part of their repertoire of staffs, it may not be used on errands. The symbol represents the proverb *Òsono kuntann gyan, adowa na òde ne man* (The elephant is huge in vain, it's to the antelope that the state belongs) (see fig. 5.1, chapter 5). This proverb contrasts the versatility and craftiness of the small antelope with the elephant's brute strength and relative lack of wits. Physical size and might are not the requisites of greatness; cleverness is the key. The elephant can be easily outwitted by the antelope, it is implied. If such a staff is taken on an errand to a superior chief, it may start a crisis, since it may be interpreted as an attempt to undermine the prevailing political order. If used on an errand to a subordinate chief, however, the metaphor may be reversed, and the staff's contextual meaning may rebound on the visiting chief. In fact, such a staff may be used only if conflict is intended.

Another staff, in the repertoire of the Kwahu-Akan of the village of Aduamoa, likewise may not be used on diplomatic errands. This is due to the message of physical aggression suggested in its motif: a snake's head trapped in a bird's claws. The related proverb is *Wosuo òwò ti a, nea aka yè ahama* (If you hold the snake's head, the rest of it is mere thread) (see fig. 5.2). It may convey the message "If we succeed in capturing your chief, or general, your whole state is doomed to defeat."

3.8. Staffs on parade in Kumasi. 1988.

This proverb suggests a military strategy of destroying first a state's military base, which facilitates complete conquest; but it also conveys an innuendo of the relative insignificance of the host chief's retinue.

Occasionally, akyeame carrying staffs on other chiefs' premises are asked by the latter's akyeame to explain the motifs on the staffs. Sometimes this is a test of wits; occasionally, it is a prelude to a diplomatic crisis. One ὸkyeame told me how his wits were challenged several times by Ashanti akyeame when he led a delegation to the palace of the king of Ashanti in the early seventies.

> They knew the message on my staff was a peaceful one, yet they tested my mastery several times over its meaning. 'What is the meaning of your staff?' they challenged. At the time, I was holding the staff of a tree motif with birds on it. And I told them the proverb it represents: *Dua bere a nnoma di bi* (When fruits ripen on a tree, birds may benefit). This was at the funeral of the former king of Ashanti, and we went to convey our sympathies. It was a message of peace and prosperity I carried, yet they wanted to make sure it was not a double entendre.

On a few occasions, staffs have led to open confrontations; one ὸkyeame told me, "In the olden days, that could lead to war." A recent incident confirms the likelihood of this. Violence nearly erupted at a funeral at Agona Nsaba when courtiers of the host chief discovered that the symbol on the staff of the visiting ὸkyeame, from Agona Nyakrom, carried a potentially aggressive message. The symbol represented a hunter struck down with his gun beside him, and an eagle standing close by. *Òkòre akye òbòfo* (The eagle has defeated the hunter) is the message. Besides the open aggression conveyed in the motif, the controversial visual symbol also appeared to encapsulate a political conflict that had raged between the two states for years.

The image of conquest depicted on the staff was not taken lightly. A fierce argument ensued over its intended meaning, and no amount of protestation of benign intentions appeared to convince the hosts. An attempt was made to seize the staff, and other elders intervened. In the end the hapless diplomat, staff in hand, escaped from the scene of controversy and hurriedly departed, retracing his steps back to his village. From the beginnings of traditional diplomacy to the present, staff rhetoric, like the intermediary's oration, has helped to minimize risks in face-to-face interchanges, but it has also held a tremendous potential of its own for sowing the seeds of political crises. The importance of discreetness in the management of public communication becomes even more evident in the articulation of public speech, to which we turn in the next chapter.

4 / ORATORY IN AKAN SOCIETY

THE SKILLFUL control of words is highly valued in Akan society; yet there is no formal training in the art, since it comes naturally with constant exposure to traditional speaking situations. According to an Akan adage, speech is free. In fact, *Ananse antòn kasa* ("The spider did not sell speech") is a saying depicted by one of the symbols on the staffs of the akyeame.

The protean spider of the Akan, Ananse, the trickster in *Anansesèm* (folktales), is believed to be the source of all cultural phenomena, and despite his greed and selfishness he did not make speaking the monopoly of one man. That is perhaps because Ananse's earlier attempt to monopolize wisdom had failed, thanks to the wits of his son, who exposed his folly:

> One day, Ananse put all wisdom in the world into a pot and decided to put it out of reach of all men. He would throw wisdom away so that the rest of mankind would be fools. With the wisdom pot on his back, he came across a fallen tree which had blocked the path except for a small gap underneath the tree. Ananse made several attempts to pass beneath the tree with the pot at his back, but to no avail. Kweku Tsen, his son, who was watching silently, at last volunteered a piece of advice to his father, "Put the load on the fallen tree, pass beneath the tree without the load, and pick up the load from the other side," he advised. Ananse complied and succeeded. Yet realizing wisdom was not his monopoly after all, Ananse in frustration smashed the wisdom pot. The pot broke and wisdom spread to all mankind.

Like wisdom, speech is accessible to all people. Noam Chomsky's claims of a child's intuition about the grammar of language appear to be supported in Akan ethnic lore. Yet the Akan, like Dell Hymes, do not assume grammatical knowledge to be the be-all of language learning. The sociocultural rules governing the use of language are considered equally significant, and Akan rituals on the birth of a child attest to this.

Naming Ritual

On the eighth day after a child's birth, when all signs of its survival are evident, the child is taken outdoors and a naming ceremony performed. One significant aspect of this ceremony involves engaging the child's most important organ of speech, the tongue. Initiating the child into the moral values of speaking, the offi-

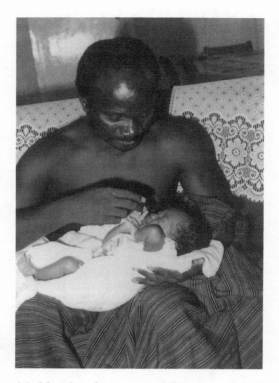

4.1. Man dropping water and liquor on a baby's tongue at a naming ceremony. Legon, 1990.

ciant baptizes the child's tongue with three drops of water (nsu) and three drops of liquor (nsa), accompanying this with the words,

Se wose "nsu" a "nsu"
Wose "nsa" a "nsa"

When you say "water"
Let "water" be your word
When you say "liquor"
Let "liquor" be your word

This ritual within the naming event initiates the child into the essence of truthful and discreet speech, the need for care, truth, firmness, and social sensitivity in the exercise of the spoken word. Water and liquor are employed in the ritual to symbolize contrastive social paradigms within the child's potential sphere of experience. The two elements (*nsu* and *nsa*), even though they sound alike, have different referents (like all minimal pairs in language) and cannot be substituted for each other. According to the Akan adage, *Nea a yède nsa yè no, yède nsuo yè a ènyè yie* (Rituals that must be performed with liquor cannot be performed with water).

As it reacts differently to the two elements, the child thereby demonstrates potential sensitivity to the vagaries of social experience, and the need to comply with the cultural rules of communication. The fact remains, however, that it is by slow degrees that the child actually learns to communicate.

The Akan generally delight in hearing their child utter its first meaningful word or phrase. Children speaking at an early age are considered potential sages. Tales of infants or fetuses speaking wise words to solve riddles or save stressful situations abound in Akan folktales. Even though such incidents are far from real, children with unusual verbal wit are highly prized, and it may be said of such a child that *òbenyin ayè kyeame daakye* (this one will grow to be a *kyeame* one day). In a few cases, such fluent children have at a very early age begun training to be akyeame.

Eloquence

The contrastive conditions of *wet* and *dry* are important metaphors for understanding how the Akan perceive fluency; for whereas wetness of the organs of speech denotes immaturity, dullness, and slurred speech, the condition of dryness allows for phonetic clarity and precision. It is said of the eloquent one, *n'ano awo* (his/her lips are dried up) implying that this speaker is capable of crisp, smooth, concise, and controlled speech—speech devoid of hesitation, mumbling, and forensic uncertainty (see also Nketia 1971). Ineloquence, conversely, is associated with wet lips—*n'ano nwooe*, "the lips are not dry, this person is not linguistically weaned." Lack of eloquence is thus equated with the salivated lips of a child (or a mentally handicapped person), capable only of babbling, imprecision, and meaningless chatter. The inability of the child to control the excesses of saliva, which naturally interferes with smooth speech, is the point implied here. Like the unweaned child, the inarticulate speaker loses control of speech situations.

Alternatively, a good speaker may attract the words *òyè aberewa nana* (this is the grandchild of the old lady), implying that the speaker's wit may have been passed on by the grandmother to whom s/he was constantly exposed (see Nketia 1971).

In another equation of wetness with defective speech, "speaking to an elder with water in one's mouth" is a habit to be avoided. Used metaphorically, it connotes speaking untruth, in apparent reference to a purposeful mumbling with intent to lie, insinuate, or abuse. Note that "water in one's mouth" conjures images of saliva, waste, and impurities. To purposefully activate or produce these during speech implies an attempt to transmit the impure–an untruth—or an attempt to denigrate the addressee. It is significant that the oath sworn by a newly installed chief to a superior king includes the statement *memfa nsuo nngyina m'anomu nnkasa nnkyerè wo* (I will never address you with water in my mouth), implying "I will never lie to you or address you with disdain," as in the following oath sworn in 1988 by a new subchief to the King of Ashanti, Otumfuo Opoku Ware II:

Pȯnkȯ Baafoȯ nana ne me
Safo Akoto nana ne me
Adȯntȯfo nana ne me
Boadu Kwadwo nana ne me
Ėnnė me nananom *akonnwa* a etȯeė yi
Otumfuor w'adaworoma
Wose mensȯ me nananom tuo mu
Na memfa nsom wo
Sė wofrė me anȯpa o
Sė wofrė me anwummrė o
Sė wofrė me anadwo o
Esum mu o
Ewia mu o
Mesuae meyi yadeė
Meremmfa nsuo nnyina m'anom
Nnkasa nnkyerė wo
Sė mede nsuo gyina m'anom
Mekasa kyerė wo a
Mesrė ntamkeseė ka ntamkeseė

I am the grandson of Ponko Boafo
I am the grandson of Safo Akoto
I am the grandson of Adontofo
I am the grandson of Boadu Kwadwo
Today, by your grace,
You the Great One have bidden me
To take over the gun of my forefathers
And sit on the stool that fell vacant
And serve you
When you call on me in the morning
When you call on me in the evening
When you call on me in the night
In darkness, in blazing heat
I swear to make illness an exception
I shall never address you
With water in my mouth
Should I ever address you
With water in my mouth
I violate the Great Oath

   In this oath, the new chief first identifies himself with his ancestry, then pledges loyal service to the superior king. Yet knowing how his new position will bring him into constant face-to-face communication with the king, the subchief swears to abide by the cultural norms of speaking. To speak in contempt of the royalty through a lie is considered a serious offense; to commit this violation on the sacred oath of the king is an even more grave breach of the law. The fact that the oath sworn by a new chief makes allusion to a communicative taboo in the royal domain demonstrates how seriously cultural speech rules are taken by the Akan.

Clan Myth

Even though the techniques of oratory are basically considered to be learned skills, the Akan believe it came naturally to one out of its eight clans, the anóna/agona clan, whose totem is the parrot, a bird of crisp "speech" well known for breaking the communication barrier between man and animal. The eloquence of the anóna/agona clan is considered to follow from the fact that it was saved long ago by the cackling "talk" of the parrot, as their clan myth relates:

> The prime ancestor of the clan was on a journey long ago when he met a murderer who stopped him, and asked whether he was alone or in company. He replied he had a following behind him. Each word spoken by the ancestor was further boosted by its echo from a parrot, giving the illusion that more clansmen followed and would seek revenge if the ancestor was killed. In fear, the murderer abandoned his scheme, and the progenitor of the anóna/agona clan went scot free, saved by the eloquence of the parrot.

Among members of ther anóna/agona clan, the associated saying goes, "When you see a lone bird, do not throw a stone; it may belong to a multitude." To the clan, the eloquence of the parrot is equivalent to the might of a multitude. Underlying this, evidently, is the belief in the supremacy of the spoken word over physical power.

Power of the Word

Unusual reticence, among the Akan, is abhorred. Absence of speech in a critical moment may worsen a crisis. The Akan say *se woankasa wo tiri ho a yèyi wo ayibone* (If you do not complain to your barber, you are given an ugly haircut); or *sè ankasa wo nam ho a ewe biew* (If you decline to complain about bad meat, you eat a bone). It is generally held that words properly negotiated may bring tense situations under control, as the following sayings attest: *Ȯkasa pa pam abufu* (Good speech drives anger away); *tèkrèma dè ma abaa tò* (The sweet tongue disarms the aggressor); *tèkrèma wò hò a èse mmò nkuro* (In the presence of the tongue, the teeth do not litigate). The tongue, lying between the two rows of teeth, literally staves off tension between the two. Furthermore, as mentioned earlier, one of the designs of the royal spokesman's staff depicts two birds with their beaks touching. The implied saying is *ano ne ano hyia a ntoto mma* (When two mouths meet, conflict does not arise).

Even though the spoken word may be used to the society's advantage, it is generally considered to have a double edge: the capacity to make or break. Good speakers are thus expected not only to know what to say, but also what not to say.

The destructive potential of the spoken word, and its power of fulfilment under

certain conditions explain the existence of two types of verbal taboos: *ammòdin*
and *ntam*.

Ammòdin refers to the unmentionable: a category of potentially destructive items
to which one may not refer by use of their regular names. Among the Fanti-Akan,
the items include *wòmma* (pestle), *waduro* (wooden mortar), *prae* (broom), *kaka*
(whitlow disease), and more. All these items may be generally referred to in speech
by use of the general referent *ammòdin*. They differ from the much bigger category
of profane words and their euphemisms, more commonly known in other languages, for verbalizing the regular designations of *ammòdin* without an apologetic
formula is believed capable of invoking a calamity. This taboo is not strictly
adhered to in present-day speech, yet elders within certain Akan communities
strictly enjoin its compliance.

Attitudes toward words here cannot be divorced from specific cultural beliefs
and practices. The belief underlying the use of *ammòdin* is that the materials out of
which certain objects are made embody powerful spirits and deities that must not
be invoked lest society become destabilized. Additional verbal taboos may appply
to devotees of certain charms and fetishes, in whose presence all mention of certain
items is forbidden. While certain *suman,* or fetishes, taboo the presence or verbal-
ization of items like *waduro* (mortar), others taboo literal references to *gyata* (lion)
or *òsebò* (leopard). Instead of these, euphemisms like *aboa kèse* (big beast) or *aboa
fufuo* (white beast), respectively, may be used. If such a taboo is violated, a particular fetish may lose its power until sacrifices are made to propitiate the offended
spirit (Rattray 1927:43–44). It is likely that verbal avoidances originally restricted
to devotees of certain fetishes eventually became generalized.

In any case, it is the power of the spoken word that is relevant here, its ability to
invoke the physical presence of the referent. It is thus not surprising that a passage
in Ashanti royal "praise" poetry about Osei Tutu, the warrior founder of the
Ashanti state, makes only an oblique reference to his ferocity, which must not be
unleashed by vain allusion to his name.

Ammò-wo-din ee
Ammò-wo-din ee
Osei Tutu, yèmmò wo din oo
Yèbò wo din a yèbò no ko so

The Unmentionable, alas
The Unmentionable, alas
Osei Tutu you are unmentionable
When we mention your name
It is solely at the battlefront

Note that the danger associated with mentioning the warrior's name is, paradoxically, neutralized by calling him "unmentionable."

The most important category of verbal taboos among the Akan is the *ntam,*
whose avoidance is rigidly complied with in all Akan societies. Traditionally, it is
the most important weapon in judicial proceedings, and may not be uttered unless it

is the wish of the speaker to begin a legal suit. A *ntam* often refers to a historical calamity—a defeat in war, a royal death, a natural affliction, or some marked unfortunate incident in the life of a venerable individual. The Akan believe that spoken reference to any such incident (often summarily referred to as *ntam kèse,* the great oath), is capable of leading to its recurrence, or of unduly stirring national grief.

The national *ntam*—that is, the prerogative of mentioning such a calamity—is thus, strictly, the property of the territorial ruler. The ruler makes it available for use by his subjects as a legal instrument to protect or claim their property, the condition being that it must not be pronounced to support a falsehood (see also Rattray 1927:205–215). Those who pronounce *ntam* are thus instantly arrested (*kye dadua*) and brought before the chief. Judicial proceedings then begin. Custom requires a costly sacrifice:

> A sheep should be slaughtered over the spot where the *ntanka* had taken place. This had a double significance, namely, (i) *religious*: the blood of the sheep was sacrificed to ward off evil threatened by the utterance (according to Akan belief), and (ii) *social*: this public ceremony (sacrifice) publicised the offence committed, and thus forestalled evasion by the culprit. Litigants who had occasioned the forbidden utterance were not penalised. The penalty was rather inflicted on the party against whom the judgment was given in the settlement of the dispute that had occasioned the mentioning of the *ntam* (Mensah-Brown 1976:160).

Indirection

The perceived power of the spoken word among the Akan calls for the deployment of various strategies of speaking that may obviate crises. These include avoidance or discretionary uses of verbal taboos, apologizing for their use, using euphemisms, or resorting to indirection.

Indirection, through the use of *kasakoa* (metaphor), *akutia* (innuendo), or an *èbè* (proverb), is one frequently used mode of controlling the potency of the spoken word. The ambiguity of indirection, in which there is often a shift from one domain of experience to the other, prevents the easy assignment of malicious motives to its user.

Indirection may find expression in circumlocution while addressing a sensitive topic, such as loan solicitation (boseabò) or other requests for favors. In such potentially embarrassing situations, the speaker may initially skirt the main subject and divert the attention of his potential benefactor to other issues. In broaching the topic, the speaker may begin from the root of the problem and work his way gradually to the circumstances that led to his need, sometimes confiding delicate but irrelevant domestic information to justify his cause. All this while, he may avoid direct eye contact with his addressee. In his reply, the addressee may adopt a similar strategy and break into a long narration explaining his own situation of need; or he may direct his explanation to a big loan he gave away to another in need, just a moment ago. The use of circumlocution in addressing sensitive topics appears to be a pervasive phenomenon in West Africa (see Tarr 1979:33).

Where the need for roundabout criticism arises, Akan may resort to *akutiabò,* where the speaker insinuates his or her reproofs while avoiding eye contact with the person who has occasioned them. *Akutia wȯ ne wura* (*Akutia* has a known target) the Akan say, implying that *akutia* always aims at someone—and that its target is expected to be aware of the subliminal frame of interpretation.

In certain domains of use, *akutia* has the stylistic trappings of the *ebè* (proverb), insofar as it constitutes a mode of indirect discourse which can be replicated in other situations. *Ebè,* however, is a broader concept, and encompasses both malicious and benign uses of indirection. The nature of the proverb as impersonal (ascribed to a third source) and as a cultural truism makes it an appropriate rhetorical device in the negotiation of delicate discourse (see Yankah 1989b), for as in all uses of indirection, there is only a minimal threat to the face of both speaker and addressee.

As discussed in this book, the use of intermediaries in public speaking is a specialized functional expression of the verbal art of indirection. The two are different facets of the same process, and it is not accidental that they merge in the oratory of the ȯkyeame, who is not only a social epitome of indirection but also displays a great fondness for verbal indirection in the fulfillment of his duties.

It would, however, be imprecise to conclude that the Akan predilection for indirection is unconditional. A few maxims point to the practical need for candor and openness in certain interactions. Proverbs like *twene anim da hȯ a yemmȯ nyèn* (When the drum is barefaced, you don't rattle the sides), and *paepae mu ka ma ahomka* (Candid words produce relief) point to the need for directness in situations where indirection may prove counterproductive. Similarly, in situations where a litigant is relying unduly on an unofficial surrogate during cross-examination in court, he may be reprimanded with the proverb *dua dum gyina hȯ a yènnyae nkȯbisa ahohorota* (We don't ignore the mighty odum tree/And seek knowledge from the mere ahohorota). While this proverb does not necessarily denounce the formal uses of triadic communication, it does decry the undue avoidance of responsibility through the use of proxies.

Related strategies used to avoid threats to face in speaking situations become evident in our discussion of formal oratory.

Formal Oratory

Opportunities for speaking abound in Akan society, and range from such informal situations as in *nkȯmmȯbo* (conversation) at home or streetside to highly formalized speaking settings at *badwam* or *adwabȯ ase* (public assembly), where *dwamu kasa* (oratory) is highly celebrated. It is important to note here that even though the word *dwamu* literally means public, it emphasizes the formality of the forum and the large quantity of discourse participants involved rather than simply the public nature of the locale. The phrase *bȯ dwa* means to cause a crowd to assemble for a formal speech event. In Ashanti royal panegyric, for instance, part of the meritorious attributes of King Osei Tutu, founder of the Ashanti state, includes his power to assemble crowds. The appellation *Osèe Tutu a wobȯ dȯm dwa* (Osei Tutu, who assembles crowds) does not only underscore the power of the ancestral king; it also implies his oratorical skills.

The challenge in *dwamu kasa*—public speaking or oratory—lies in exercising such speaking skills as can persuade two or more individuals at a formal forum. For as soon as speech moves from the domain of few and familiar to larger and less familiar audiences, the speaker is tasked to deal with a more complex social context, audiences of greater social variety. In this way, he puts his social and rhetorical integrity at greater risk. *Dwamu kasa* typically occurs at a public location such as an *ahenfie* (chief's palace) or *abusuafie* (house of a lineage head), which are spatially designed to cater to large audiences. Within individual households, though, various degrees of formal speech may take place, depending on the nature of the speech event under consideration.

The Akan do not have a consistent, elaborately devised taxonomy of speaking, yet "casual speech" (*kasa a emu da hɔ*) stands out as the unmarked style of speaking. It is the everyday mode of speaking, such as to friends and equals or relatives in purely informal settings. It is also the style to be used in articulating the prosaic forms of verbal art: *anansesɛm* (storytelling), *nsekuo* (gossiping), *nkɔmmɔbo* (chatting), etc. This mode of speaking is more open, direct, and sincere, and typically uses the home as setting. It differs stylistically from *mpanin kasa* (speech of elders) in the intensity of poetic devices used.

The label *mpanin kasa* marks a style of speaking and the social group that is its best exponent, as well as a speech setting. But *mpanin kasa* is not necessarily the exclusive preserve of elders, nor is it the only mode of speech adopted by them. The social group with which *mpanin kasa* is typically associated is also the nucleus around which formal discourse revolves. This mode of speaking typically situates the speaker within the public domain (*dwamu*) or formal assembly, where sociopolitical issues are debated before a consensus is reached. It is the constituent of formal speech and the stylistic touchstone of *dwamu kasa,* oratory. The speech of elders is essentially what is employed in oratory.

Speech events requiring the use of formal speech include *asenni* (judicial deliberation), *awaregye* (marriage rites), *awaregyae* (divorce proceedings), *mpaeyi* (libation prayer), *nkurobɔ* (litigants' statement at court), *amanneebɔ* (statement of mission by a visitor), etc.—indeed the gamut of verbal interaction, including greetings, at all formal assemblies.

Devices Used in Formal Oratory

Dwamu kasa, which is the province of elders, is too broad a notion to briefly characterize, particularly since it covers a very wide range of formal speech taxonomies. Even so, one can sketch some of its basic salient features, bearing in mind that the same stylistic devices may be used, but only to a lesser degree, in informal speech. *Dwamu kasa* is characterized by a greater density of ornate expression (such as proverbs and metaphor), honorifics and politeness formulae, and metacommunicative signals. Above all, a formal address has to be routed through an ɔkyeame, who receives the message and conveys it to the intended addressee.

4.2. Elders at a formal meeting. Agona Nsaba, 1988.

Politeness Devices

Since the risk to face is great in public speech, not only is speech often routed through proxies by the Akan. They may also resort to a speech form termed *obuo kasa* (polite speech). This refers to speech suffused with terms of politeness, or courteous addressives expressing deference or solidarity. In formal speech, where audiences are more often of high social status or imbued with political power, speakers make an extra effort to mark asymetrical social relations between them and the addressees through various deferential honorifics and phrases. In situations where the expression of social solidarity is desired, on the other hand, speakers may resort to in-group identity markers.

Expression of deference in formal speech includes the use of traditional titles, appellations, or honorifics in reference to dignitaries. In such formal settings, the use of titles or appellations is common, such as *Nana* (Elder or Chief), the stool name referring to a chief, or an appellation such as *Otumfoȯ* (The All-Powerful), *Ȯsagyefo* (Savior at War), and *Ȯdèefoȯ* or *Daasebrė* (The Magnanimous One). Such deictics have an evocative effect ,and mark a degree of social distance between the speaker and the dignitary.

Another significant mode of reference is the use of terms of respect such as *oburu, aberaw, akudȯntȯ, amu, ayisi, awo, apeaw, esȯn, ahenewa,* and *anyaado,* which are often suffixed to greetings, expressions of thanks, or requests. Their use denotes the addressee's identity or affiliation with a respectable social class or family. Unlike the honorific addressives above, these are used only at the end of an utterance, often as an assurance of respect and peaceful intent in ambiguous contexts. The speaker may, for example, add *aberaw* or *oburu* to an illocution to soften its force, if it runs the risk of being misinterpreted as a command. This is, of course, in addition to the use of common politeness phrases such as *mepa wo kyɛw, mesrɛ wo* (Please, I beg your pardon). The following statements thus differ in illocutionary force, the first being a command, and the second a request:

Fa ma me   Give it to me
Fa ma me aberaw Give it to me (with due respect to your social class).

Good examples of the use of the terminal deference addressive as a softener in formal discourse can be found in the following statement by Ɔkyeame Baafuor Akoto (one of the spokesmen of the King of Ashanti) during the formal installation of the Chief of Chiraa in June 1988, prior to the latter's pledge of allegiance to the king. Such pledges are often preceded by remarks by the king's councillors, who make formal pleas to the king to release the ancestral stool to the new chief. ("Gun" is used in the passage instead of "stool" in reference to the military duties of the chief in former times.) Ɔkyeame Akoto's words ended with a formulaic plea to the king:

Mese wo oburu, Nananom se w'adaworoma
Ɔne ne mpanimfoɔ ne n'amanfoɔ nyinaa aba sɛ
Ɛnnɛ ɔrebɛsrɛ ɔnana tuo ama no a
W'adaworoma, wonntan no
Wo nana ne no
Nti fa ma no a, oburu.

I tell you, oburu, the elders say
If by your grace
His councillors and people are here today
To plead on his behalf for the gun of his forebears
By your grace, he is not your foe
He is your grandchild
Give it to him, oburu.

Through the use of deference formulae such as *w'adaworoma* (By your grace) and the polite terminal addressive *oburu,* any appearance of imposition on the king is reduced considerably.

The terminal addressive may also be used in response to formal greetings. Instead of merely responding *Yaa* ("I acknowledge your greeting"), one may add a politeness addressive, as in *Yaa oburu, Yaa ahenewa,* in recognition of the distinguished social status or affiliation of the greeter. Occasionally, the greeter may immediately follow his formal salutation with a quick metacommunicative reference to his appropriate or preferred greeting addressive. Thus after greeting, he may quickly add *wɔgye me anyaado* (*anyaado* is my greeting response), to which those greeted may respond, *Yaa anyaado* (I acknowledge your greetings, *anyaado*).

In certain modes of formal speaking, politeness addressives may also be added to phrases of thanks, to emphasize the speaker's acknowledgement of his distinguished addressee.

It is not only deference terms of address that mark formal speech. Where group solidarity or commonality of interest with the addressee is the speaker's point of emphasis, s/he may use in-group identity markers or kinship labels such as *me ba, me wòfaase, m'agya, me nana* (my child, my nephew/niece, my father, my grandchild, respectively). These could be used in the literal sense of blood affiliation, but more often they are employed to denote metaphorical kinship proximity to the referent. Generally, individuals may be categorized within a set kinship scheme in formal speech.

Another stylistic mark of politeness in formal speech is its saturation with apologetic formulae and disclaimers. By apologetic formulae, I refer to pre-sentence disclaimers used by a speaker to key an imminent or apparent profanity, verbal taboo, or proverb. In this sense, apologetic formulae are metacommunicative, since they refer to aspects of an ongoing discourse. General metacommunicative devices in formal speech will be discussed in more detail below.

The principal apologetic phrase is *sèbe* (apologies), or where an emphatic apology is meant, a reduplication of the above, *sèbe sèbe sèbe,* or *sèbe mpèn aduasa* (apologies thirty-fold). The phrase and its related forms disclaim any possible impression of irreverent or offensive intent in the use of language. Alternatively, an apology may aim at narrowing the referential focus of a remark or apparently offensive language, and properly define the ratified addressee. "My words are not directed at the entire august congregation," the speaker may imply, "they have a narrower target." Or instead of initial apologies, a speaker may use a euphemism. Generally, euphemisms and apologies lend a measure of refinement to speech; they are rhetorical filters that aim at decorum and politeness in formal interactions.

In their use to key an imminent proverb, apologetic phrases disclaim a didactic intent and convey the humility of the speaker. Since proverbs may be used in part to convey a moral to the less sophisticated, they run the risk of affronting a cultivated audience. The speaker's quick apology, therefore, reassuringly implies that the proverb following is not intended to teach wisdom to the addressees, who are themselves repositories of wisdom. We shall see a good example of this verbal hedging a few pages down.

Beforehand, however, let me allude to a very significant stylistic feature of Akan formal speech—the profuse use of tropes: metaphor, proverbs and ornate expressions.

Metaphor/Proverbs

Speakers in public forums often seek to display their verbal artistry through the use of *kasakoa* (veiled speech or metaphor), *tete kasa* (archaisms), and *ebè* (proverbs). These are often the highlights of a good public speech. Audiences pay close attention to a speaker's turn of phrase and his use of ornate figures of speech. Such devices may be used both to animate and embellish orations through their poetic luster and to touch on themes of sociocultural delicacy that may otherwise offend dignified audiences in a public forum. In this case, it is the trope's obliqueness that the speaker may count on. The speaker may in fact decide to obstruct a clear understanding of his metaphor or proverb by omitting the contextualization cues that index meaning (Gumperz 1982, Yankah 1989a:130).

Such uses of proverb and metaphor agree with the general tendency to protect the vulnerability of face in formal discourse. In this case, as in all uses of conventionalized indirection, the speaker avoids responsibility for any potentially damaging interpretation, since he may plausibly disclaim an offensive intent.

As observed above, archaic expressions (*tete kasa*) may also saturate formal speech. Their use lends unusualness to the discourse while implying that it is in line with traditional thought and sentiment.

Generally, formal speech is more condensed and obscure than casual conversation. In indigenous terms, *emu pi*, "it is thick," not given to ready interpretation, or it is *tete kasa*, "speech of ancient times." Speech can be made even more intensely formal through the extensive use of metacommunicative devices.

Metacommunication

In using metacommunicative devices, the speaker makes exegetical remarks about the ongoing formal discourse; he makes the art of public speaking the focus of his comment, and thereby drops hints of the esthetic norms of his community. Thus, apart from filtering potentially offensive speech, metacommunicative devices in Akan formal speech may comment on the structure or esthetics of speech itself.

By metacommunicative references to structure, I refer particularly to the use of organizing signals by the speaker to ensure the structural integrity of his address. These include the use of itemization formulae such as *nea edi kan, nea eto so* (first, secondly), and terminating phrases such as *m'ano ato* or *m'asem ara nyen* (my speech is ended). As will be seen, speech about speech characterizes formulae used by the okyeame.

Besides references they make to the structure of an oration, metacommunicative markers may draw attention to the esthetics of speech. The speaker may indulge in self-cautioning, to demonstrate his sensitivity to the need for brevity, with the remarks *mennka mma no nnwa* (I will not make a lengthy remark) or *kakra a meka ne se* (the little I will add is as follows). Alternatively, members of the audience may advocate the abbreviation of a long, uninteresting oration with the words *ntiantiam, ntiantiam* (in brief, in brief).

It is only when a speech is formal that evaluative remarks may be made at its conclusion by the audience. Such remarks as *mmo ne kasa, mmo apeaw, w'ano huam* (well spoken) are made quite openly and are intended to be on-record evaluations of formal speech.

Any description of formal speech is incomplete, however, without reference to the required kinesic comportment on the part of the speaker. These norms include non-exclusive use of the left hand in gesticulating; baring of the shoulders; removal of footwear in addressing the chief or the chief's proxy; and finally, not placing oneself too close to the chief. It is not enough to route one's formal address through an ɔkyeame; the speaker's gaze and theatrics must draw and satisfy the public eye and ear. The ɔkyeame is the principal focus of all formal discourse. In the absence of an ɔkyeame, a public discourse risks losing its formality.

The above characterization of formal speech as polite, systematic, and conditioned to minimize threats to face would appear to justify Bloch's view (alluded to earlier) of formal oratory in traditional society as predetermined, impoverished, and deprived of innovative rhetoric (Bloch 1975:13). However, as will be seen in interactions cited in this book (chapters 6-9), it is within formal forums that creative wit in speaking finds its utmost fulfillment. The existing norms of formal speaking only provide a frame within which speakers may operate; there is great scope for recreating existing rhetorical patterns and creating new ones. This becomes more evident in the orator's conscious attempt to ornament the chief's word through proverbial metaphor and artistic elaboration that both surprise and satisfy expectations. Besides this, the formalization of public speech often challenges the creative wit of speakers who are up against the establishment. The challenge becomes that of creatively registering dissent, protest, or displeasure within the scope of the politeness frame. It is on such paradoxes that a greater part of creativity in formal rhetoric thrives. Speakers may burst forth in angry orations while still complying with every rule and maxim of politeness.

Then also, there are instances where orators have taken the opposite tack, registering protests through a discretionary avoidance of the existing norms of formal communication. In this case, a transgression of the norms may itself constitute a veiled political statement.

Amanneɛ̇ (Telling a Mission)

Speech skills and the control of situations through effective oratory are not necessarily restricted to public locations. It is true that within individual households, speech is basically informal among relatives and friends in their day-to-day interactions. Significantly, however, speech assumes more formal overtones during the reception of a visitor, whether it's a neighbor, a friend, a relative arriving from a journey, or a complete stranger with a formal mission.

In the construction of typical traditional houses, provision is often made for a speech setting or parlor (*dampan*) situated close to the entrance of a house. This space is commonly reserved as a forum for both private and "public" talk within the household. (Bear in mind that *dwamu,* "public," does not necessarily index a public location but rather a large number of discourse interactants, be it at home or at a public place.) Among other events, *dampan* provides a setting for *amanneɛ̇bo,* mission telling by visitors.

Cultural norms require that one visiting be properly seated, and the *amanneɛ̇*—the visitor's mission—formally solicited. If it is friends or relatives who are visiting, informal speech among interactants may prevail from the moment of arrival until a formal meeting is called to order. Thereupon social relations and speech registers are transmuted, and interactions assume greater formality.

After the visitor is seated, he is served with water and/or drink, on the assumption that he is exhausted from a long trip. Greetings of welcome are addressed to the visitor, and formal speech begins from this point. The host begins by narrating the prevailing domestic circumstance into which the visitor has walked, and concludes on a peaceful note: *Ɛha deɛ bɔkɔɔ, amannee?* "There is no bad news here, what's your mission?"

It is significant that even in situations where the meeting is prearranged and the host knows the visitor's mission in advance of his visit, *amanneɛ* is still solicited, with the remark *mpaninfoɔ se yɛnim nso yɛbisa,* "The elders say, though we know one's mission, we still inquire." This adage underscores the Akan's delight in creating opportunities for the celebration of eloquence in formal speech. The host here expresses interest not necessarily in the content of the message, but in the mode of narration, the verbal artistry with which the message will be presented, and the visitor's knowledge of the norms governing formal speech. The *amanneɛ* is presented with the initial formula *menkura no bɔne,* "I hold no bad news." If the news really is bad, a proverbial phrase may be used or hinted at—for example, "Family conflict is like a goat fight; horns are raised in fury, but softly lowered"—to denote an anticipated peaceful outcome. After the principal narration, the narrator concludes with the remark *Mebae a amanneɛ ne no* "That is the mission on which I have come."

In such domestic settings of *amanneɛbo,* use may or may not be made of an ad hoc ɔkyeame, depending on the nature of the mission, the availability of a third party within the household, or the social status of the speech interactants. Where one is instantly appointed to act as ɔkyeame, it is often one socially inferior to the host, sometimes a nephew. He becomes the focus of the speech interaction, receiving all messages and passing them on to the potential addressees. Playing ɔkyeame in such domestic settings is only a temporary role; for the office of ɔkyeame, as well as structural indirection in communication, properly belongs to the royal and associated domains.

Below, I exemplify *amanneɛbo* in a real-life situation (Asuom, 1984), where a man of 30 has returned from a journey and goes to a remote elderly relation, a woman of about 70, with a prayer drink. The young man pays the visit in the company of an older adult of 60. After the initial exchange of greetings, the young man is properly introduced by his older companion, who concludes his brief introduction with an invitation to the young man to tell his own mission to the old woman. The older adult justifies his call for direct speech, instead of the use of an intermediary, with the proverb *Yɛnnom aduro mma ɔyarefo,* "We don't drink medicine for the sick man." Whereupon the young man speaks his *amanneɛ* (note his use of proverbial speech, and his adherence to the prescribed protocol):

I hold no bad news
My apologies,
We don't dispense with the thumb
In tying a knot.
Thus if one visits home
And does not see the elders

He defaults
I visited So-and-So and met So-and-so
From whom I sought your whereabouts
I thus found it fit to come for a visit
And, if nothing at all, to seek traditional lore
For it is said,
It's when you get closer to the stream
That you hear a crab's cough
Mere visit is what has brought me here
Yet I haven't come empty-handed
I have brought you something
Receive this drink and say a prayer for me
Today is the fortieth-day festival
And I haven't come empty-handed
For it is said,
If Mr Let-Go is your name
We don't necessarily allow you
To ignore the demands of custom
As custom demands, I have brought a drink
Take, and pour libation
That's the news I have brought.

As is typical of the *amanneè* speech event, the mission teller opens and concludes his speech with the appropriate formulae, states his mission succinctly, and enriches it with relevant proverbs. He vividly compares the old lady with the thumb that is indispensable in tying a knot. This correctly establishes his addressee as an important social entity, a significant source of traditional wisdom, who cannot be ignored by the still-learning young man. Even though the proverb is a normal rhetorical device in the *amanneè,* the speaker significantly apologizes for its use, acknowledging the sapiential sophistication of his addressee. By prefacing his proverb with an apology (*sèbe, sèbe*) typical of formal speech, he implies, "I do not seek to teach you wisdom by my proverb, for you cannot be surpassed in traditional lore." This way, he displays sensitivity to the social context, and steps down the didactic tone of the proverb; after all, his speech is essentially a plea.

Note also the speaker's use of a second proverb, one that underscores the logic of his earlier one. Having noted the indispensability of the addressee to his social progress, the speaker further justifies the pains he has taken in his quest for unalloyed truth (authentic traditional lore) with the proverb image of the curious one who ignores hearsay and personally verifies the crab's physiological habits through a visit to its habitat. There is no substitute for authenticity and empirical evidence, he implies.

From this point, the speaker's *amanneè* moves to a more solemn phase and to its conclusion. He alludes to the religious significance of the day (it's a festival), and offers a drink for a libation prayer to be performed. Explicitly advocating adherence to traditional mores, the speaker combines his formal speech with a formal act, implicitly acknowledging their mutual interdependence.

Even though the above event does not take place at a public forum, the speech it inspires has formal overtones, indicating that a degree of formality may permeate certain speech genres even within the domestic setting. Evidently, the dual paradigm private/public is not necessarily coterminous with the informal/formal dichotomy.

Communication Functionaries

The best forum for the display of *mpanin kasa* ("elders' speech") or *dwamu kasa* (oratory) is evidently within the public domain, where speech skills are most important in the deliberation of public affairs. Public speech may be freely exercised by a wide array of individuals within the society: ordinary men and women may speak, as well as specific communication functionaries within the society, including the akyeame. To put this in a better perspective, I discuss below both the Akan social system and the communication intermediaries who serve it.

Sociopolitical System

The Akan social system, consisting of the *abusua* (lineage group or groups), *òman* (state), and *abosom* (gods), involves a system of intercommunication which the Akan consider crucial for the material and spiritual well-being of the state.

Each *òman,* or state, consists of subdivisional wings and *abusua.*

The term *abusua* refers to a social organization based on blood ties. Every Akan, by definition, identifies himself with one out of seven or eight *abusua* groupings. All members of one *abusua* are supposed to have descended from a common ancestress. *Abusua* is a wider concept than the nuclear patrilineal family consisting of father, mother and children, yet is a smaller concept than village or town. In order to coordinate and control the affairs of members of one lineage group, as well as maintain links with the spirit world, other *abusua,* and the *òman,* each *abusua* has its leader, the *abusuapanin.* He is the coordinator of the *abusua* and custodian of *abusua* property. He convenes and presides over all formal meetings of the lineage, at the *abusuafi,* home of the lineage head, where intra-lineage conflicts and problems are resolved in an open forum. The *abusuapanin* is the occupant of the sacred lineage stool, which represents the spirits of all deceased members of the lineage. He is thus the intermediary between the *abusua,* on one hand, and the outside physical and metaphysical worlds, on the other. In a sense he is a communication intermediary, representing the lineage in its interaction with the state and the ancestral world. Whether deliberating on intra-clan affairs or representing the clan at a higher administrative level, the *abusuapanin* relies heavily on communicative and forensic skills.

The biggest political authority, however, is the *òman* or state. This is administered by the *òmanhene* (king), who exercises political power through divisional chiefs, who often represent traditional military wings. These chiefs are autonomous in their administration over the divisions they control. Divisional chiefs in turn

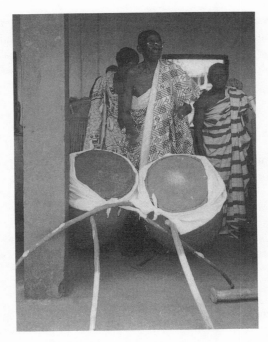

4.3. The talking drummer, a key communication
functionary. Kumasi, 1988.

exercise their control indirectly through *ahenfo,* if the localities are townships, and
adekuro if these are villages or hamlets.

All of the above functionaries have communication specialists—akyeame—who
may execute, ratify, or transmit their speech. The existence of a speech intermediary, however, does not excuse a chief's ineloquence. Chiefs are expected to be
adept in the handling of words, for in most cases, the chief's message, even if it is
reconstructed by his or her orator, is audible to the audience. In some instances, too,
the chief's words are transmitted by the ȯkyeame with merely a token formula
added. Thus the chief must speak reasonably well or be exposed to public censure.
Indeed, ineloquence on the part of a chief has sometimes led to destoolment (Saah
1987).

Each chief or king also has an *ȯkyerėma,* talking drummer, who through his
drumming is able to transmit messages over long distances, to recite the appellation
of the chief and other important personages, and to invoke ancestral spirits during
festivals and other special occasions. He is considered divine. The *ȯkyerėma* may
also recite state history on drums. In smaller villages, another important communication functionary is the *dawurubȯfo,* or gong beater, who is the public announcer
and informs the public, outside formal settings, about those decisions by the chief
and the chief's councillors that directly affect public interests. Moving from ward
to ward, the *dawurubȯfo* beats the metal gong to summon villagers, then announces

4.4. Village public announcer with a
bell (gong), an important communication functionary. Gomoa, 1982.

the chief's message, be it on communal labor, taxes, or impending celebrations.
Unlike the òkyeame, who is part of the chief's counselling body, the gong beater is
only a street announcer with no executive privileges.

In spite of the existence of other specialists, the chief or king is the key custodian
of tradition, key arbitrator of conflict, and key communication intermediary, even
though, as is evident, this latter function may be delegated.

Every unit within the hierarchy has a council of elders, *mpanimfo,* consisting of
all heads of the unit directly below, who may be chiefs in their own right. For
example, the king's council of elders comprises all the divisional chiefs, whose
council of elders also consists of the lineage heads, and so on.

The functionaries above also have religious duties; for since the Akan world is
made up of human and supernatural worlds, chiefs combine political and religious
functions. The latter consist in keeping touch, through libation prayer and other
religious rites, with the spirit world of gods and ancestors.

The *abosom,* gods, represent one of the supernatural dimensions of the Akan
world, standing next to the Supreme Being, *Onyame.* They are responsible for
linking the communities of the living, the dead, and the spirits, as well as for giving

moral and spiritual guidance to the living. Between Akan society and the pantheon of gods, the principal intermediaries are *akòmfo,* priests, who receive and transmit messages between the two worlds.

It is evident from the above that by the very nature of the Akan world view and its socio-political systems, communication intermediaries are indispensable for state survival and integration. It is significant that even though the above functionaries perform significant communication and intermediation duties, they do not attract the title *òkyeame.*

Outside the above political and religious hierarchies, general intermediation occurs within the society at large, between individuals or units, where the need arises. In general terms, one in need of representation to plead a cause may look generally for *òkamafo,* a term loosely applied to any person making a representation on another's behalf. This ad hoc position may be assumed by any relative, kinsman, or volunteer on behalf of anyone in need of representation to plead a cause. Such a surrogate is not the same as an òkyeame. Indeed, dirges sung on the occasion of death may lament the deceased as an *òkamafo,* often in reference to the deceased person's role as a friend of the needy. The allusion here is not necessarily to the individual's forensic or rhetorical skills, but rather the extent of his socio-political influence.

The general predilection for interveners or mouthpieces in Akan society explains the institutionalization of plea intervention within the Akan judicial system. In the absence of lawyers or judicial advocates within the judicial system, one proven guilty by a court may plead for leniency through an elder or a political functionary. In certain Akan groups, this position is appointive and institutionalized as a *dwanetoahene* (chief intervener) or a *dwanetoahemmaa* in the case of a female appointee. The verb *dwane toa* literally means "run to engage." The *dwanetoahene/dwanetoahemmaa* is thus the official under whose office one in trouble with the law may seek refuge. Such an advocate is not a lawyer (in the Western sense); he represents a litigant only after judgment has been passed.

Alternatively, any respectable functionary may intervene at the request of a guilty one. In most cases, the intervener occupies a stool, or holds political office. Ultimately it is often not the individual personality under whom the refuge or intervention is sought but his sacred stool, *n'akonnwa,* which inspires greater political and religious awe.

Thus after judgment has been passed and a penalty announced, the guilty one may say *Medwane toa* . . . (I seek the intervention of . . .), after which the intervener may publicly announce, "So and so has come to hold my stool" (*Wabèsò m'akonnwa mu*). Not much persuasive speech is expected of a judicial intervener; he may plead for leniency in a few words, but is expected to make an extended plea only in critical situations. The plea, in many cases, is a pro forma gesture, institutionalized to create room for leniency in the award of penalties.

But even if judicial interveners do not have much room for oratory, other elders, jury members, and political functionaries may be entitled to deliver extended and persuasive orations at formal meetings. Such functionaries, whether or not they are akyeame, are often masters of public oratory in their own right.

Below, I exemplify the use of formal oratory by an elder (not an ɔkyeame) representing his wing of the Ashanti state, during court proceedings in Kumasi, the seat of the state. This was during the heated discussion of a disputed succession to a stool in one of the Ashanti towns.

The speech was directed at a dissident subchief (called "A" below), who had expressed opposition to the manner in which the new chief of his town had been installed. In expressing his dissenting views, the dissident had made remarks that appeared to impugn the integrity of the great king of Ashanti Otumfuor Opoku Ware II, who presided over the meeting. Such a show of insolence was a sacrilege the elders would not countenance. In one speech after another, they argued for the instant arrest of the dissident and his supporters, and the levying of appropriate fines for the blasphemy. Representing his traditional wing, this elder spoke against a background of tension and highly charged emotions (Kumasi, Manhyia Palace 1988).

Manwerė
Deė yėsrė yėka ne sė
Nana A, wama yehunu sėbe n'adwene
Ene sė, wahuri atra ogya
Ama wira agu n'ani   5
A, sėbe, wama n'ani atra n'anintɔn
Aniėmmɔwoho a wayė yi
Yėhwė no
Wo nko ara na woyė hene wɔ fie ha?
Edi kan, Abontendɔmhene   10
Ommaa ne ho ntɔɔ no da
Etɔ so, ɔpė sė ɔkyerė sė
Tafohene nkyėn Benkumhene biara
Yėse wosa asa kyee a
Yėhunu ɔkraa ba   15
Yėpė sė Nana A, ɔte aseė sė
Bebrebe yi, kuntann kuntann
Bebrebe ne booboo yi
Yėabrė no
Na wo X—hene ne X—hene   20
Sėbe oburu, modi n'akyi yi
Bosomtweni, ɔdi kwaku tire?
Mo a sėbe, moretia Otumfuor yi
Mosuaee Daasebre nsamu
Moanya amane   25
Yėnkye mo dadua
Yėmmɔ mo ka a ėso!

We of the Manwere subdivision
We beg to say as follows:

Nana A, *my apologies,* has betrayed his thoughts
He has jumped over a conflagration
And blown cinders into his own eyes   5
A, *my apologies, has allowed his eyes*
To outstrip his eyebrows
We are all witnesses to his vicious conduct
Are you the only chief at this assembly?
First of all, he has never allowed the chief of Adonten   10
To have peace of mind
Next, he seeks to demonstrate that
The chief of T is superior to none
In the left wing division
It is said, *If you dance too skillfully*   15
You betray your slave parentage
We want A to understand
That we are fed up with his excesses
His arrogance and rowdy comportment
And, to you, Chief of B   20
And Chief of T
My apologies, Oburu
You who are supporting his cause
Does the Bosomtwe affiliate not taboo the monkey's head?
You who, *my apologies,* are violating Otumfuor,   25
Remember you swore an oath
In the hands of *the Magnanimous One*
You are in violation of the law
Arrest them, let's impose a heavy fine!!

In this speech, the speaker presenting the views of his subdivision begins with a performative, metacommunicative phrase to imply his modesty and deference to the august assembly, including the king. *Yɛsrɛ yɛka* (We beg to say), he pleads, almost apologizing for his contribution. This is followed by a more overt apology, *sɛbe* (lines 3 and 6), and later on by *sɛbe oburu,* the latter word being a term of respect for the king. Each use of the apologetic phrase frames the referential focus of the speaker's impending rebuke, lest it be misconstrued as a verbal assault on the general assembly: "My rebuke is exclusively directed at the defendant," he implies.

In saying A has been burned in trying to leap over a great fire, the speaker metaphorically depicts the defendant's wounds—his present precarious situation— as self-inflicted, the result of a miscalculated risk. "Dealing with the powers that be requires extreme caution, or else you are destroyed by your own schemings," he tells the culprit. The addressee has stepped beyond the bounds of acceptable behavior. To underscore this further, the speaker recalls the image of the eye that has reached beyond its natural limits. Such violations of the natural order may spell chaos.

The use of veiled speech here is in cognizance of the delicacy of the action—rebuking a fellow elder in a public forum—but it is also an attempt to assert the speaker's own social status. As an elder, he has to demonstrate his preference for elegance and obliqueness.

Following this, the speaker indulges in an overt organization of his address through formal enumeration, acknowledging the essential role of structural order in public speech. This is followed by the proverb of the skillful dancer who unwisely overindulges in his talent (lines 16-17). Public exhibition of dancing skills is highly appreciated, yet this may betray one's undignified ancestry. While this proverb is not a direct replication of the earlier metaphors, it still sustains the image of unwitting self-betrayal which the speaker associates with the defendant's demeanor. Note that at the beginning of his speech, the speaker literally proclaims the offender's act as self-betrayal—"he has laid bare his thoughts unwittingly."

This statement, which subsequent images underscore, indicates that obliqueness in word and behavior, or the concealment of one's intentions, is a widely accepted norm in Akan society. The Akan say *Etire nyè borófere na yèapae mu ahwè* (The head is not a pawpaw fruit that can be split to reveal its contents); in other words, human motives and thoughts can never be surely discerned from external appearances. Since obliqueness and ambiguity are highly valued modes of behavior, the defendant's rash and arrogant openness about his intent betrays the baseness of his motives.

The speech continues with frequent interspersal of apologies, appellations, and other honorifics directed at the king, whose august presence cautions the speaker to convey his aggressive theme in an elegant and oblique style. Each reference to the king is prefaced with an apology or a term of deference, another way of helping to mark the discourse as far from ordinary. Getting to the end of his speech, the speaker lends yet another measure of formality to his address through a proverb that once again charges the offenders with a violation of the natural order. The proverb "Does the Bosomtwe affiliate not taboo the monkey's head?" suggests that the offense the culprit and his accomplices have committed—their show of insubordination to the king before whom they had sworn fealty—is comparable to a breach of religious norms. Indeed, to pledge allegiance to the king and at the same time engage in an act that impugns his integrity is as serious a religious violation as a devotee of a spirit (a Bosomtwe) breaking a food taboo (by eating monkey flesh). Collectively, the proverbs emphasize the extent to which social order has been threatened by the culprits, a situation that calls for propitiation rites that alone can restore the balance.

5 / WOMEN AND RHETORIC

THE PREVIOUS chapter, in which we dealt with the socio-political base of oratory, made little or no reference to the relationship between gender and oratory. Yet it was assumed that most roles requiring rhetorical skills are assigned to males. This chapter deals with women's relevance in rhetoric within the royal domain, as well as their commonest modes of self-expression.

In the three decades of the contemporary women's liberation movement, a great deal has been written on language and gender—particularly in the United States and Europe—and several attempts made to efface male-dominated biases in the use of language (see, for example, Penfield 1987). In Africa and third world cultures [particularly, as well, where the gender gap appears to be culturally circumscribed,] the period has witnessed a slow but steady upsurge in the study of gender roles in agricultural production, literature, politics, and other spheres the West has traditionally associated with men (see Christine Oppong 1983).

Even though not much has been done in the study of gender attitudes in self-expression, the expressive power or limitations of the African woman cannot be easily separated from an assortment of social, political and artistic inhibitions, which are largely prescribed by tradition (see Bisilliat 1983, Ottenberg 1983, Arhin 1983). The fact is that aside from gender-specific art forms, where women have a monopoly over certain spheres, the historical tendency has been toward male domination.

Bearing in mind the close relationship between established political roles and the exercise of public speaking, one is particularly interested in the relevance of gender in political authority. In some parts of West Africa, it has been suggested that colonial rule, with its bias towards patrilineage, precipitated the submergence of female roles in traditional politics (Arhin 1983; Okonjo 1983). One cannot, however, overlook constraints in communication that have been imposed by indigenous cultural norms—the general expectation of reticence on the part of women in certain contexts (Hymes 1972:45). The restriction on women's expression, whether culturally or psychologically conditioned, appears to apply in most African cultures. However, a few cultural idiosyncracies prevail in different regions.

Among the Akan of Ghana, who are the focus of this discussion, male domination does not express itself in grammatical structure; gender is of little structural relevance. There are, for instance, no gender-based pronoun distinctions, even though nominal suffixes occasionally distinguish female names. An underlying gender tension, however, asserts itself in Akan oral traditions, where one occasionally comes across maxims, songs, or other expressive forms that appear to project one gender's view or another. From the male viewpoint, there are such song refrains in folktales as, "Women like ready-cooked foods/Women like ready-cooked foods;/Women, your mouths are as big as boiled yams." In proverb lore, there are maxims from female perspectives also, such as "When a polygamist is ill, he is starved to death" and "A man with thirty wives has thirty tongues," which are subtle protests against male polygamy.

In speech styles of Akan men and women, it is hard to identify significant areas of difference in the absence of thorough research, except for stereotypical characterization of women's speech as imbued with less diplomacy and more emotion (see also Keenan 1975 on Malagasy women). One can discuss, though, the institutionalized channels for Akan women's rhetoric, and examine the extent to which this affects their expressivity.

Gender Restrictions

First, the relationship between gender and verbal art. The existence of gender-specific genres in Akan makes it possible for women to assert their verbal wit in art forms for which women are traditionally considered to be favorably disposed. This includes the *nsuie* (dirge), which is half-spoken and half-sung amidst sobbing; and songs such as the *adenkum,* the *nnwonkorò,* and the *mmobome.* Significantly, the latter genre has militaristic overtones. Though Akan women generally do not go to war, they may sing and dance to *mmobome* in support of the warriors.

Certain genres, on the other hand, belong specifically to the male domain, either because their very nature is held to require masculine enactment (such as the *apae,* a royal panegyric energetically dramatized by bards to instill fear in the king's foes) or because their performance is ritually identified with male functionaries, such as the *mpae-yi* (ancestral prayer) communicated to the spirits.

These restrictions cannot be divorced from general practices and taboos regarding certain channels of communication, often restricted to men. I have in mind here major communication functionaries in the Akan society, as well as typical locations for oratory and formal argument.

In theory, it is true, formal meetings within lineages are not restricted by gender, even though in the presence of men, women are relatively mute during heated debate and argument. Key communication functionaries, however, such as chiefs, counsellors, lineage heads, akyeame, diplomats, public announcers, and so on have typically been male. The drummer of the talking drums, a key functionary in the communication system, must also be male. Besides this women, as a rule, must not touch the talking drums when they are in their period, since the sacredness of the drum is considered capable of being violated by an "unclean" woman. Furthermore, the chief's palace, which is the most common forum for oratory and formal argument, is not always open to women; they are prohibited from entering the premises or sitting over the judgment of a case when they are "unclean." The rationale behind such taboos is that uncleanliness in women is believed capable of weakening spiritual immunity. Thus by direct or indirect contact with her one becomes spiritually vulnerable.

The woman's freedom to exercise verbal wit appears, then, to be relatively limited.

The domination of the prime modes of artful communication by males is reinforced in Akan society by the following maxims (or proverbs) which emphasize the
woman's social subordination: *Obaa tò tuo a èda barima dan mu* (When a woman
buys a gun, it is kept in a man's room); *Obaa twa bòmma a ètwere barima dan mu*
(When a woman makes a talking drum, it is kept in a man's room); *Obaa tòn
ntoròwa, na òntòn atuduro* (A woman sells eggplant, not gunpowder); *Akokòbere
nim adekyeè, nso òhwè onini ano* (The hen knows the dawn of day, yet she looks to
the cock's crow). These proverbs underscore the woman's traditional deference to
man in situations requiring valor, initiative, and assertiveness.

In more recent times, however, this view has been changing, particularly among
the female elite, as is vividly demonstrated in the following dynamics of proverb
meaning. The symbol associated with Volta Hall, the women's hall of residence at
the University of Ghana, has traditionally been the hen. Whereas in the past the hen
symbol stood for the proverb "The hen knows the dawn of the day, yet she looks to
the cock's crow," the same symbol now stands for the proverb *Akokòbere nso nim
adekyeè* (The hen also knows the dawn of day), conveying a sense of equality with
man. Interestingly, the proverb *Anomaa antu a òbua da* (If the bird does not fly, it
sleeps on a hungry stomach), has been progressively modified in recent discourse to
emphasize female dependency on male as in, "If the male bird does not fly, its wife
and young ones sleep hungry." This revision has now been rebutted by women
with another: "If both mother and father birds do not fly, they and their young ones
sleep on empty stomachs."

Traditional Wisdom

The Akan society has from time immemorial not ruled out women in the political
structure. Indeed within traditional lore itself the *aberewa,* the old lady, is considered the epitome of wisdom, oral history, and eloquence. This is true of other
African cultures as well. The kingdom of Dahomey during the eighteenth and nineteenth centuries, was said to have 28 women chroniclers, who recited genealogies
on important occasions (Argyle 1966).

Among the Akan, men stepping out of a formal meeting to deliberate and take a
decision are, in idiomatic terms, said to be consulting *aberewa.* As noted earlier, an
eloquent and witty youth well versed in traditional lore and logic is referred to as
aberewa nana, grandchild of the old lady, implying that wit and wisdom have been
passed down to the youth by his or her grandmother. This identification of woman
with wisdom is further evidenced by her recognized role within the Akan political
hierarchy. In the villages, the official counselling body to the chief often includes
an *aberewa,* an older woman, or an *òbaapanin,* a female functionary responsible
for women's affairs (Arhin 1983:93). Besides this, though chiefs are typically male,
their positions are meaningless without an *ohemmaa,* queenmother, often a sister or
mother of the chief, who has a hand in the choice of a royal successor and partici-
pates in the legislative processes. The queenmother is the only one among the
chief's counsellors that can reprimand him publicly. She has her own court, where

she sits in jurisdiction over certain domestic issues; she also has her own body of counsellors and akyeame, orators who are mostly female. Within the female domain, then, there appear to be ample opportunities for formal talk by women. In Ashanti history, the role of queenmother once acquired military connotations. It is the military leadership of the queenmother of Ejisu, Yaa Asantewa, that inspired the war with the British Army in 1900, in a war that has been named after her.

Within the male-dominated royal domain itself, the female symbol is occasionally in evidence. Besides the occasional existence of female chiefs, proverb symbols on the staffs of orators of male chiefs sometimes depict some feminine attributes in chiefs in positive terms, in spite of the preponderance of the imagery of power and authority in such symbols. I have in mind here the symbol of the mother hen surrounded by its chickens, depicting the chief as a caring, loving mother; and another image of the hen with one foot on one of its chickens, symbolizing the proverb *Akokò nan nkum ne ba* (The hen steps on its young one, not to kill it). The latter proverb depicts the hen's care in disciplining its young ones; in other words, penalties are applied by the royalty as tenderly as the hen deals with its young ones; we punish not to destroy, but to correct.

The typical female expression of wit can be observed in the following situations: a) all-female forums; b) rare situations where typically male roles, like those of chief and royal orator, have been given to women in competition with men; and c) women's management of interpersonal conflicts in domestic settings.

Royal Court

Though the roles of chief and royal orator in Akan and many other parts of Africa are generally held by males, there are a few instances of women chiefs and orators among the Akan. There is the classic case of one of the Akan states of Ghana, Agona, which during the colonial times was known to have been ruled from time immemorial by a queen, an unusual custom in the Gold Coast. According to Ellis, she was not allowed to marry, but could purchase slaves as paramours. Successor to the stool was the eldest daughter of the queen who, at puberty, could also purchase male slaves. Any male children of the queen were sold (Ellis 1969:81). This custom was, however, not typical of the Akan in general; and among the Agona, it has ceased. Women generally do not advance to such positions of power.

Nonetheless, in recent times, there have been a few women chiefs and akyeame among the Akan; the chief of Agona Nsaba traditional area was a woman up to a few years ago, and so is the chief of Ekumfi Atwia, a village in the central region of Ghana, whose assertiveness is very well known. This chief provides an example of indigenous rhetoric at its best. Her official orator, whom she often outstrips in eloquence, is male. For female akyeame, I cite the example of Kwahu Aduamoa in the eastern region of Ghana, where a male chief has a woman as his *akyeamehene,* head orator. This is besides several instances of queenmothers, like that in present-day Ashanti, whose cluster of speech intermediaries is sometimes headed by a woman.

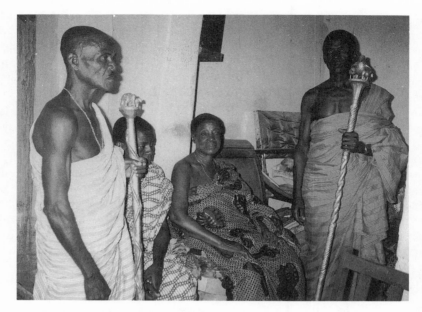

5.1. The chief of Agona Nsaba traditional area, Nana Agyemfra Nyama I (a woman), flanked by her three male akyeame, one sitting, two holding staffs. The left staff depicts an elephant with an antelope beside it: "The elephant is huge in vain, it's to the antelope that the state belongs." The right staff depicts a hen surrounded by its chicks: "Mother hen with her chickens," also called, "The hen steps on its young one not to kill it." Nsaba, 1988.

Chieftaincy

The chief of Atwia, Nana Baah Okoampa III, whose title means "true fighter," a few years ago explained her ascendancy to the royal throne as follows. Note the density of traditional lore and proverbs in her speech: "We belong to the *dehyena* clan; our totem is the lion. When my great-grandfather settled here, he was later joined by his kinsmen; for as the elders say, 'One person does not stand in council.' There are seven clans in this village. But 'the path your ancestors paved to your village, whether good or bad, becomes the only access route for strangers.' My grandfather constructed a good path; and that explains my success as a woman chief.

"When the stool fell vacant, my brother was the next in line; but he was a truant. I was a baker; I didn't intend to be a chief, because I was a mere woman, and never went to school, but I was chosen to succeed my grandfather. I didn't buy my way to the throne; and my manner of wearing the royal cloth clearly shows I am not queenmother, but a chief.

"As to my verbal wit and knowledge of traditional lore, I learnt that from my mother, who lived in a locality where there were several chieftaincy disputes. My brothers and I sat through most of those deliberations, and I learnt to speak well. As far as chieftaincy matters are concerned, my mother is my mentor. 'He who carries the leper knows the cure for leprosy'; and 'If you see a cripple at the outskirts of the town, do not take him to be handicapped.' I am a woman chief, but not to be taken for granted."

The eloquence of this chief does not express itself only in casual chat; it finds its best fulfillment in public speech, where she completely displaces her male orator. The official inauguration of a storytelling theatre at her village provided one such opportunity for oratory. She delivered a moving libation prayer whose speed, metaphor, and historical allusions set her audience nodding in appreciation (Atwia 1988).

Otwediampɔn Kwame
Yɛkyerɛ wo nsa na yɛmma wo nsa
Ndɛ adzesaa yi, Atwia kodzi o, Atwia kodzi o
Wɔwo ba a wɔto no dzin
Na yɛreto no dzin ndɛ   5
Na dzin a yɛroto yi
Yɛndze no mbusu
Ɔdɔ nko
Yɛdze nsa rekyerɛ wo
Ma ehyira do ama hɛn   10
Ma wo mba kuw a yɛwɔ kurom ha nyinaa yeanya siar
Fa wo tum na w'ataban fa hyira do ma hɛn
Finfin na ase mba wɔmbɛgye
Okatakyi, Okatakyi bɛgye nsa nom
Bɛgye nsa nom awisi   15
Nkyɛ yɛyɛ mbofraba a
Nkyɛ wɔrekeka a yɛnka bi
Nanso sɛ mbre fir siw do
Na sɛ ankɔto no ntsɛm a
Ɔyɛ dɛn araa benya kor wɔ mu   20
Adan w'ekyir egya
Ei, mo nkonguafo nyinaa, wombedzidzi wɔ ha
Ndɛ adzesaa yi, yɛrefrɛ Nananom
Yɛrefrɛ nkan mpanyimfo a wɔboa kodzi yi
Nkyɛ yɛma wɔ eyiadze eyiadze wɔ ha   25
Na mamma kwan
Medze korɔ Nkran
Mankɔ sukuu a nna maayɛ gyan menam Ekumfi?
Nyame kyɛ me adze bi a wɔfrɛ no ndze
Ma medze yɛɛ adwuma wɔ radio do   30
Ɔyɛ Kwaku Donsuro
Na sɛ akɛyɛ yei wɔ baabi a
Nkɛyɛ yei wɔ wo kurom

Kȯbena Adu
Mo nyinaa mongye me bom   35
Na momboa mbofraba no,
Na ndė kodzi yi yėayė nkȯdaa
Finfinimba aba mu
Ekyirmba so aba
Sė ikofua ȯdze na ȯbȯ na itu a   40
Edze kyerė amanfo
Ntsi ndė yėrotu bayer yi
Yėdze akyerė amanfo
Otu Amanfo, na n'ekyir
Nana Maanan Ntofur   45
Ndadzeban
Odum Kweku
Amoako Kwesi,
Owo na sė wȯdze kėntsėnpan mpo ba wo do a
Wȯdze nam kėntsėn kȯ fie   50
Gye nsa nom. . . . .

The Dependable God of Saturday
We only show you drink, we do not serve you drink
This evening we celebrate
Atwia storytelling, Atwia storytelling
When a child is born, it is named   5
Today, we are naming it
We are not naming in the name of evil
It's for love's sake
We are showing you drinks for your blessing
That your children in this village   10
Would live in prosperity
Protect us under your wings
The middle wing, the southern wing
Receive drinks
The valiant one, receive drinks, *awisi.*   15
Children were we, unfit to speak in public
Yet "when mushrooms sprout on a hilltop
And you arrive too late for a good harvest
There is at least one to count on"
Come all ancestors of the stool   20
Today we invoke you all
Come and dine with us
We invoke all ancestors that nurtured the tale telling
Our stories were originally restricted to funerals
Yet I wouldn't allow us to stagnate   25

I took it to Accra
If I didn't go to school,
Does that make me hopeless in Ekumfi?
God gave me the gift of voice and tongue
Which I put to good use on the radio   30
It's me that started the Kweku Donsuro (tale program)
On the radio
Would you not better prosper in your home
Than in another's?
I thus brought home my voice   35
And the enterprise has thrived
Kobena Adu and his following, lift me up
Help the children
Some are middle-aged, others are youths
"A matured yam is dug out and displayed"   40
Today we have dug out the yam to display
Otu Amanfo and his following
Nana Maanan Ntofur,
Ndadzeban, the Iron Wall
Odum Kweku,   45
Amoako Kwesi
It's you whom the poor person visits with an empty basket
And returns with a basketful of fish
Good parent and widower
Receive drinks. . . .   50

This performance was a combination of effective delivery and drama. The chief's loud, agitated voice, rumbling low tone, restlessness, gesticulations, and dramatic pauses heightened the theatrical effectiveness of the rendition. Combined with the proverbs, appellations, and historical allusions therein, the prayer had a highly evocative effect on both performer and audience, and was greeted with a unanimous *Mo ne kasa* (Well spoken)! Moved by the lineage history and deities she had recalled during the prayer, the chief, completely overwhelmed by her own performance, instantly asked for a drink.

In this prayer, one also notices a gradual integration of the performer's personality with the message; she partly embeds her own sociocultural history, obliquely depicting her social progress from a youth unqualified for public speaking to an indispensable voice in public debates. Note also the oblique comparison of herself to a sole mushroom at the hilltop, in part a reference to her role as a pioneer in female leadership.

Even though this chief has an official male ȯkyeame, her natural capabilities in public speech oftentimes overshadow the rhetoric of her orator (who in normal circumstances should have said the public prayer), sometimes reducing him to silence in public forums.

5.2. A woman ȯkyeame, Eno Asuama, with a staff depicting a bird with a snake's head under its claw: "If you hold the snake's head, the rest of it is mere thread." Aduamoa, 1988.

Orators

The concept of female akyeame is a rarity in Akan, but need not be so, owing to the traditional association of women with wit, fertile memory, and traditional wisdom in Africa. Indeed, there are clues that orators or the speech intermediaries of the king of Dahomey included women. According to Dalzel, "If the chief officers wished to speak to the king, they first kissed the ground, then whispered their pleasure into the ear of an old woman, who communicated to the king and brought his answer" (Dalzel 1793:35).

In present-day Ghana, there are a few cases of male chiefs whose akyeame are female, and several instances of queenmothers having a combination of male and female orators. Considering the wide range of roles played by akyeame, from diplomacy to prosecution, this provides ample opportunities for self-assertion, even though the cultural limitations imposed on women sometimes interfere.

A significant example is Eno Asuama, the orator of the male chief of Aduamoa, in the Kwahu district of Ghana. The chief, Nana Bediako Akenten, has four akyeame, among whom is this 60-year-old woman of 20 years' experience. The woman told of the circumstances of her appointment:

"My brother was the chief's ȯkyeame; when he died, I was asked to step into his position. I was at first not interested, but the chief thought I would be capable. For even as a woman, I had played a leadership role in opening the branch of a church in a nearby village, and he thought I could transfer my leadership qualities to the royal court. They say, 'It is a good marksman who is asked to guard a game animal's trail.' After all, my father Yaw Gyimah was himself an ȯkyeame; and if I, child of an orator, have been chosen for the position, why should I decline?"

Eno Asuama takes a leading part in prosecution and public debates at the chief's court, moderates verbal exchanges between the chief and his audience, and occasionally settles cases all by herself. Despite her gender, she appears to be the chief's favorite orator, due to her unusually fertile mind and her effective control over words—attributes that are indispensable in an ideal elder. "From my birth to date, there is nothing that has happened before me I cannot recollect; there is nothing I ever forget. It's God's talent. He has also given me a talented tongue to cool tense situations. . . . My tongue has no pepper on it. It's a gift from God."

Like her male counterparts, Asuama holds the orator's staff when speaking in public; unlike them, however, she is prohibited from saying a libation prayer on the chief's behalf.

The Akan queenmother more normally has female *akyeame*. Though the queenmother is often, in reality, the chief's sister, she is considered the "mother" of the chief and readily makes her experience and historical knowledge available in the management of crises, a fact which corresponds with her image as mother. Besides playing a crucial role in appointing a chief, she has jurisdiction over certain cases pertaining particularly to marriage and divorce. Her public duties require the use of counsellors, orators, and diplomats, whose number often depends on the range of her responsibilities. Almost all queenmothers have a female *ȯkyeame*. Where a queenmother has more than one orator, the group may include men. Like orators of chiefs, queenmothers' akyeame stand up when their patrons speak; unlike them, however, they do not use *akyeamepoma,* orators' staffs. I cite three examples of the rhetorical responsibilities and limitations of queenmothers and their orators, from Ashanti and Kwahu.

The queenmother of Ashanti, Nana Afua Kobi Serwaa Ampem III, has jurisdiction over certain specified towns and villages in Ashanti. She presides over cases ranging from land disputes to curses, marriage, and divorce problems emanating from the villages under her jurisdiction. Her counsellors include men, some elderly women, female courtiers, and surviving wives of former kings of Ashanti. She has six akyeame, two of whom are women, and four men.[1] Her *akyeamehene* (head orator) is Nana Adwoa Pinaman, a woman of 60, who is herself queenmother of another village, Ėserėso. Indeed, by heredity, every queenmother of Ėserėso is automatically the head orator of the queenmother of Ashanti.

"We are kinsfolk," she said, "the Ashanti queenmother and I. In the olden days, when the queenmother of Ėserėso visited the state capital, the Ashanti queenmother invited her to be her orator."

---

1. Even though the queenmother of Ashanti has positions for six akyeame, only three are active: two men and one woman. A second woman orator had become too elderly and infirm to perform her duties at the time of this research in 1988.

5.3. The queenmother of the Ashanti, Nana Afua Kobi Serwaa Ampem III, arriving at the funeral of her brother, Nana Bonsu. 1990.

Being the chief spokesperson, she does not only take part in judicial proceedings at the Ashanti queen's court; she is the only ōkyeame privileged to enter the hallowed stool room with the queenmother to perform rituals, including libation prayer. "It all begins during installation. To inaugurate your access to the sacred room of the ancestors, you go through sokanhyire rites; you slaughter the sheep with which your initiation rites will be performed; it is after those rituals that one qualifies for continuous access to the stool room. I went through all that to earn the exclusive privilege of access."

Even so, as a woman, she is considerably limited in her duties. "I neither enter the sacred stool room nor go to formal meetings when my fingers are bruised [that is, when menstruating]. In that case, I am represented by one of the other akyeame."

The female orator of the queenmother of Kwahu Aduamoa has even more severe limitations; unlike her Ashanti counterpart, she has no access to the stool room at all. In the words of the queenmother, Nana Akumwaa Sapomaa: "Yaa Mansa is my sole orator; yet for the purposes of rituals at the stool room I have appointed a male, who is solely responsible for the rituals and does not speak in public. He is not officially an ōkyeame, but is called in only on festival occasions to make sacrifices and pour libation in the stool room."

Besides cultural limitations imposed on female akyeame in the exercise of their public duties, their rhetorical potential is often not fully fulfilled when their coorators are male. They tend to be dominated by the males in public functions, and assert themselves either when they are their chief's sole orators, or in the absence of their male counterparts. This concession has been made by the female head orator of Ashanti, and also the female orator of the queenmother of Agona Nsaba.

If limitations on female orators, whether psychological or cultural, restrain their expressiveness in male-dominated public forums, one could turn to other areas where the expressive wit of the woman has unlimited fulfillment. I refer to rhetoric within domestic settings.

Domestic Tension

Even though women among the Akan have been stereotyped as emotional, less discreet, and relatively undiplomatic in speech, a close look at communication in periods of tension reveals a concentrated use of verbal and behavioral tropes in the management of stressful situations. In an attempt to obviate open confrontations among co-wives or couples, Akan women have been known for incisive use of various modes of indirection, particularly *akutia*—a mode of ambiguous innuendo or malicious comment in which the speaker avoids eye contact with, or direct reference to, the target. In its various reflexes, this mode of communication may find expression in *ebebuo,* proverb speaking, where the metaphorical and impersonal nature of the proverb lends considerable style and ambiguity to the message. In discourses involving delicate themes this mode of speaking is ideal, since the speaker wishes to save the interaction from degenerating into chaos.

Uses of *akutia* by women may be exemplified from a few proverb verses narrated by a professional proverb custodian, whose function it is to document and keep new proverbs that have been composed in the heat of domestic discourse. After a speaker has composed or effectively used a proverb, particularly in a conflict interaction, she may register it with the custodian and narrate the circumstances that triggered the proverb (Yankah 1989:183–213). The custodian then moves from ward to ward narrating the proverb and the circumstances of its original use to the public.

Here are a few examples of such well-crafted, reflective statements by women, most of which were triggered by matrimonial conflict and stress:

Amma Bisiwaa of Kwahu Asaaka
She spoke her proverb
That "man is not a pillow
Upon which to rest one's head."
She got married to a man
Who bought a lot of things for her
When things didn't work out and they divorced
The man took back everything he gave to her
Leaving her with nothing
She spoke her proverb

"Man is not a pillow
Upon which to rest one's head."
She will never again put all her hopes in a man.

Here the woman is compelled to convey her disappointment in metaphor. The experience she has undergone is personal, yet it provides useful lessons for society in general. The image she conjures to state her case is also in partial critique of the traditional Ghanaian overdependence on man by woman, for material support. Woman should assert her economic independence and fend for herself, or else man will forever hold her to ransom, she implies. The above situation is closely related to the following, where another woman, disappointed in the sour turn her marriage had taken, composed the following in a heated discourse with her husband:

The deceptive sugarcane fruit:
Sweet at the bottom, tasteless on top.

That's how marriage is, the woman adds in explanation; it's sweet at the beginning, and gets progressively sourer. In a similar vein another woman, Akua Dufie, was said to have spoken the following to her husband, remarking on a marriage which, to her surprise, had turned problematic:

The ripening pepper fruit I thought would be sweeter;
I hardly realized the more it ripens the spicier it gets.

Appearances are deceptive, the women imply in their witty remarks.

In some instances men, returning to wives they had earlier divorced, are rebutted with proverbial remarks, either drawing their attention to an ideal they had ignored or criticizing them for their lack of foresight. Consider the following verses from the custodian's corpus:

Adwoa Oode
She comes from Brekuso in Akwapem
It's she that spoke her proverb,
"If you support the plantain tree
Support the banana too
For in times of hunger, you cannot tell
Which your savior will be."
She married some man,
But the man divorced her,
And returned soon after, pleading,
"I have returned to marry you."
The woman replied,
"Me whom you jilted for another woman?
I will not marry you.
If you support the plantain tree

Support the banana too;
For in times of hunger, you cannot tell
Which your savior will be."

The plantain and banana trees bear similar fruits; indeed they are both similar in substance. Having weak fibrous stems, both should normally be given supports against stormy weather. But the banana (eaten only as a snack) is often ignored by the imprudent farmer, who pays greater attention to the plantain. Yet in hard times, the banana is an important substitute, and it may be the only source of sustenance. The woman here compares her state of neglect to that of the banana, which her negligent husband now seeks as a substitute. "You don't deserve me as a last resort because you neglected me," she implies.

Finally, note the following proverb, inflicted on a man who became wealthy through his wife's help and then took more wives, neglecting the original; the latter insinuated:

Even as it blossoms, the apurokuma tree has killed the monkey;
Oh, how dangerous it will be when it bears fruits!

The apurokuma tree is poisonous, particularly its fruit. Because they live in trees, monkeys are especially apt to be victims. Here, the woman sneers at the man, cautioning that there is indeed more to come of the havoc her ungrateful husband has unleashed upon the world.

Textile Rhetoric

Among the channels that Ghanaian women typically employ to express themselves, there is one on which they hold a virtual monopoly. I refer to the use of cloth design, along with the mode of wearing it, not just to praise political heroes, to commemorate historical events (Spencer 1982), and to assert social identities, but also as a form of rhetoric—a channel for the silent projection of argument.

Use of garments as a mode of argument by women exists in most African cultures. It is found not only in Ghana, Nigeria, Kenya, Uganda, Tanzania, Zaire, Mozambique, and other African countries, but also in the Caribbean, where it has been noted among the Paramaribo of Surinam (see Amory 1985; Herskovits 1936:3–9).

In general, various clothing domains that communicate messages include sandal designs, head scarves, hair braiding patterns, and textiles. Among textiles in Ghana, the traditional silk (*kente*) cloth (woven on a loom) and the stamped funeral cloth (*adinkra*) convey messages based on the designs in them. The cloths may be named after individuals, events, and social messages, including proverbs (Rattray 1927:236–268). These generally may be worn by both men and women on special occasions, though a few designs are restricted to royal wear.

The most popular channel for textile rhetoric is, however, the modern wax print, introduced from Europe at the end of the last century. Africans acquired a taste for these through their introduction by traders of the Dutch East India Company. In addition, West African men who had served as soldiers in Indonesia brought back batik cloth (Spencer 1982:8). Since the 1960s, modern wax print cloth has been produced in Africa in large quantities, supplemented by imports from Switzerland, Holland, and England.

Whether imported or not, the wax print is generally less expensive than the traditional cloth, and is worn on a wider variety of occasions, both in domestic and public settings. More important, it is an invaluable rhetorical asset for women, owing to the messages their names convey. In East Africa, the *kanga* cloth is the most significant mode of female textile rhetoric; its messages, however, are not encoded in the design but are written in the Swahili language (Amory 1985). Among the Paramaribo of Surinam, the rhetoric is expressed mainly in the style of wearing the headscarf or its design. There is often no direct link between a headscarf's design and its associated name; the connection is arbitrary (Herskovits 1936:7). In Ghana, by contrast, there is usually a direct link between design and message—the name often embodying a visible image in the design.

Textile rhetoric is women's lore in Ghana, partly because women wear the wax prints more often than men; but also because the retail outlets for wax print cloth are controlled by women. The specific names assigned to modern wax prints rarely originate from the factories where the cloths are manufactured. Cloth manufacturers introduce the design and the local retailer seizes the opportunity to give it a name based on a current happening, popular phrase, idiom, satirical statement, or existing proverb. Foreign manufacturers have, of course, studied the taste of African consumers, and accordingly introduce designs that are likely to appeal. In the words of Spencer (1982:8),

> European manufacturers have continued to export cloth to Africa up to the present. Aware from the outset that African buyers are discriminating, they have designed fabrics for these markets with local tastes in mind. Regional color preferences, for example, are well known and reckoned with.

Even so, the responsibility of naming the fabrics rests with the female retailers. Commercial appeal is partly based on the extent to which consumers identify with the textile's message. Thus the guiding principle in the naming process is often cultural appeal allied with simplicity: long proverbs and idioms are truncated so that customers can more easily remember them.

Cloth names in Ghana, for example, range from simple Akan phrases such as *Akyekyedeè Akyi* (Shell of a Tortoise) or *Kwadu Sa* (A Bunch of Bananas) to proverbs. Thus a cloth with a staircase design attracts the proverb name *Owuo Atwedeè Obaako Mfo* (Death's Ladder is Not the Monopoly of One Man), a way of saying "we shall all die one day," which makes it very appropriate for funeral garb. Another design, featuring an object that looks like a worm, has been called *Aboa bi Reka wo a* . . . (The Creature Biting You . . .). This is the truncated form of the longer proverb, *Aboa bi reka wo a efi wo ntama mu* (The creature biting you belongs to your own cloth), implying that your worst betrayers are often your best friends, for these know your vulnerable points. This cloth serves as an appropriate insinuation directed at unfaithful colleagues.

The most significant aspect of textile rhetoric is, perhaps, its use to express domestic conflict in polygamous households; for behind the facade of daily smiles between co-wives are often deep-seated tensions. In the words of one woman, Baanee of Nyinahini, who registered a proverb with the proverb custodian, "Rivalry between co-wives is like cow dung, crusty on the surface, messy at the bottom." This surface harmony is maintained by a tacit agreement to manage conflict through indirect communication, the most convenient of which is the wearing of proverb-embedded wax prints.

The existence of this unspoken code between rivals is even confirmed in meta-communicative terms via the wax cloths themselves; for one of the most popular designs used to negotiate conflict between co-wives is *Ahwene Pa Nkasa* (Precious Beads Are Silent). This is a design of bead-like objects strung together. The wearing of beads around the waist is a common female habit among the Akan, particularly after initiation into womanhood. The beads hold in place the woman's undercloth worn between the thighs during menstruation. Outside its practical use, the wearing of beads is also of aesthetic value. Yet beads are of different qualities. Akans put a higher premium on precious types, such as the *bota* and the *gyane,* which are more solid, heavier, and less noisy. The textile proverb above thus commends the reticence of the wearer and ridicules the rival's fondness for empty talk; "empty barrels make the most noise," it is implied. A courteous woman is less garrulous. Moreover, silence is itself an effective mode of rhetoric.

A woman celebrating her success in drawing her husband's attention at the expense of her rival may tease her co-wife by wearing the textile *Borofere a eye De na Abaa Da ase* (It's a Sweet Pawpaw Tree under Which Lies a Stick for Plucking)—in other words, "It is my sweetness that has attracted the man's attention." Another textile design, *Woko Aware a Bisa* (Seek Counsel before Marriage) may also be used to comment on a co-wife's sense of indiscretion. Other textile innuendoes are more blunt, for example, *Me ho ye fe kyen me kora* (I Am More Attractive than My Co-wife). Occasionally, the lower cloth may be wrapped around the waist with a terminal knot at the back to communicate the innuendo *Okwasea bi Di M'Akyi* (A Fool Follows Behind Me), in reference to the co-wife.

When a proverb statement is expressed through a non-oral channel like the cloth, indirection is achieved twofold: first through the very use of a verbal metaphor (proverb), and also through the subtle shift from a verbal to non-verbal channel of discourse.This way, the art of persuasion attains its utmost realization, as a nonviolent means of crisis management; after all, in the use of such ambiguous modes of rhetoric, the user always has available to her institutionalized avenues for retreat, should she be challenged by the law of slander. Among the women of Ghana, rhetoric is muted but, like the precious bead, extremely treasurable.

6 / ORATOR AND CHIEF
The Politics of Immunity

THIS CHAPTER discusses the nature of the link between the chiefs, their orators, and third parties, with a view to putting into a wider perspective the ethnographic rationale for the avoidance of face-to-face encounters with a chief. As has already been noted, the Akan have a whole system of avoidance rituals that promote indirection in communication. This is contrived to minimize hazards of face-to-face engagements, but it also provides opportunities to lend finesse and elegance to formal communication.

The issue is better perceived through a closer look at the two allied institutions, chief and ɔkyeame; the process of appointing an ɔkyeame; and the nature of the bond that links the two functionaries, as well as the assignment of responsibility in such joint enterprises. If an ɔkyeame is the chief's proxy in discourse, the question may arise as to who takes responsibility for flaws or acts of indiscretion, and who takes credit where this is due?

Answers to these unfold from a closer look at the sacredness of royal space and its implications for accountability in Akan communication theory. As will be seen, the issue revolves on what may be called *the politics of avoidance,* which imposes constraints on the organization of word and space in discourse within the royal domain. Also relevant is the issue of nonvocal behavior such as gazing, which here is not simply a means of obtaining sensory information but is itself a social act (Goodwin 1981:30, Goffman 1963:92, Simmel 1969:358-359). The bodily and visual orientation of the discourse participant is conditioned by the royal presence, as is the chief's spatial orientation in respect of his or her addressee. The object is to avoid penetrating the royal ego-boundaries, whether by word or by deed, and thereby ensure the chief's physical and spiritual sanctity. In all such transactions of avoidance the royal surrogate, the ɔkyeame, becomes the locus of interaction, ensuring smooth exchanges between the two discrete domains.

The first part of this chapter discusses the ɔkyeame, the process of his appointment, and the ritual contract between him and the chief.

The Ɔkyeame

The ɔkyeame is the most conspicuous functionary in the chief's executive wing, performing duties in several spheres of activity—social, political, religious, and rhetorical—on the chief's behalf. In addition to being the chief's orator, diplomat, envoy, prosecutor, protocol officer, and prayer officiant, the ɔkyeame is also the chief's confidant and counsellor. Thus his duties require an uncommon familiarity with traditional lore, custom, and history, as well as wisdom, experience, and skills in the forensic arts, oratory, logic, diplomacy, and public relations. To command credibility in his representation of the chief, he is also expected to be the quintessence of moral virtues: sincerity, loyalty, probity, and selfless devotion should guide his behavior at all times.

The very powerful position occupied by the ọkyeame within the political hierarchy, naturally lends him greater visibility than the chief. This, however, does not reduce the chief to a mere ceremonial figurehead; neither does it necessarily pose a threat to royal supremacy. Indeed, an Akan maxim emphasizes the prohibition against combining the roles of chief and ọkyeame: *Okyeame dane ọhempa a yẹkyi* (It's taboo for an ọkyeame to become chief). If, on the other hand, a chief unduly usurps the ọkyeame's role, the Akan apply to him the derogatory title *ọhene-kyeame* (spokesman-chief). It's a cultural prohibition, then, for either functionary to usurp the other's duties, except in cases where the chief's voice must be heard by all.

The chief is the moral, political, and religious leader of his people. His responsibilities require a combination of wisdom, probity, and a deep knowledge of custom and traditional matters; for even though he holds consultations with a council of elders before taking decisions, he should command a high level of political sophistication and personal charisma in his own right. Moreover, verbal wit and effective control of words are no less expected of a good chief than of other public functionaries. Indeed, the chief's roles as arbitor-in-chief and chairperson of all formal meetings of the state require careful and effective use of speech, as well as exemplary compliance with the aesthetics of communication. The existence of a speech intermediary does not necessarily eliminate opportunities for royal oratory: besides presiding over formal meetings, the chief may partake in prosecutions and take an active part in other formal deliberations.

In order for a chief not to feel upstaged by the eloquence of his orator, it is in his own political interest to be a good speaker. Besides this, the rhetoric of an ọkyeame is mostly expected to be an extension of the principal's rhetoric, not a complete substitute.

Very few chiefs have only one orator; their number often ranges from two to twelve, depending on the size of the chieftaincy or state. While many *adekuro* (village heads) have one or two orators, bigger paramountcies have four or more. The king of Ashanti, who controls the biggest traditional state in Ghana, has positions for twelve, each of them in charge of maintaining liaison between the king and specific townships, among other duties. In some parts of the Akan area, one specific ọkyeame, the *ọmankyeame* (state ọkyeame, or chief protocol officer of the state), is appointed, among other things, to serve as liaison between the people and the chief, both in protocol and communicative matters. Such an ọkyeame is the people's spokesperson, and he belongs more to the people than to the chief.

Other akyeame have specific areas of control. For instance, Baafuor Akoto, the oldest of Asantehene's orators, is responsible for maintaining liaison between the king and the townships of Dwaben, Nkoranza, and Kokofu, along with the Agona and Ankòbea divisions. "All envoys from the selected towns or divisions seeking audience with the king come through me" he explains, "and all messages from the king to these towns go through me." The existence of more than one òkyeame facilitates the systematic flow of information to and from various units within the king's control and helps to maintain a balance of political power within the communication hierarchy of chiefs and subchiefs. Moreover, a chief's pool of orators itself has a prevailing hierarchy, and roles are apportioned on the basis of seniority of rank.

The Making of Akyeame

The confidence and competence akyeame acquire, whether in their performance of ritual prayers, in their maintenance of liaison between the chief and his visitors, or in their public oratory, are not overnight gains. Akyeame acquire their skills or potential over a long period of time, either prior to their appointment or on the job. In any case, skills in traditional communication come with constant exposure to traditional meetings, first as an observer, royal attendant, or courtier, and then as a constant participant in formal meetings—either as a political functionary or as a subject of controversy.

Hereditary Akyeame

Akyeame in hereditary positions, like chiefs, are occupants of *akonnwa tuntum,* or *punnwa,* black stools on which ritual sacrifices may be performed. On the death of an orator in a hereditary position, a chief is obliged to ask the particular lineage to nominate a fitting successor, subject to the chief's final approval. Successors to akyeame stools may or may not necessarily have prior oratorical skills. In a few cases, the professional skills are passed on to favorite youths before the incumbents breathe their last. But if the skills in public speaking are lacking in newly installed akyeame, they may be acquired from continued exposure to formal meetings as well as close understudying of experienced akyeame.

The case of Òkyeame Baafuor Akoto of the palace of the Ashanti king provides a fitting example. He was installed as òkyeame, somewhat reluctantly, in August 1935, when he was 31. Now in his nineties, Baafuor Akoto has served two Ashanti kings over a period of six decades. He tells his own story:

> My grandfather who sat on the stool in my youth, Baafuor Mensa, was succeeded by his younger brother Baafuor Yaw Nnum. He served under Prempeh II. He served the stool faithfully until he went blind. In Ashanti, a blind okyeame is a taboo. He was therefore removed. At the time, I was about the only male left in the lineage, and the lot fell on me. I was an apprentice auto mechanic then, and I found it hard leaving my lucrative job for this position. I kept declining it, until the elders threatened to transfer the stool from my lineage into another. My father then persuaded me to take it up, or else future generations would never forgive me.

Most of my knowledge about traditional lore and history was acquired from my predecessor (my grandfather). Owing to his visual handicap, he was at home most of the time, and I started learning from him.

Said one of the akyeame of the king of Kwahu traditional area, Ọkyeame Kwadwo Akuoko, a 30-year-old orator of five years' standing: "I was a full-time farmer until I inherited my uncle's stool as ọkyeame . . . Nobody really taught me traditional lore, customs, or the art of oratory. I learnt it through constant exposure on the job."

More striking are instances of akyeame installed or appointed in their youths who have acquired competence over the years. An example is Ọkyeame Kwasi Yeboah, one of the six orators of the chief of Pepease-Kwahu. He is 85, and has been an ọkyeame for 70 years. He became an ọkyeame at the age of fifteen:

> My uncle died and I succeeded him. I was installed at that young age for rather pecu-
> liar reasons. I had four uncles, but as soon as my uncle the ọkyeame died, the others
> began dying one after the other at about three-week intervals. In a matter of three
> months, all my uncles had died. I, the child, was the only male left; the rest were
> women. I was then asked to succeed my uncle as ọkyeame. . . . The deep knowledge
> I have about traditional lore and the art of oratory was not formally imparted to me. I
> learnt it informally, by gradual exposure to deliberations at the chief's court.

Appointed (Gyaase) Akyeame

Where an ọkyeame has been directly appointed by the chief, this has been through careful observation of the nominee's public speech comportment, conduct, and knowledge. Akyeame directly chosen by chiefs are normally known as *gyaase akyeame*; their choice is often independent of their lineage or divisional affiliation, and they may or may not be replaced on their death by a kinsman. At traditional meetings, where verbal skills are highly celebrated, a chief may appoint an ọkyeame on the basis of his personal observations of a speaker's oratory and char-acter. In other cases, the chief relies on the recommendation of his counsellors. In a few cases, orators in appointive positions have had their office converted by the chief into a hereditary one. One such example is that of Ọkyeame Antwi Boasiako, who was previously a courtier, but was directly appointed by the king of Ashanti, Nana Otumfuor Opoku Ware II, for his good conduct and knowledge of tradition.

In one other case, the chief's appointed ọkyeame had excelled as a royal servant and public speaker, and had been known to have solid knowledge of royal affairs as well as competence in oratory. The paramount chief of Agona Nsaba had no alter-native but to appoint him as his ọkyeame. Kofi Amoakwa is his name. He grew up in a neighboring town, Agona Duakwa, where his father comes from. He told me his story thus:

> When I was a child, I always accompanied the elders to meetings and on trips. I used
> to accompany my grandfather, who was the chief of Duakwa at the time, on formal
> trips; and I acquired a lot of confidence and experience through meetings and partici-

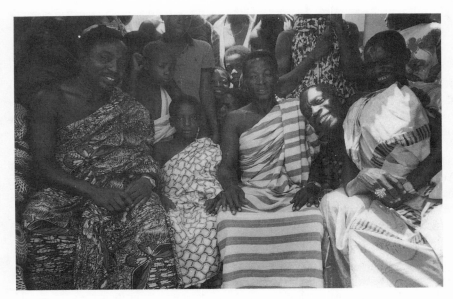

6.1. Ọ̀kyeame Agyei of Nwamase, eleven years old, flanked by elders. Kumasi, 1988.

pation in festivals. Apart from this, my father was a ritual specialist for the same Duakwa chief, and I understudied him. I therefore reached a point where I became the chief consultant on royal customs. The paramount chief of Agona Nsaba, where my mother comes from, noticed my talent and informed my father he was interested in appointing me as his ọ̀kyeame.

In one extreme case, an ọ̀kyeame was directly appointed by the chief at the age of seven. Still a primary school pupil, Ọ̀kyeame Agyei is one of the akyeame of Nwamase in the Ashanti traditional area. I first noticed him among a group of elders paying respects to the king of Ashanti during an Adae festival in June 1988. The chief of Nwamase, who appointed him at that age, explained:

Most of the very knowledgeable elders in Ashanti here are slowly passing away. I therefore decided to appoint a child to second my steps, so he can learn the art over several years. When I am no more, there will then be somebody, my orator, who can also impart the knowledge to future generations.

This juvenile ọ̀kyeame currently does not actively participate in public debate; he is apprenticed to the older akyeame. But he attends all formal meetings and witnesses all ceremonies. Even at this age, he appears to know the subtle norms of formal communication and comportment, and has begun using idiomatic speech.

The death of a chief does not mark the termination of an ọ̀kyeame's tenure. Only death, dismissal, or a sense handicap or disability (such as deafness or blindness) may end his profession. On the installation of a new chief, the previous orators continue to serve him, even though the new chief may decide to add to the existing pool of orators.

The Akyeamehene

One significant functionary in the pool of royal orators is recognized as a chief in his own right. He is the *akyeamehene,* royal orator-in-chief. He is the chief among the orators. Besides occupying a hereditary position (like one of the two types above), he is recognized as a chief (roughly equivalent to a divisional chief), and may go through royal installation rituals like his master; he also has a stool name by which he is addressed, and may have his own ọkyeame if he chooses.[1] If he is *akyeamehene* of a whole traditional state, he is strictly speaking the king of all the orators, including other head orators in the various divisions of the state.

The *akyeamehene* has exclusive access to *nkonnwafieso,* the ancestral stool room, where he accompanies the chief on ceremonial occasions and performs rituals on his behalf. In the presence of junior orators, he is not very active in public transactions; he may direct his subordinates or oversee their work. He is also in charge of the *akyeamepoma,* the staffs used by the royal orators, and selects fitting proverbial staffs for relevant missions and occasions. Moreover, "in the olden days," says Nana Asiedu Kwaben III, the *akyeamehene* of the paramount chief of the Kwahu traditional area, "the head orator was solely responsible for pronouncing a death sentence at court."

Ritual Wedlock

The crucial significance of akyeame to the chief is made evident by the nature of the rituals performed prior to an ọkyeame's appointment. The greater part runs parallel to wedding rites. Indeed, an ọkyeame is traditionally referred to as the *ọhene yere,* the chief's wife (distinguished, however, from the chief's real wife).[2] Even though this metaphor originally applied to the chief's own chosen ọkyeame, it is generally applied to all akyeame, whether in appointive or hereditary positions. The metaphor implies mutual accessibility between the two functionaries, enjoining mutual loyalty and unanimity in word and deed. Its fuller implications become more evident in the strict interpretation of the chief's word by his ọkyeame in public forums.

---

1. Besides the orator-in-chief, other akyeame may also hold titled positions, particularly if the royalty is a king. This is true of some akyeame of the king of Ashanti. These have stool names in their own right, and they may delegate the holding of the orator's staff to an assistant while serving the king. When such titled akyeame are speaking in the king's presence, their words may be answered by assistants, just as the king's words are, particularly if they hold a high chiefship position.

2. Even in cases where a chief is female and her ọkyeame male, the ọkyeame is still a "wife"; and the chief, a "husband."

I shall now take a closer look at the rites of matrimony observed in the making of an ȯkyeame and their political implications. When an ȯkyeame is being appointed by the chief, the normal procedure for arranging a matrimonial engagement is observed. The details of the procedure differ slightly from one Akan group to the other. Ȯkyeame Kofi Amoakwa of Agona Nsaba explained to me the procedure in his own case as follows:

> It's just as if the chief has seen a woman he is interested in. He first seeks your consent, and informs his council of elders of his intention to "marry" you, then sends a drink through an envoy to your father. The latter in turn presents the drink to your maternal lineage and informs them about the chief's intentions. If they also agree to the proposal, the father sends a positive reply to the chief. After this, the chief makes final preparations for the marriage. If he is a paramount chief, he presents Schnapps (gin) drinks and a token cash amount to your father. In the olden days, items presented included an *amoase* [undergarment worn by women between the thighs]. Part of the drink, plus the *amoase,* are given to the ȯkyeame-to-be, and the cash is distributed to key members of the lineage. A day or so after this, you are presented to the chief as his "wife," and in the presence of his elders, you pay a drink fee to the state drummers and hornblowers, after which it is announced, "This person, So-and-so, is henceforth the chief's wife; if you slander or verbally assault him, the law will deal with you accordingly."

Widowhood Rites

When the chief dies, akyeame may be put through the same rituals as the chief's wife (or wives). Again, this has been relaxed in some parts of Akan over the years. In some areas like Ashanti, though, the orators undergo the normal widowhood and confinement rites. Among the Agona, the orator-in-chief alone may be confined on behalf of his subordinates, but is released after just a week (earlier than the wives). The Agona royal lineage after the confinement is expected to present him with a new cloth, a cock, and a drink, the normal rites in widowhood.

The metaphor of matrimony used in depicting the relationship between ȯkyeame and the chief, which is ritually reinforced, is a token of their mutual ties, loyalties, and interdependence. Above all, it underscores the ȯkyeame's subordinate status in the alliance, and puts him at the service of his lord. Political subordination to the chief, however, does not necessarily imply inferiority in wisdom; for, as will be noticed, the ȯkyeame also pledges wise counsel and guidance to the chief. The major point of emphasis is the bond between the two functionaries.

In conformity with this ritual linkage, the royal spokesman on ceremonial occasions may dance to communicate his loyalty to the chief.

Mutual Access

It is in the execution of the ȯkyeame's duties, however, that the spousal metaphor is more vividly brought to play. Among the chief's counsellors, the ȯkyeame has the sole right to enter the chief's chambers with little or no ceremony, and to wake him up if there is a crisis. He indeed has unlimited access to the chief, and knows him better than any of the chief's other counsellors. No wonder it is the ɔkyeame that is charged to interpret the chief's word in formal forums. One ɔkyeame explained this with the proverb *Awerewerewa na enim anadwoboa kasa* (It is the cockroach that best understands the language of the night beast).[3] Even while the chief is sitting in state on ceremonial occasions, the ɔkyeame has the exclusive right to walk to him without ceremonies, and whisper in his ear.

Like a wife, he may receive the chief's official visitors and serve them as guests. No guest has direct access to the chief except through his ɔkyeame. Consequently, no matter may be brought before the chief if it has not been processed or cleared by the ɔkyeame. Guests coming to the chief must first report to his orator, announce their mission and, if the orator finds it fitting, be taken to the chief immediately thereafter. In some cases the ɔkyeame, after listening to a guest's mission, may on his own discretion advise on the issue if it is relatively trivial, or he may instruct the guest to comply with certain norms before appearing before the chief. The guest may be asked to go home and come back again, this time with all ritual items originally omitted. In cases demanding a judicial sitting, the ɔkyeame takes an oral statement from the plaintiff and accomplishes all preliminary judicial transactions before presenting the case to the chief.

Were a formal matter discussed with the chief without having been channelled through an ɔkyeame, the outcome of the proceedings could be declared null and void, since it had not been officially mediated and witnessed. This is precisely what happened at a sitting of the Kumasi Traditional Council (Ashanti), when a defendant-subchief at a court sitting argued that his rebellious position against a superior chief's installment was in compliance with a decision taken at a meeting between him and the king of Ashanti. As far as the jury was concerned, that meeting was void since the defendant did not present the matter to the king through an ɔkyeame, who would have been witness. During the heated debate that ensued, one of Asantehene's akyeame took advantage of the opportunity to address the defendant on the protocol he was ignoring (Kumasi, Manhyia Palace 1988):

Otumfoɔ adaworoma
Akyeame da mo ano mmaako mmaako
Biribi kyere wo so a
Na woakɔ ɔkyeame fie
'Nana Kyeame, asɛm sei atɔ m'ani
Na yɛbɛyɛ no dɛn?'
Nana Kyeame, ɔwɔ ahenfie ha da biara
Adeɛ bɛkye da biara a
Yɛne Otumfoɔ na ewɔ hɔ
Yɛrete, yɛrete, yɛrete, yɛnhunu
Nti deɛ yɛbɛteɛ no
Woba a na yɛne wo atena ase

---

3. Spoken by the ɔkyeame of Afrisipa, in the Bono region.

Yėaka sė 'yė no sei, yė no sei'
Na nteaseė ayė n'adwuma
Na wose worebó atra akyeame
Na woakó de a
Na sėbe, worekósi ogya mu!

By the grace of Otumfuor,
Various akyeame have been appointed
To liaise between him and the various divisions
Should a problem arise, it's for you
To call on the ókyeame at home and plead,
"Nana kyeame, a cinder has fallen into my eye
How do we solve this?"
Nana kyeame is always at the chief's palace
We are at the chief's palace each day with Otumfuor
We only hear again and again all that happens
Yet we don't see
So what has reached our ears, it is for you
To sit down with us and discuss
So we would suggest, do it thus and thus
To promote mutual understanding
But if you decide to jump over akyeame
And go directly, then, my apologies,
You are bound to land in the fire!

Like the chief's wife, ókyeame is the chief's confidant and informant. He has access to all confidential information about his patron, and is obliged to pass on any intelligence he comes across. Apart from executive counselling, he may also advise the chief on appropriate wear for relevant occasions, what type or design of cloth to wear, sandals, ornaments, etc.

In a few cases, an ókyeame may live in the same compound as the chief or queenmother to facilitate their easy access to each other. This is true of the queenmother of Ashanti and her akyeame. Even where they live apart, the ókyeame is obliged to report at his patron's premises each morning and be apprised of the day's agenda. During formal meetings, the orator sits near the chief, holding his staff of office, another index of their mutual bond.

The Ókyeame's Oath

The bond between the ókyeame and his patron, ritually established by wedlock, receives a more potent booster by oaths, binding on the ókyeame, and carrying fatal consequences in case of violation.

In one such ritual, called *nom abosom* (drink the gods), an ókyeame may be given a concoction to drink while the following solemn oath is said to him by a priest (Rattray 1927:277):

Ọkyeame, receive the gods and drink,
We give you this stool
That you may speak the truth
If you do not speak the truth but lie
And if you accept bribes
And if the chief does wrong
And you do not advise him
But keep urging him on to evil
And if you walk between two nations
If you do these things
May the gods slay you
For you are in breach of the great oath.

Even where he is not put through this solemn ritual, he is required to swear an oath of allegiance to his chief, promising truth, loyalty, and dedication as part of the installation process. In some cases, an ọkyeame's oath may literally include a vow never to alter the chief's word or message, a fact which underlines the importance the Akan attach to precision in relaying the chief's word (see next chapter). The following, for instance, are part of the words used in one Akan township in the Bono region:[4]

I stand before you, chief and elders,
And solemnly swear as follows:
In blazing heat, in the morning or evening
I shall respond to your call
What the chief has said
I shall not add to it
I shall say only as he says
If I add to the chief's word
I violate the great oath

This is not all. When a newly installed chief has to pledge his allegiance to a superior chief, the chief's pledge is preceded by that of his spokesperson, who says as part of his pledge:

Anọpa, anwummrẹ
Sẹ mankọsọ ne nsa
Ammẹgye no taataa
Amma wammẹsom Otumfoọ
Amfa ansom Asanteman a
Meto Ntankeseẹ

---

4. Spoken by the ọkyeame of Afrisipa.

Whether morning or evening,
If I don't hold the chief's hand
And guide his footsteps
So he might serve you [the king]
That you accordingly serve the state
I violate the unspeakable oath.

The reader will recall that violating the unspeakable oath (*ntam*) means making formulaic reference to a specific historical calamity, behavior which constitutes a serious religious breach currently punishable by a heavy fine. In the olden days, such a breach could result in capital punishment.

This is hardly the only punishable offense for an ȯkyeame. Potential misdeeds range from acting ultra vires, indiscretion in speech, or wrong interpretation of the chief's word to any manner of performance flaw (see also Adjaye 1984: 105-110). "Our duties are the most difficult in the palace; for when we default, we are considered to be in a position to have known better," said Akoto, one of the Asantehene's akyeame. He recounted one such incident in his own experience:

> The king I formerly served, Nana Agyeman Prempeh II, once sent me and other counsellors on a formal mission to Domaa. This was not long after I had been installed as ȯkyeame. I had a confidential chat with the king before the journey, which I unwittingly included in my formal presentation of his message. I was instantly reported to the chief, who sent envoys to withdraw me from the mission. On my arrival, I was instantly arrested, and fined heavily.

Other reasons for punishment or dismissal include accepting a bribe intended to influence one's judgment, or serious performance flaws in enacting a libation prayer. One such incident occurred in a village in the Fanti area of Ghana, where, in communicating a prayer, the ȯkyeame of a subchief made an error of omission during the invocation segment. This section, which is often part of the introduction of libation prayers, requires the celebrant to call on God, mother earth, deities, and ancestors of the relevant lineage. One elder explained the error:[5]

> You see, we have several hierarchies within the lineage—the head, the mother, etc. During annual festivals, you cannot be excused for omitting the name of the lineage head during the invocation. That should have been the first name before the others. They say, *Aboa akyem ne buw aduasa akrȯn; adze kye a okyin ne nyinara do no, na ȯmansiesie ntsir a* (The weaverbird has 39 nests, yet it is for the sake of nation building that she pays daily visits to all).

As a result of this serious lapse, the elders convened a meeting to consider sanctions; but they gave him a severe warning and spared him a fine.

---

5. Said by the chief of Ekumfi Atwia.

The Politics of Immunity

The above discussion of the bond between the chief and his orator summarily points up the political significance of the ȯkyeame, but it also demonstrates the hazards of his profession, the serious implications of breaches in his contract with the chief. Yet, a professional transgression on the part of an ȯkyeame is not the only source of risk. Whereas the above risks are based on professional indiscretion or performance flaws, the more significant hazards are intrinsic. Such intrinsic hazards constitute an integral part of any situation of surrogation where the principal functionary is sacred. In the case of the chief and his ȯkyeame we have a sacred principal with a secular surrogate, one protected by cultural rules of immunity, the other exposed to ritual and interactional hazards. Here, the secular surrogate becomes the virtual target of all dangerous interaction otherwise directed at his sacred principal.

The hazards in an ȯkyeame's vocation as a royal proxy become more evident when one considers the social and religious awe in which the chief is held, along with the steps taken by the Akan to reinforce his distinctiveness.

Royal Space and Ego

The chief speaks with the voice of the ancestors and must not be challenged or contradicted. He is the ȯkasaprėko (speaker of the last word). According to an Ashanti maxim, *Otumfoȯ kyekyere ade a yėnnsane mu* (When Otumfuor wraps a parcel, it is not unwrapped for scrutiny). This implies absolute trust in his judgement, partly because of his wisdom, and partly because he acts with sacred authority. The serious consequences of challenging a chief's word are evident in the following account of a speech given by an ȯkyeame in Ashanti. He reprimands a group of three subchiefs for their exaggerated insistence on custom in deliberations at the royal palace, pointing out that they themselves have been in clear breach of custom (Kumasi, Manhyia Palace 1988).

Otumfoȯ se woabȯ n'ano abira
Nso wose mėka mėka
Woka kȯsii sėn?
Na ėkyerė sė Otumfoȯ asėm a ȯreka no
Wone no redi asie?
Wonni kwan sė woyė saa
Wokȯte kȯmfo ano asėm bėka
Na wose aboa wo a
Woboa!
Wose amanneė nti na yėwȯ ha
Wonim amanneė kyėn Otumfoȯ
Ȯno a ȯte amanneė nyinaa so no?
Nana X mpo deė ȯdii adeė mpo nkyėree

Kòtò foforò ekyim mpo nni n'aperè mu
Nanso èwò sè woto wo bo ase
Na wosua amanneè no yie
Kumasi abòntene ntokuro ntokuro
Woanhwè a na woakòtò mu
Na wo serè abu.

The king warned you
You were contradicting his word
Yet you insisted
What did you profit by your words?
Does it mean you are challenging Otumfuor?
You have no right to do that!
If you hear a priest's word, and you report it
Thinking it helps your case
You are mistaken!
And your insistence on custom!
Do you surpass the Otumfuor in customary lore?
He who presides over all custom?
Nana X, the other defendant subchief,
Was only recently installed
A baby crab with no marrow in its claws
You have to take time to learn the custom.
The streets of Kumasi are full of potholes
The careless pedestrian may fall
And break his limbs.

The speaker fortunately finds the circumstances partly extenuating, since one of
the offenders is still fresh on the job and appears to be ignorant of tradition. However, the speaker's warning about the need for caution in spoken transactions at the
palace is important, for appearing to contradict or challenge the chief's word
attracts heavy sanctions. Another elder compared matters at the chief's palace with
the mound where the thorny yam plant grows: "You don't fall in it and go
unscathed" (Ahenfie asèm te sè ahabayerè amona, yèntò mu mfa yèn ho toturodoo).

The chief's sacredness is based on his being the intermediary between the human
and spirit worlds. Òte nananom akonnwa so (He sits on the stool of the ancestors),
the Akan say. He is the custodian of the blackened stool, the shrine of the royal
ancestors on which ritual sacrifices are made and libation poured for the welfare of
the people. During a chief's installation, he is lowered and raised three times upon
the stool to depict his close contact with the ancestors. His sacredness is empha-
sized by taboos that take effect upon his installation. He may not walk barefooted
lest a misfortune befall his community. He should walk with care, since a stumble
may spell calamity for his people. Further, a chief's buttocks may never touch the
ground (Busia 1951:26-27).

Significantly, the chief may also neither strike anyone nor be struck. The power of the chief is such that he must not be provoked to physical aggression, for his slap is believed capable of causing madness, and his curse on any individual may be fulfilled. The forces the chief is believed capable of unleashing are such that considerable self-restraint is expected of him; but the society stands in even better stead if this force is contained through the avoidance of face-to-face behavior. On the other hand, society needs to institute steps to protect the chief from vicious forces outside the royal realm.

The chief's revered position requires that society accord him the highest possible level of veneration, and also acknowledge the sacred space he occupies. One of the ways in which this is expressed is physical avoidance, to protect the chief from the risks of face-to-face interaction.

The chief's unique position as a distinctive political personage is marked in various ways. In processions, he may be carried high in a palanquin, or distinguished by a majestic overhead umbrella topped by a proverbial design projecting his authority. His clothing and adornment while sitting in state are usually unique. Indeed, in such states as Ashanti, certain ceremonial cloth motifs may be worn by the chief or king only, and there are craftspeople and weavers who exclusively craft royal regalia. Several motifs in the famous Ashanti woven silk kente cloths are named after the eminent kings and queenmothers with whom they were uniquely identified in the past (see Rattray 1927:236-268).

Where no such restrictions in clothing prevail, chiefs still ensure that their uniqueness is evident on formal occasions. One òkyeame in the Agona area told of how he would normally sneak to the parade grounds and observe the textile designs and motifs worn by the subordinate chiefs before advising his chief on what to wear for that occasion.[6] While walking to formal meetings or ceremonial grounds, the chief may be preceded by a long entourage of royal functionaries, including court minstrels, *abrafo* (praise poets), executioners, traditional bodyguards, porters of royal regalia, and religious functionaries, giving him physical and spiritual protection.

His majestic steps may be heralded by his courtiers and talking drummers—not only to praise them but to ensure their safety, since an accidental fall by the chief may spell disaster. Even when he sits, the courtiers may loudly comment on the grace and majesty with which he has seated himself. An excellent example of this is the verse passage in the prologue of this book, which contains the comments of the king of Ashanti's herald as the king was in the process of taking his seat at one formal meeting in Kumasi. (Recall the cautionary tone of the messages, admonishing the chief to be careful lest he stumble.) A chief's rising from his stool after a meeting is similarly heralded. A courtier shouts, "Nana rises!" The whole congregation rises to its feet; the chief is helped to his feet, and he gracefully leaves the assembly.

As the chief sits, he is normally flanked by royal functionaries, including the akyeame. The latter are all holding their staffs of authority, whose proverbial symbols convey the chief's supremacy and generosity. There are also attendants that fan him to cool him and keep flies away from him. If the occasion is ceremonial,

---

6. Informant: Òkyeame Amoakwa of Agona Nsaba.

6.2. The King of Ashanti, Nana Otumfuor Opoku Ware II. 1990.

poets and court minstrels may chant his noble deeds and those of his predecessors. Dancers may also communicate their humility to the chief, and gesture his political supremacy over all the wings of the traditional state. These modes of communication, oral, instrumental, and visual, are all meant to mystify the chief's ego and shroud his personality in awe.

Physical Avoidance

In formal settings, the above mystifying performances are further reinforced by acts and avoidances aimed at preserving royal space and ensuring the chief's physical and spiritual safety. This is partly achieved through physical and communicative distancing. It is a prohibition to engage the chief in a *focussed interaction,* by which I refer to any situation in which "individuals extend to one another a special communication license and sustain a special type of mutual activity that can exclude others who are present in the situation" (Goffman 1963:83). Exceptions to this rule are artists such as poets, singers and dancers entering into artistic communication with the royalty; his personal confidants and counsellors whispering or passing on messages to him; or a subordinate chief or functionary swearing an oath of allegiance. All these situations, entailing few or no uncertainties, permit limited face-to-face engagements with the chief, and may join the chief and these benign personalities in a single focus of visual and cognitive attention without threat to royal face.

During the installation of a new chief, subjects greeting him may shake hands

6.3. A chief bows to the King, a deference gesture.
Kumasi, 1988.

only with the *òkra* (soul), often a youth who sits in front of the chief and acts as his proxy, thereby absorbing any spiritually potent contact otherwise meant for the chief. Similarly, as a queenmother walks, she may be preceded by her *mmòdwoafoo,* youthful maids who stand between her and imminent evil. Walking in public processions, the queenmother may be flanked by maidens holding large fans that protect her from direct contact with any evil eye.

In Ashanti tradition, the rule prohibiting physical contact extends to all formal occasions. All subchiefs, functionaries, dignitaries, and subjects filing past may convey only a distant greeting, by a low bow. The bow is preceded by two other acts of humility—slipping the sandals off one's feet, and baring one's shoulders. No functionary may shake hands with the king while he sits in state, except his military general (*bantamahene*), who is the keeper of the royal mausoleum. While the latter complies with all norms of greeting, he is exempt from the rule of physical avoidance. Indeed, the general's handshake may be supplemented with an embrace.

Verbal/Visual Aggression

The above strategies of distancing and the preservation of royal space find their utmost fulfillment in formal communication with the chief, where messages have to be routed through a third party, the ȯkyeame. The rationale for this is partly to give opportunities to orators to display rhetorical skills as they pass the message on. But the rerouting routine is also meant to minimize the hazards of face-to-face engagements—verbal, rhetorical, or visual—which direct speech involves.

Verbal hazards are based on the power of the spoken word and its potential for instantly destabilizing interactants, if it is unguarded or if malice is the motive. Verbal shocks may arise from verbal abuse or from physical or spiritual aggression. In these cases, the rerouting process may have the effect of stepping down their potency, through delay, reformulation, or the power to absorb shock. When the chief speaks, the orator equally removes from the message any possible shock based on the chief's fury or indiscretion.

The minimizing of rhetorical hazards also involves reformulation, but the primary focus is on the stylistic elegance of the message. The chief must not be seen to be rhetorically incompetent. Royal messages should be presented in elegance; the rerouting of the message enables the orator to do this.

There is still a third dimension to the possibility of hazards, this time based on ocular aggression, which is inevitable in face-to-face communication. In formal assemblies the chief's orators are seated beside him, and those addressing the chief are expected to obey the relevant proxemic and visual norms of communication. The speaker must avoid not only bodily but also visual confrontation with the chief, since mutual eye contact is often a prelude to face-implicating engagements. The speaker, with his shoulders and feet bared, faces the chief's orator directly and should not stray into occasional side glances at the chief. One such violation by a visitor announcing his mission to the king of Ashanti instantly brought his courtiers and orators to their feet: "We don't speak thus to the king!" they warned.

The fact is that among the Akan, one's gaze, whether in itself or as a supplement in communication, can be used as a form of attack. The concept of *anibȯne,* evil eye, is believed by the Akan to be capable of altering reality. Thus a direct concentrated focus may constitute aggression, and instances of visual dueling are not uncommon. Gazes meant for the chief, particularly during a speaker's presentation, would be an integral part of the verbal message, and have to be channelled accordingly. This is also true of formal communication among the Samoans of the Pacific islands (Duranti: personal communication).

The significance of gaze in the norms of communication is further evinced by gaze avoidance by children, particularly when they are being rebuked by adults. To stare directly at an adult under such conditions is a sign of juvenile insolence.

Spiritual Immunity and Ritual Uncleanness

The lore of certain craftsmen among the Akan illustrates the way spiritual potency is held to imply vulnerability. These craftsmen's wives may not speak directly to their husbands when they are in their menses (Rattray 1927:75). Even when she is in the same place as her husband, a wife in this situation must communicate with her spouse only through a child, whose innocence constitutes an immu-

6.4. An ɔkyeame relaying a message to the next in rank. Agona Nsaba, 1988.

nity in itself. The condition of menstruation is considered capable of breaking down the spiritual immunity of direct addressees. Where such addressees, through their vocation, are in constant interaction with spiritually powerful animals or trees, a collapse of spiritual immunity may spell occupational disaster. Menstruating women must not go to the royal court for much the same reason: the sanctity of royal space must not be violated.

In a way, this type of avoidance rule affects the chief's orator himself. Even though he generally has unlimited access to the chief, an ɔkyeame in confinement from the death of his own spouse is prohibited from entering the royal premises until ritually cleansed. Until then, he is considered spiritually unclean and could contaminate the royal sphere. This norm is rigidly enforced, for the pre-cleansing condition in widowhood, like menses, implies vulnerability. Since spiritual immunity is needed for the effective protection of the chief, a spiritually vulnerable ɔkyeame is technically unfit to protect his master.

Ɔkyeame Baafuor Akoto of the Ashanti royal court explains the ɔkyeame's role as a spiritual buffer thus:

> The chief relies on the ɔkyeame to dispel all contamination and evil attacks directed at him through speech, for he is not as clairvoyant as his ɔkyeame. We akyeame (yɛaben) are spiritually potent; we inherit very powerful stools. So when you speak through us, we absorb any incidental contamination that could affect the chief, for that has no effect on us.

It is this condition of spiritual invincibility which is compromised during the period of ritual confinement in widowhood and must be restored through cleansing rites. The spiritual potency of akyeame is confirmed by others. One ɔkyeame of Agona Nsaba spoke of how he would sometimes alert the chief on noticing an evil presence in a formal assembly:[7]

> If this is unnoticed, you would sometimes find the chief suddenly falling ill in public. This may be due to a spiritual attack by someone in his presence, who would want to embarrass the chief, or remove him from the stool he inherits. For this reason, I have every right to reprimand anybody who directly speaks to the chief, or goes to his premises without passing through me.

Liability

Whether or not he is spiritually potent, the ɔkyeame faces considerable occupational hazards, being the surrogate focus of all interaction within royal space. These hazards are reinforced by other acts of surrogation. On official trips, for example, food eaten by the chief must first be tasted by his orator, to protect him from potential poisoning.

Being the royal prosecutor and advisor, the ɔkyeame also suffers the consequences of a judicial mishap. For he has considerable influence on the final verdict reached by the chief, since his judgement is informed by his vast knowledge and judicial experience. He investigates cases, interrogating and cross-examining witnesses. After the ɔkyeame has stated his opinion on a case, all the jury members express their own opinions in order of rank, before the chief says the last word. The chief's last word may or may not agree with the judgement of the jury. But it is the ɔkyeame who announces the verdict. It is significant, though, that norms of court transaction require the conveyance of felicitations to the chief after the final verdict has been announced. The congregation, either individually or collectively, conveys to him greetings of *di bem,* denoting fairness, justness, or lack of judicial bias. *Di bem, oburu; di bem, esɔn* members of the jury greet the chief, one after the other.

Despite this, it is the ɔkyeame, not the chief, that is held liable if an appeal against the royal judgement is upheld by a higher court. Ɔkyeame Baafuor Akoto explained to me how the situation affected akyeame in the Ashanti state,

> If after a court judgement the litigant is not satisfied, it is the ɔkyeame the litigant swears by *ntam* [the unspeakable word] to challenge, and not the king. As soon as the litigant uses *ntam* to challenge the verdict, the akyeame of Mampon, Nsuta, Dwaben, and Bekwai, constituting an appeal jury, are summoned to hear the case. After they have spoken, we also explain the basis of the court decision. If on the appeal hearing the contestant's guilt is upheld, he may be liable to severe punishment. It means he has wrongly challenged our word. If the contestant is proclaimed innocent, we [the Ashanti king's akyeame] are arrested and heavily fined.

---

7. Informant: Ɔkyeame Amoakwa of Agona Nsaba.

Penalties faced by akyeame were even more fatal for other acts of indiscretion in the past. R. S. Rattray writes,

> Anyone committing adultery with the wife of the king of Ashanti's ȯkyeame was liable to be killed; if the co-respondent himself was a chief, then that chief's *ȯkyeame* himself was liable to be killed, as the adviser and counsellor of his master and keeper of his conscience. (Rattray 1927:227)

Protecting the chief also means that the ȯkyeame must pronounce on his behalf, all curses that have the potential of calling catastrophe on their utterer's heads. The Akan call such a curse a *nsedie*—an oath invoking a supernatural power to witness what has been said and to impose a supernatural sanction should the statement be false. If a royal *nsedie* misfires, the relevant supernatural sanctions are borne by the ȯkyeame who spoke the curse. While this further demonstrates the sanctified position of the chief, it also underlines belief in the power of the spoken word and its performative potential (Fernandez 1987).

Linguistic Avoidance

The Akan further ensure the sanctity of royal space through lexical avoidance— the use of euphemisms for certain words and concepts considered indecent in collocation with the chief. A reflex of this was seen earlier (chapter 4), when, in addressing a formal assembly, a speaker profusely used formal apologies and disclaimers (*sèbe oburu*, "my apologies," *mesrè meka* "I beg to say") to disclaim any possible impression of irreverence or offensive intent in an impending phrase. Besides the heavy use of apologies and euphemisms in general to minimize the incidence of vulgarisms and ensure decency in speech, extra steps are taken where the chief is the subject matter of discourse.

In formal speech, the chief may often be addressed by an appellation, such as *Daasebrè* (The Generous One), or *Ȯsagyefo* (Savior at War), which are elegant bynames that depict the virtues he represents. The most neutral term is often *Nana,* a general term of address for a chief, elder, or grandparent. It is not very common for the chief's real or stool name to be used in formal reference.

Norms of reference are even more rigid if a chief's name has to be associated with death, sickness, or misdemeanor. Euphemisms used here are more elaborate. The chief's death is reported metaphorically as *Nana kȯ akuraa* (Nana has gone to his village) or *Odupȯn atutu* (A great tree has fallen). Alternatively, the word "ȯkyeame" may be substituted for chief, e.g., *Ȯkyeame ho dodo no* (The ȯkyeame is indisposed); it is significant that the condition of indisposition is itself a euphemism for death. It is a verbal taboo to literally proclaim a chief's death. The above euphemisms refer exclusively to a royal death, for there are other euphemisms for death in general. The avoidance of a literal statement here implies the traditional unacceptability of the death of an indispensable one.

In their day-to-day duties akyeame make a very conscious effort to avoid vulgarisms in speech, the more so when a chief is the subject matter. If it is a public forum where his linguistic skills are being publicly appraised and sanctions may be applied in case of rhetorical flaws, the ɔkyeame's test is even greater. Ɔkyeame Amoakwa of Nsaba recalled the euphemistic statement he made when on behalf of the chiefs of the central region of Ghana, he expressed condolences to the bereaved on the death of a king in 1973:

> Ɔkyeame, listen so the elders may hear. Here come the paramount chiefs of the Central region. We heard the ɔkyeame is indisposed (*ɔkyeame ho dodo no*), and the elders have sat today to baptize him (*bɔ no asu*), so we are here for nothing else but to bid condolences.

There was no literal mention of the chief, death, nor funeral; euphemisms were used throughout.

The phenomenon of linguistic protection of royalty in certain contexts is even more strikingly illustrated in the earlier-cited discussion at the court of the king of Ashanti, in which a litigant, explaining his opposition to a subchief's installation, sought somehow to implicate the king presiding. He had argued that he had the support of the presiding king himself in his opposition to the installation. This support, according to him, had been lent by the king in a private meeting he had with him. While the king admitted having met with the litigant, he denied having encouraged him. The elders, of course, would not hear the king's name dragged in the mud. Even so, they made sure that in discussing the delicate topic, there was not the remotest association of the king's name with a negative allegation. Idioms were the order of the day. Said one elder, "Do you challenge the Magnanimous One? Who are you? When the Magnanimous has spoken, *you thrust his lips to the floor* [that is "disgrace his word"]? Another avoided literal reference to the allegation against the king by substituting "ɔkyeame" for the king's name: "You are in serious violation of the law—attributing to the *ɔkyeame* a statement he has not made (*Asɛm a ɔkyeame nkae)!*" Here, lexical avoidance ensures that the royal realm is not even in remote collocation with a misdemeanor.

In the same vein, another member of the jury delivered a lengthy pronouncement, making euphemistic references to the chief while reminding the litigant that his misdemeanor amounted to a breach of the oath he swore on his appointment as subchief (Kumasi, Manhyia Palace 1988):

> Nyɛ sɛ wo nipadua na yɛtan no
> Na ade a woyɔɔɛ no na
> Yɛrehwɛ ho abɔ wo mmrane
> Otumfoɔ adaworoma
> Nipa a ɔyɛɛ adeɛ no
> Wamfa kwan pa so
> Na wode asɛm bɛto obi so a
> Ɛnyɛ Nana Kyeame a!

Wo ne, sėbe, aboa kėse da a
Baabi a ne tiri kȯ no
Mma wo werė mfi
Na ȯkȯm de no a, wo na ȯbėkye wo
Ȯgyina hȯ yi, ȯno na bere biara
Yėreka asėm a,
Ȯse amanneė na yėreka
Wone Nana Kyeame kȯdi nkȯmmȯ wȯ dan mu
Na sė yėbȯ asėm pȯ a
Yėnka no abȯnten
Sė polisini koraa na ėbėkye wo ho a
Ėsė sė wosesa w'ano
Kum na yėbėkum wo a
Na yėaku wo.

We bear you [the defendant] no grudge
The appellations you have earned
Are based on your own deeds.
By your grace, Otumfuor,
The man's action deviates from the path of
propriety
You may bear false witness against anyone
But the ȯkyeame!

If you lie beside a big beast
Never forget where its head lies
For it's you it will devour
When it's hungry!
It's he, the defendant,
Who always insists on compliance with custom
Whenever we meet here
Custom indeed!
If it's custom you really advocate
Why do you leak the news
After you have spoken with *Nana Kyeame* in chambers?
When you are in chambers with *Nana Kyeame*
And together, you deliberate on a matter,
We do not divulge it in public
Even if arrested by the police
You have to change your word while in public
If it's death you have to face for lying
Be prepared to die!

Note, in the above speech also, the substitution of ȯkyeame's name three times
for the chief's. But note also the proverb used by the speaker to emphasize the need

for caution in interacting with the mighty one—or his surrogate. The forces the chief in his passion is capable of unleashing are so deadly that those in his environment stand the danger of being engulfed. While this underlines the royal power, it is also a subtle comment on the need for strategies to be devised to avoid such social disruptions. This would necessitate the presence of a third force to mediate between the two domains.

In short, in playing the role of stand-in, the ɔkyeame easily becomes the most vulnerable functionary within the executive committee of the chief. In acknowledging the dangers to which ɔkyeame stands as a ritual and linguistic proxy, however, one cannot ignore the professional benefits accruing to him from his proximity with the chief. Whereas he does not receive a fixed salary from the chief, an ɔkyeame occasionally receives an allowance from his master, based on revenue from court hearings. Besides this, the chief may apportion to him a piece of land on which to farm to sustain himself and his family. Those in hereditary positions also inherit land or other real property.

The power and political honor the ɔkyeame derives from his position are, however, priceless. Having been "wedded" to the chief, he shares a measure of the sacredness attached to his master's position. He is immune from physical or verbal assault, for any attack on him is construed as an attack on the chief.

Nonetheless, this affinity with the chief, from which the ɔkyeame derives both material benefits and tremendous sociopolitical respect, has double-edged implications. Whereas he receives little public credit for the chief's success and good decisions, he may be liable for some executive failures. No wonder the Akan have a maxim that addresses the apparent thanklessness of an ɔkyeame's profession, the fact that credit due to him is not only denied, but also emphatically replaced with its exact opposite: *Ɔkyeame a wasiesie ɔman na ayɛ yie no na yɛfere no nkontomponi* (An ɔkyeame who has successfully built a state is often called a liar).

7 / "LISTENING SO THE CHIEF MAY HEAR"
The Circuit of Formal Talk

THIS CHAPTER discusses the norms of formal oratory in the royal domain, and examines the structure of interaction between the chief and his ɔkyeame, on one hand, and their interlocutors in a public forum, on the other. Here one is interested in the extent to which the structure of power relations earlier discussed is brought to play in a public forum, where the interaction is more focused and role participants are all linked in time and space. The strategies employed, in principle, follow the basic pattern observed in situations where the interactants are not situated in one spatial continuum: formal interaction with the chief must literally be channelled through the ɔkyeame. The ritual, social, and linguistic forms of surrogation we found at play in the previous chapter find their ultimate realization in public speech, where the threat to royal face is more immediate and must be contained through various strategies of control.

But discourse mediation in royal domain should not be viewed only as a face-control device, but also an opportunity for the display of embellished oratory. The situation fits squarely into the Akan penchant for nondirect speech—indirection, ambiguity, and circumlocution—where opportunities are created for the glib-tongued to deploy obliqueness, poetic metaphor, and proverbs for stylized communication. An informant dismissed direct, literal communication with the words, *Sɛ wopa asɛm no ho ntama a ɛnyɛ dɛ* (Speech is not sweet if you strip it of its garment). Thus, just as literal speech is dull, so is all direct communication. Routing speech through another creates opportunities for a dull message to be given a new lease of energy, through stylized manipulation of the code.

Royal Speech Act

Just as the content of one's *amanneɛbɔ* (telling one's mission) may not be as important as the style of telling (see chapter 4), the point in a relayed message is often not at issue, since the message may have been heard anyway. It is the strategy of retelling by the ɔkyeame that arouses greater interest.

But the animation of the chief's discourse by the ɔkyeame is also a public reflex of the system of democracy that permeates the political structure. *Ɔbaako mmu man* (One man does not rule a nation); *Ti koro nkɔ agyina* (One head does not stand in council), the Akan say. When speech is faithfully relayed by another, an impression is conveyed that the opinion embedded is shared. Relating this to the monarch, we see that the chief should not be seen as an autocrat, taking and executing decisions all by himself. The message he conveys in a public forum should be seen as literally going through a ratification process. A token confirmation of his word by another implies that his message, at least, has normative support. As a corollary, words meant for the chief must be witnessed; passing them through the chief's ɔkyeame makes this possible. It lends formality to the transaction and implies that the message is public knowledge. Where the proper circuit of transmission is ignored, a message cannot be considered as having been formalized.

Akyeame are quick to point out the incompleteness of a formal message, if it has not been routed through them. One ɔkyeame told me, *Adwabɔ ase, woamfa asɛm amfa me so a, ɛnni mu* (In a public setting, if you don't route a message through me, it is not valid). Confirming this, the chief of Abetifi (in the Kwahu district) also stated, *Amansɛm ba a yɛde fa akyeame so; anaa sɛ ebia yɛpɛ mu kena. Ɛfa ɔkyeame so a daakye na yɛde ayɛ asɛm aka* (Public matters are routed through the ɔkyeame, and also matters that need to be distinctively marked. When it goes through the ɔkyeame, it can then be later used as testimony). Thus going through an ɔkyeame is not only necessary in a formal call on the chief, or in seeking access to his judicial infrastructure; it is also necessary in the subsequent discourse interaction over which the chief presides. Indeed, ɔkyeame is the focus of all formal interaction in the royal domain, whether social or verbal.

Between the chief's word and that of the ɔkyeame, nothing short of concord is expected. Whether acting as a royal delegate or interactional intermediary, the ɔkyeame is not expected in public to convey sentiments contrary to the chief's own position. He may disagree with his master in their private deliberations over public matters; but any such differences of opinion need to be sorted out before a formal meeting.[1] With reference to the chief, akyeame often say, *wonntumi mmɔ n'ano abira* (you cannot contradict his word); or *memmfa n'ano nnsi bɔne* (I will not pervert his word). One ɔkyeame added, *Wonntumi nntu n'ano asɛm ntwene; yɛka biribi na yɛsusu ho wie na ɔno nso kasa wie a na ɛkyerɛ sɛ wasi no prɛko* (You cannot reject his word; when all arguments cease and he speaks, it's final). But while the content of the chief's word is final, its articulation by him is only part of the speech act; the ultimate voice box of the royal speech act is the ɔkyeame. It is said, *Ɔkyeame kasa ɔhene ano* (Ɔkyeame speaks for the chief).

But prohibition of open disagreement with the chief's word does not make the ɔkyeame an inert medium. As noted earlier, the chief's words addressed through the ɔkyeame may be repeated verbatim by him, analytically transmitted, or passed on by a summary formula. Regardless of the strategy of transmission, however, the phrase used by the akyeame to depict their own speech role is *sɔ so,* as in *mesɔ*

---

1. This does not completely rule out occasional differences in opinion. The chief may, for instance, overrule the verdict of his akyeame in a legal deliberation and pardon an accused. To this, his akyeame may in various ways express dissatisfaction. Writing on the Ewes, Verdon notes frequent open disagreement between chiefs and akyeame (Verdon 1983:262).

Nana kasa so (I supplement the chief's words). The phrase *sò so* literally means to continue, supplement, add to, or make complete, an etymology suggesting an intrinsic "incompleteness" in the chief's words. *Nsòso* lends wholeness to an incomplete act of speech, through animation.

Seen schematically, a royal speech act requires two role participants at the production end. First is the chief, who is the addresser and source of the message, one from whom the message officially originates. Not that the chief's voice in the royal speech act is obligatory. He may exercise his part of the transmission by being present and speaking, may be present but not speak, or may be completely absent from the scene of interaction and make his views represented. Should he speak, his word is still considered incomplete without the ὸkyeame's *nsòso*.

Akyeame in general are considered more experienced and knowledgeable than the chief. That is why a chief's downfall is sometimes attributed to the incompetence of his akyeame. It should therefore not be surprising that both their presence and their voice is obligatory in a royal speech act.

Royal speech is referred to as *adehye kasa*; this is typically hurried and laced with occasional stuttering. In some realizations, *adehye kasa* is soft (*bòkòò*), and has a slight nasal resonance, the likely effect of its calculated low volume. A chief may speak in an undertone, whisper, or speak with moderate intensity. In any case, his voice need not be aimed at the ears of the entire audience. He directs his speech at his ὸkyeame, who sits or stands adjacent to him. The entire audience, or a greater part of them, may also hear his word if they are not spread out in large numbers. The chief's word may be brief or extended, depending on the subject matter and the chief's own strategies of public speaking. The generally low-keyed nature of the chief's word is meant to signify its incompleteness as a speech act.

As the chief speaks the ὸkyeame, with his staff of authority in his left hand, rises to his feet as a mark of respect, and also to signal his attentiveness. Ordinarily, he sits close to the chief, either facing the same direction as him, or facing his side view. The chief and the ὸkyeame thus redirect their focus in a mutual gaze as the chief speaks. The two engage temporarily in an internal dialogue, even though they are allied role participants in the macro communication model. In the course of the royal speech, the ὸkyeame answers with token confirmatives, such as *sio*, *ampa*, *saa saa saa* (yes, it's true, in truth in truth in truth), in solidarity with the chief's word. These replies are designated in Akan as *ngyesoò* (responses) or *mmemaho* (embellishments). Where the chief has several akyeame and they are all present, they all rise and articulate the *ngyesoò* in unison.

The responses to the chief's word are often the beginning of the animation process; they lend support and vitality to the royal speech, enhance its rhythm, and set the pace for the *nsòso*, supplementation of the royal voice, that follows.

If the ὸkyeame is the ultimate voice box of the chief's message, he is also the speech act's strategist. Holding his staff of authority in his left hand, the ὸkyeame completes the royal speech act by analytically reporting the chief's message, paraphrasing or elaborating it. His performance is more foregrounded than the chief's. His speech is often louder and fuller and he is more lively in his gesticulation and histrionics. His voice is also more expressive than that of his principal. In some parts of Ghana, the òkyeame draws even more attention to his relay duties by walking a few yards closer to the other party for whom the message is meant, delivering the message and returning to his seat.[2] This style of presentation ensures that the message is fully heard.[3]

Message Reception

Having discussed the role participants in the delivery aspect of the royal speech act, I now turn attention to interlocutors for whom the message is meant. In making this dichotomy between speakers and listeners, I am aware of its shortcomings as a model for the real phenomenon of communication. As Bakhtin rightly points out, distinctions between speaker and listener are only linguistic fictions.

> Any understanding of live speech, a live utterance, is inherently responsive, although the degree of this activity varies extremely. Any understanding is imbued with response and necessarily elicits it in one form or another: the listener becomes the speaker. A passive understanding of the meaning of perceived speech is only an abstract aspect of the actual whole of the actively responsive understanding, which is then actualized in a subsequent response that is actually articulated. (1986:68)

The fluidity of participant roles in speech is epitomized in the merger of speaker/listener roles in the òkyeame. The receiving end of communication in the royal domain may also have two constituents. If the listening party is a group, or contains a dignitary, such as a chief, it is likely also to have an òkyeame of its own. In this case, the second òkyeame is the receiver of the message, and has to be distinguished from the addressee (dignitary or group) for whom the message is meant. The speaking òkyeame thus directs the message he relays to the listening òkyeame, who receives it and passes it on to the principal or group he represents. A message from the addresser to the addressee then has the potential of going through three phases: From Addresser (source of message) to Òkyeame 1 to Òkyeame 2, to the addressee. If there is a reply, the reply must trickle back in a reverse order—also as a three-part relay.

The distinction between the two akyeame has to be made clear. The interaction between Òkyeame 1 and Òkyeame 2 is not the same as that between a principal and his surrogate; it is ostensibly between two surrogates from different parties, one analytically reporting, and the other receiving on behalf of his own principal.

In cases where the other party has no surrogate orator, the chief's òkyeame becomes the sole focus of the interaction. He relays his principal's message as well as the other party's, even though he is not bound to imbue the transmission of the two messages with the same artistic finesse.

The phenomenon of formal communication may thus be schematized as follows:

---

2. This practice has been noted among the people of Nkonya.

3. In the court of the king of Ashanti, the contrast between the chief's delivery and that of his òkyeame is further sharpened by the latter's use of the microphone when the court is overcrowded.

1	2		3	4
Principal→	Ȯkyeame→	/	Ȯkyeame→	Principal
Source of	Animator		Receiver	Addressee
message	Speaker			Goal of Message
Addresser	Strategist			

In this schema, the slash sign marks the boundary between two parties in a discourse interaction; thus participants 1 and 2 belong to the same party, while 3 and 4 also belong together. 1 is the source of the message, or addresser; and 4 is the addressee or the final goal for which 1's message is intended. 2 and 3 are the discourse animators (akyeame), an interaction between whom could constitute a royal speech event.

In our schema above, direct communication between the two polarities, 1 and 4, is not permitted by the norms of formal communication. It has to be mediated by either 2 or 3, or both consecutively.

There are instances, on the other hand, where within one segment of the communication unit, the message passes through two or more animators before reaching the interlocutors. In that case, the schema becomes:

$$1\longrightarrow \quad 2\longrightarrow 3\longrightarrow \quad 4\longrightarrow \quad / \ 5$$

Such a situation, however, does not undermine the basic bipartite constitution of a royal speech act. It only shows the possibility of multiple frames within the second part of the speech act.

Before the structure of formal talk is exemplified, let's look at a summary of the various modes in which a message from the principal may be animated by the ȯkyeame.

Modes of Animation

I classify the various modes of animating a principal's speech under two broad categories:
1. Supplementative
2. Substitutive

The supplementative mode of animation refers to all situations where an ȯkyeame's words follow that of a chief's (or principal's) on the scene of interaction, such that the orator's words complete (*sȯ so*) the speech initiated by his master, and it is possible to juxtapose the two texts spoken. Here, the ȯkyeame's animation has an audible frame of reference, the chief's words, within which it operates. The substitutive mode of animation, on the other hand, refers to situations where the ȯkyeame's words completely substitute for the chief's, who may or may not be present on the scene of interaction. Here, the ȯkyeame performs alone, and his words have no audible frame of reference.

Supplementative

Modes of completing a principal's words may be divided into three, *verbatim*, *analytic*, and *formulaic*, depending on the style in which the chief's words have been relayed.

VERBATIM

There is a sense in which a strict word-for-word, monolithic style of animation in reported speech is impracticable (even in authoritative discourse), since certain forms of emotional/affective speech, for instance, resist exact reproduction and have to be translated from form into content via a process of analysis (Hanks 1989:6; Volosinov 1973:128, Goffman 1974:529). "Analysis is the heart and soul of indirect discourse" (Volosinov 1973:129).

Even so, akyeame's modes of animating a principal's speech, in some instances, aim at a near replication of the original. Here the principal's message may be relayed almost verbatim, as he speaks one sentence after another—a type of simultaneous interpretation. This type of animation has been noticed, among other modes, at the palace of the king of Ashanti. Where he has a long message, the king speaks softly and slowly, pausing at the end of sentences (see also Moerman 1988:49-67); his ɔkyeame faithfully relays his message after every sentence or so, sticking as closely to the chief's words as possible. The fragmented relay is often a repetition of the chief's words, whose integrity and authenticity are mostly preserved (see chapter 8).

ANALYTIC

Analytic animation appears to characterize most of what the akyeame do. By this, I refer to the discretionary paraphrasing, elaboration, or embellishment of the principal's message without altering its logical focus. In this case, the principal makes an entire speech, which is then analytically reported by the ɔkyeame. This is a complex operation, as Volosinov explains:

> Language devises means for infiltrating reported speech with authorial retort and commentary in deft, subtle ways. The reporting context strives to break down the self-contained compactness of the reported speech, to resolve it, to obliterate its boundaries. (Volosinov 1973:120)

This type of animation may be thought to present a dynamic tension between the reporting and reported contexts—a situation that appears to transgress the ɔkyeame's vow not to change the chief's words. It should be clear, however, that despite the high reverence in which the chief is held, his word is not necessarily religious dogma that has to be repeated verbatim, with all its stylistic contours. Embellishing the words spoken by the chief is the ɔkyeame's prerogative, and he is considered to have been faithful to the chief's word so long as its logic has not been undermined.

Where changes are made in the chief's words, they are presumed to be in the interest of improvement. Even so, the decision to manipulate the chief's words is based on several factors, such as the occasion and the type of speech event. Generally, however, the extent of analytic animation rests on the appeal of the chief's own words. Ọkyeame Yaw Koranteng, orator to a wing chief of the Kwahu traditional area, states:

> You often need to take your time and explain the chief's message. In certain cases, a brief statement by the chief should be relayed in brief. In certain situations, it should be elaborated. In the absence of elaboration, some speeches sound incomplete (*ẹnwie pẹ yẹ*). If in your opinion, the chief's message is incomplete, you may add your own. If his talk sounds complete, it may not be necessary to add on. You only pass it on by a formula.

Another ọkyeame of Kwahu, Kwasi Yeboa, added. "If the chief's message is long and without blemish, I just pass it on. If there is a blemish, I add my own words to make it wholesome." Ọkyeame Akuoko confirmed this, "If whatever the chief says is true, you relay it in brief. An ọkyeame has every right to abbreviate the chief's message. If his message is long, you may decide to highlight the main points (*woyi mu nea ẹyẹ titiriw no*)."

This informant also stressed the fact that the chief's message is supposed to be brief, affording the ọkyeame the opportunity to fill in. The ọkyeame may thus insert an anecdote, recall a historical precedent, or make reference to customary norms, to sharpen the focus of the chief's message. The image this informant used in depicting the often fragmented nature of the chief's message is particularly significant: *Ọpọnepọne tire, ọbobọ so kyerẹ ọkyeame* (He peels off the head, he only gives the highlights to the ọkyeame). The act of peeling off the head is in reference to any edible root with a head (*tire*), such as a yam. Peeling off the head implies recognizing the most important section of an item (head), and carefully breaking it off in bits. The broken-off parts are therefore fragmented, and need to be reassembled into a unified whole. The chief thus highlights the most salient aspects of the message and imparts them in bits to his ọkyeame who, on the basis of his past experience, is expected to reconstruct them into a coherent whole.

But the coherent narrative is also expected to please the ear. Akyeame are very sensitive to the aesthetics of discourse animation—the fact that the relayed message must be sweet. To many of them, it is the most delightful aspect of their duties. *Ọkyeame tumi de bi ka ho ma asẹm no yẹ dẹ* (The ọkyeame may add his own words to sweeten the message), said Ọkyeame Akuoko. This is in accord with other statements from informants, such as *Yẹfeafea ọhene kasa ho* (We embellish the chief's words). One ọkyeame of Asuom compared the art of treating the chief's words with the act of eating fufu, a pasty Akan dish made of pounded plantain and cassava. The fufu paste has to be softened by the hand to facilitate swallowing. The image here recalls Chinua Achebe's depiction of Igbo proverbs as "the palm oil with which words are eaten" (1959:10). Similarly, the chief's words have to be worked and sweetened for the enjoyment of his audience. In this sense, the ọkyeame raises the aesthetic level of the chief's discourse to suit the sublimity of the royal context.

TOKEN/FORMULAIC

If the ȯkyeame considers the principal's word audible and well articulated enough, he may simply draw the audience's attention to it by a token relay formula—in the local parlance, *ȯma nsèmpa*. He may tell the party for whom the message is meant *Mo nsèmpa o* (It's for your consideration) or *mon asomu a* (you heard it all). It is presumed that the message was clear enough not to bear meticulous relaying. The practice of relaying a message with a token formula is sometimes not seen in a favorable light. The Akan consider it an escape route for the incompetent ȯkyeame, incapable of discourse embellishment. This explains the existence of the proverb, *Okyeame a ȯnnim asèm ka na ȯse Nana wo asomu a* (It's the ineloquent ȯkyeame that says "Nana, you heard it all") (see Adu Amankwa 1988).

Substitutive

By *substitutive animation*, I refer to situations where the ȯkyeame's words have no objectifiable point of reference. The principal may or may not be present on the scene of interaction. Where present, he may whisper his words into the ȯkyeame's ear (*ȯwasa no*), or speak in an undertone to him. He may, on the other hand, only deliberate privately (*tu agyina*) with his advisors, leaving it to the ȯkyeame to publicly proclaim the chief's decision. In any case, it is the ȯkyeame whose delivery goes on record; his speech substitutes for, not supplements (as in earlier cases) the chief's.

There are also instances where the ȯkyeame, without prior on-scene deliberation with the chief, speaks his words using his own discretion. Certain segments of formal events follow such a routine format that akyeame need not consult to make verbal proclamations on behalf of their principal. These include presenting a drink (*to nsa*), accepting a drink presented, or welcoming a party (*ma akwaaba*) and seeking their mission (*bisa kwan so*). Here, akyeame may compose words of welcome, or formulate a drink acceptance or presentation speech, and attribute these to their principal.

In the modes of animation discussed so far (both supplementative and substitutive) the ȯkyeame frames his speech as *attributive*, or rather uses phrases indexing reported speech (see also Urban 1989). Such report forms (sometimes quotatives) include *Nana se* (The chief says), *ȯkyerè sè* (He means), *Sè Nana seè ne no* (So says the chief). These report forms may be used whether or not the principal really spoke.

There are, however, certain situations where the ȯkyeame's rhetoric may be presented as non-attributive, whether or not his principal is on the scene of interaction. In this case, the ȯkyeame assumes a quasi-autonomous status and sheds all linguistic clues of representation. He presents the utterance from his own perspective but, of course, based on the understanding that he is a royal surrogate.

This happens on formal occasions such as judicial hearings, where it is the ȯkyeame's duty to directly interrogate litigants and express his opinion about a judgment. In other situations, such as oath-swearing by a new chief or presentation of a new chief to the king, the ȯkyeame may offer advice to the new monarch. On other occasions, he may educate the general audience on traditional custom or history. Such situations may also see the ȯkyeame saying a libation prayer (*yi apae*), or contributing directly to public debate. There is, evidently, a sense of representing a principal in the above instances, insofar as the ȯkyeame institution itself is a surrogate for royalty. Even so, by the very nature of those specific duties, to give the semblance of reporting would be highly inappropriate.

The above modes of animation are not bounded in their occurrence. In one single speech event, they may be combined in various ways by one or more akyeame.

Metacommunicative Signals in the Ȯkyeame's Message

The nature of the royal speech act becomes even clearer when one takes into consideration the metalinguistic component of the speech of akyeame. As discussed in chapter 2, almost the entire formal duties of the ȯkyeame may be subsumed under metalinguistics, since he mostly treats language as an object of reference or comment. In compliance with this, words spoken by, or directed at, the ȯkyeame have a greater metalinguistic component than other speeches. In this section, I discuss the general metalinguistic signals used in formal speech, paying particular attention to those that bring the formal communication model to the fore.

Since formal speeches are invariably routed through the ȯkyeame, they are preceded by addressives referring to him. Thus one making a formal speech first alerts the ȯkyeame by an addressive, then starts his message. The introductory formula used in the address often suggests the intended route of the message's transmission, and the party for whom the speech is meant. The speech may simply begin with *Ȯkyeame wȯ hȯ?* (Is Ȯkyeame alert?), where the speaker checks the channels of transmission and the perception readiness of his target. Here, the ȯkyeame's role as potential recipient of the message is highlighted. To this he may signal his readiness, *Mewȯ hȯ* ("I am alert" or in functional terms "the lines of transmission are open"). One would then continue with a relay formula, *Ȯkyeame, tie ma ȧnto Nana sȧ . . .* (Ȯkyeame, listen so it may reach the chief . . .); or *Wobȧte ma Nana ate* (You will listen so Nana may hear). The speaker here overtly distances himself from the chief or dignitary; he clearly distinguishes two participant roles at the receiving end of his message: the recipient of the message (ȯkyeame), and the party for whom the message is meant (the chief). Indeed, the speaker maps out an operational model of communication; he verbalizes a pragmatic model of formal talk.

Alternatively, one may say, *Ȯkyeame, kyerȧ Nana sȧ . . .* (Ȯkyeame, tell Nana that . . .), which once again distinguishes the recipient from the addresser, and also uses a report form, *kyerȧ* (tell), that highlights ȯkyeame's intermediary role. In cases where the expected points of message relay are more than one, the speaker provides an exhaustive list of the intermediaries along the relay path, and then names the eventual goal of the message using some such formula as, *Ȯkyeame W, tie ma ȧnto X na Y aso nte, na ȯmma Z nte sȧ . . .* (Ȯkyeame W, listen and pass it on to X, that Y may hear and in turn relay to Z that . . .). Here the speaker, through the use of serial constructions encodes in his pragmatic model the multiple frames of reporting expected.

This type of multiple relay may be exercised where more than two different parties, all having akyeame, are represented in a formal forum, and a message delivered is relevant to them all. In this case the message may be picked up serially by their various akyeame and passed on to the parties. The multiple relay formula may also be used where two or more of a chief's akyeame are present at a forum of considerable importance. Such a forum may be as special as a festival, where all the akyeame would want their presence felt. In this case, the message to the chief may proceed from the lowest to the highest ranked (who often sits closest to the chief), and the message from the chief may be channelled in a reverse order, the lowest ranked being the final medium of relay. (In some parts of the Akan area, however, only one ȯkyeame may relay a message, even if all are present.)

Where a message has to travel a multiple course, the speaker, whether or not he is a guest, has to be familiar with the parties represented and the required path of transmission, since he has to reckon with these in his initial greetings and introductory formulae. Indeed, like a war general, the speaker has to map out, ahead of his speech, the intended path of transmission and its eventual destination. Where a guest is unfamiliar with the ground norms of formal communication, he may ask to be represented by a local ȯkyeame, since a breach of communication mores may attract a fine.

Ending a speech directed at an ȯkyeame, a speaker may use the formula *Ȯkyeame, mepaee wo a amanneė ne no* (Ȯkyeame, if I called you, that's the message), which contains a deictic reference to the discourse.

After a message from the chief or another has been received by an ȯkyeame, he animates it through one of the modes discussed above, and may end his speech with another metacommunicative formula, *Sedeė Nana seė ne no* (So says the chief). Here the source of the message is named. Instead of animating his principal's speech, the ȯkyeame may opt for the token relay formula *Mo nsėmpa* (For your consideration) which directs the message to its goal.

Illustration: Two Courtly Exchanges

The entire journey of a formal talk, with its various modes of animation and metacommunicative signals, is exemplified with real-life examples below. Subsequent chapters illustrate this in further detail. I begin with a basic relay, where each message goes through one or two modes of transmission.

This occurred at the chief's palace in Pepease in the Kwahu area during a "fortieth-day" (*Akwasidae*) festival, an occasion when the chief sits in state, offers libation to the ancestral spirits, and individuals pay respects to him through presentation of drinks. The drink presentations may be made by subchiefs, guests, or individuals within the community, and are accompanied by brief speeches by those presenting or their akyeame.

In the following example, a subchief's drink for the chief is presented on his behalf by an ọkyeame; the chief gives a brief thank-you reply, which is relayed by his ọkyeame. The voice of the subchief presenting the drink is not heard here. He has communicated off the record to his orator (OKY 1), who now addresses the chief's ọkyeame as follows (Kwahu Pepease 1988):

Nana Kyeame, Kwasi Addae, Tease Adehyeẹhene
Ọse, ọno nso ọnte apọ a mpanimfoọ nim
Onua panin nso nte apọ
Nanso Adae asi yi
Gye sẹ ọbọ mmọden ara bẹkyia nananom
Waba, Nana atena ase a ọredi Adae
Sẹ wanka biribi a ẹnyẹ yie
Ọse ne nsam abrẹmpon nsa baako
Nana nsọ mu ẹ
Na ọmfa mmoa n'adae die no   10
Na nkọmmọ a ẹwọ họ ne no

OKY 2: Nananom, yẹn nsẹmpa

CHIEF:
Yẹbẹda Opanin Adae Ase
Ayẹyẹde a obẹyẹẹ yẹn
Nti woama wọn aso ate

OKY 2:
Nananom mpanin, sẹnea Kurotihene ka ne no
Ọse ade fẹfẹ a saa nipa yi yẹ maa yẹn no
Mo adaworoma.
Pepease mpanin, momma yẹnna no ase.

OKY 1:
Nana *Kyeame*, Kwasi Adae, a subchief of Tease township.
He says the elders are aware he is indisposed
His elder brother is ill too
On such a festive day, however,
He considers it necessary to come and greet the elders
He is here, and has seen Nana in state celebrating *adae*.
It is not proper to witness this without saying a word.
He says he holds in his hands
One bottle of gin, made for men of honor
Nana may take it to help celebrate   10
That is the message.

OKY 2: Nana, *it's for your consideration.*
CHIEF: We shall thank Opanyin Adae for the honor he has done us,
Let this reach him.

OKY 2: Elders, *so says the chief*
He says for Opanin Adae's wonderful gesture,
By your grace, the elders of Pepease should help us thank him.

Collectively, the entire congregation gives thanks to the donor in unison, *daase ahenewa.*

Each of the messages above does not exceed two steps of relay:

OKY 1→/ OKY 2→ CHIEF
CHIEF→OKY 2→ PUBLIC

Note the words italicized in the passages denoting each speaker's awareness of the metacommunicative frame in which he speaks: the fact that his speech is either meant to be relayed by another, or constitutes a relay in itself.

The first speaker, an ɔkyeame, speaks for his principal, who is present but does not himself put his message on record. The ɔkyeame's speech is presented from a third person's perspective, and overtly indexes reported speech; note the recurrence of the quotative "he says." The chief's ɔkyeame he addresses, OKY 2, picks up the message, and using a relay formula, passes it on to the chief. The latter goes on record with a brief statement of thanks, which he drives home with a metacommunicative formula distinguishing the intended recipient of his message from the addressee. This "incomplete" statement from the chief is forwarded to the other party by his ɔkyeame.

In the illustration that follows, the relay process is multiple, executed by three akyeame representing one chief and a fourth in a special role. It represents part of a formal interaction at Agona Nsaba, during another fortieth-day festival in 1988, and captures the interaction process when this writer and his team of researchers were presenting drinks to the chief. There were four akyeame present altogether. One was the ɔmankyeame (the state spokesman, hereafter OKY 4), Ɔkyeame Agyei; he was not the chief's orator as such, but represented the Nsaba traditional state (or its people). It is often through the ɔmankyeame that the people may reach the chief's akyeame to take their word to the chief. The chief's message to the people also passes through her akyeame, and from thence to the people's spokesman before it reaches the people, or citizens. Strictly speaking, any message for the chief has to be routed first through the state/people's spokesperson before it reaches the chief's spokesperson.

The other three akyeame at the forum represented the chief. They were the *Akyeamehene* (Ɔkyeame-in-chief, hereafter OKY 1), whose stool name is Nana Ɔteng Kwabeng VII; Ɔkyeame Kofi Amoakwa, the second-ranked (OKY 2); and Ɔkyeame Kofi Gyan, the third-ranked (OKY 3). The chief, Nana Agyemfra Nyama I, sat facing the main entrance of the palace courtyard; her three akyeame were on her left, sitting in order of rank with the most senior closest to her. Six yards across from the chief was the ɔmankyeame (the state ɔkyeame), behind whom sat various sections of the townspeople, whom he represents. On another wing were the court drummers.

A group of visitors from the university working on this project (this writer included) were on their way to present a drink to the chief. They chose one of the chief's akyeame to be their spokesperson, reducing the chief's relay team to two. The drink to be presented was to the chief and her people, who both had akyeame. The speaker's message was first picked up by the people's ɔkyeame and relayed to the people. The same message was then taken over by the chief's lowest-ranking ɔkyeame, who relayed it through two more mediums before it reached the chief.

Note here the introductory formulae used by the speakers, which often lay out the intended path of the messages' transmission. Some of the speakers begin by greeting relevant sections of the congregation to get their attention, and also establish a commonality of purpose (Agona Nsaba 1988).

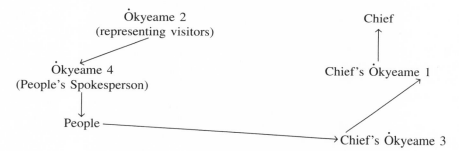

OKY 2: Ɔmankyeame wɔ hɔ?

OKY 4: Meretie

OKY 2: Wobɛtie ma Nsabaman ate
Ndɛ yɛ Akwasidae, yɛanya aban edwumayɛfo
Ɛyɛ University mpanimfo a ɛwɔ hɔ no
Wose wɔpɛ sɛ wɔhu Ghana yɛn amanneɛ
Ahenfie akyeame, ɛkwan a yɛfe so a yɛyɛ adwuma
Wɔabɛdu ha, yɛabɔ wɔn amanneɛ
Wɔn nso abɔ wɔn kwanso de
Sɛ wɔadu ha nnɛ Adae yi a
Na ɛwɔ sɛ wɔaba yi,
Na wɔmba no kwa   10
Wɔkura wɔn nsa mu Hyenapo akɔtowa
Ade a wɔde rebɛbue kwan
Nananom wɔngye na wɔde bi abɔ mpae
Na wɔanya kwan akɔ wɔn dwumadi no so
Ɔkyeame, wɔbae a
Asɛm a ɛwɔ hɔ ne no

OKY 4: Nsabaman mfrė yie!

Response: Yie mmra!

OKY 4: Mon nsėmpa

Response: Yėn nsėmpa yė   20

OKY 3: Mpanimfo mfrė yie!

Elders: Yie mmra!

OKY 3: Ȯkyeame panin, tie ma ėnto Nana Akyeamehene
Na ėnto Nana Agyemfra Nyama
Ėyė yėn wuranom a wȯyė nhwehwė mu
    Wȯ ahenfie akyeame dwumadi ho no
Wȯabėdu Nsaba ha ndė Akwasidae yi
Wȯabėhu sė nananom reyė amanne
Amanne a wȯreyė no ėwȯ sė wȯn nso wȯyė Akanfo yi
Wȯn nso wȯyė wȯn de
Nti wȯkita wȯn nsa mu Hyenapo tumpan baako   30
Ėsi akyeame nsa mu ėkȯ Nana Akyeame hene hȯ
Ade a wȯde rema Ȯdėėfoȯ ma ȯde abȯ mpae
Ma wȯn amanne a wȯrebėyė no wanya kwan ayė
Mepae wo a amanneė a ėwȯ hȯ ne no

OKY 1: Ȯdėėfoȯ, asėntia a ėwȯ hȯ ne se
Ėyė mbarima bi, wȯfi aban mu
Wȯwȯ yėn sukuu kėse no mu
Sukuu biara nni ho a ėsen no
Wȯaba ha, wȯwȯ nhwehwėmu bi a wȯpė sė wȯyė
Akyeamefo dwuma ko a wȯdi wȯ ahenfie   40
Na wȯde som ȯman
Wȯpė sė wȯhu
Na sė ėte saa de a
Na wȯaba a wȯnne wȯn nsapan
Wȯkita wȯn nsa tumpan baako
Ȯdėėfoȯ ngye ė
Ȯmfa mma Nsabaman
Na wȯanya kwan adi dwuma no
Na wȯnhu deė ėbėsi
Wȯde akȯ abrȯn mu nyinaa   50
Obiara agye ato mu
Aka sė ėdu wo Odėėfoȯ anim
Nti Ȯdėėfoȯ, wo nsėmpa ne no

CHIEF: Megye to mu

OKY 1: Nsabaman wɔnyɛ kor mfrɛ yie!

Response: Yie mmra!

OKY 1: Mpanimfo, adehye, wɔnyɛ kor mfrɛ yie!

Response: Yie mmra!

OKY 1: Ohemmaa na mpanimfo, wɔn nyɛ kor mfrɛ yie!

Response: Yie mmra!   60

OKY 1: Asokwafo na mpintinfo
      Wɔnyɛ kor mfrɛ yie!

Response: Yie mmra!

OKY 1: Ɔkyeame (Amoakwa),
Mede asɛm yi refa wo so
Na woama Ɔkyeame Gyan n'aso ate
Na ɛdu Ɔkyeame Agyei hɔ
Na ɛdu ne hɔ a
Woama Nsabaman ate
Asɛntia a ɛwɔ hɔ   70
Ɛyɛ Ɔdɛɛfoɔ,
N'asɛm ara ne sɛ
Nipa atitiriw a ɛte saa yi
Wɔaba abɛpue Nsabaman yi mu a
Wɔagye wɔn nsa no a wɔde bae no
Yɛde bɛyɛ amanne
Na wɔn nso deɛ wɔrehwehwɛ no
Wɔn nsa aka
M'asɛm ara ne no.

OKY 3: Ɔmankyeame, wo nsɛmpa.   80

OKY 2: Ɔmankyeame (The state/people's spokesperson), are you alert?

OKY 4: *I am listening.*

OKY 2:
  Listen so the people of Nsaba may hear.

Today is the Adae festival.
We have important visitors from the university

They want to observe our customs and traditions
And how akyeame perform their duties
They are here today
We have told them the news here
They have also told us their mission
If they have come for this Adae festival
They consider it improper to do so with empty hands   10
They hold a bottle of Schnapps gin
That is their way of clearing the path
That the elders might hear
And utilize it to say a libation prayer
So they can go on with their work.
Ȯkyeame, if they are here, *that's their message.*

OKY 4 (greets first):
  The people of Nsaba, unite to invoke prosperity!

People's response: Let there be prosperity!

OKY 4: *For your consideration.*

Response: *Ours indeed.*   20

OKY 3:
  May the elders invoke prosperity!

Elders: Hence prosperity!

OKY 3:
  Senior Ȯkyeame, *listen so it might reach the head ȯkyeame*
  For him to convey to Nana Agyemfra Nyama, the chief.
  Research dignitaries from the university working on akyeame
  Are here today, the day of the Akwasidae festival
  They have realized the elders are observing custom
  Being Akan themselves they know they have a part to play.
  In their hands, they hold one bottle of Schnapps gin
  It lands in the hands of akyeame   30
  And thence to the ȯkyeame-in-chief
  That is what they have *for* the Generous One
  To pour libation, to enable them to start their work.
  If I called you, that's the news.

(Ȯkyeame 2, for whom the message is meant, happens to be the same as the one representing the visitors. He finds it improper to receive the message he himself started. The message is therefore received directly by the ȯkyeame-in-chief, the highest ranked.)

OKY 1:

Magnanimous One, the *brief message* is as follows:
Some gentlemen have come from the Government
They are from the university
That is the foremost school in Ghana
They are here
Their mission is to conduct some research   40
On how akyeame perform their duties
In the service of the state
And if they are here today,
They did not come with empty hands
They have in hand one bottle of gin
May the Generous One receive it
And give it to her people of Nsaba
So they can perform their duty
And see what can be achieved.   50
The *message has gone through all the various wards*
They have all accepted it
It has come finally to you, Ȯdèèfoȯ,
It's for your consideration.

CHIEF: I accept it.

OKY 1:
People of Nsaba, unite to invoke prosperity!

Response: Let there be prosperity!

OKY 1: Elders, royal lineage, unite to invoke prosperity!

Response: Let there be prosperity!   60

OKY 1: Queenmother and elders: unite to invoke prosperity!

Response: Let there be prosperity!

OKY 1: Asokwafo, hornblowers and drummers,
   Unite to invoke prosperity!

Response: Let there be prosperity!

OKY 1:
Ȯkyeame the second,
I pass this message through you,
So you may let it reach Ȯkyeame X (the third in command),
When he hears it, it would then reach Ȯmankyeame,
The people's ȯkyeame,   70
Who will let it reach the ears of the people of Nsaba.
The brief message is that
The Magnanimous, her word is that
If such men of eminence have arrived at this state of Nsaba
She accepts the drink they have brought
It will be used to perform custom
That everything they have come to seek
Be achieved
That's all I have to say.

OKY 3:
                                                                   80
State ȯkyeame, *it's for your consideration.*

The pattern of relay above would normally characterize all messages to or from the Chief of Nsaba, except that if the guest party had their own ȯkyeame, OKY 2 would take his normal position next to OKY 1.

The above passage is a vivid demonstration of the handling of formal messages in transit, and the overt display by the speakers of their sensitivity to the model of formal communication. The speeches are replete with relay formulae. The speakers ensure that the norms of message relay are strictly adhered to, by a strategy of naming at each point of reception the next route of the message. This way, speech receivers are constantly reminded of the ground rules of communication, and the proximity of the message to its final destination is closely monitored.

The first speaker, speaking on behalf of the visitors, has no textual frame of reference. Words from his principal (us) are not heard on the scene of interaction. Indeed, his principal had in private only told him to present the drink on the group's behalf. The speech is entirely the speaker's own improvisation, even though it is attributed to a principal.

He begins with a greeting to the elders, then alerts the potential recipient of his message, the people's ȯkyeame, since the message has to be heard by the bigger congregation through their spokesman first, before its journey to the chief's ears commences. Thus the speaker maps out the journey of the message, pointing out that its initial goal is the bigger congregation. The ȯmankyeame, spokesman for the congregation receiving the message, does not repeat or elaborate it; he passes it on to the people with a token formula.

The third-ranked ȯkyeame then starts the next step of the relay. He picks up the message and sets it on a course to the chief's ear. This indeed is a very crucial part of the message. Being the beginning point of the message to the chief, any error in

7.1. A party addressing a group of akyeame, so the king may hear. Kumasi, 1988.

mapping the message's course may have a ripple effect on the entire communication process.

He addresses his immediate superior, and lays down the path to be travelled by the impending message: through the next recipient to the highest ranked ɔkyeame, and thence to the chief. Note here the distinction he makes between the ultimate goal of the message, the chief, and the rest of the relay functionaries. Significantly, the speaker projects a parallel course to be followed by the drink gift announced. The drink, he proclaims, goes to the junior akyeame and thence to the ɔkyeame-in-chief, and thereafter to the chief. Both the spoken word and the gift have to travel parallel routes, observing the same protocol of transmission, for their passages have to agree with the existing communication hierarchy, where the chief sits at the pinnacle of power. Like all Akan chiefs, this chief is *Kasa Prɛko,* Ultimate Speaker (and decision maker).

The second-ranked ɔkyeame to whom the message is addressed does not pick it up, since he is also the person representing the visitors; the message is thus received by the ɔkyeame-in-chief (OKY 1), who addresses his talk to the chief.

The ɔkyeame-in-chief begins his relay with a formula promising brevity of speech, yet indulges in some analytic animation of the previous speaker's speech. Significantly, this relay ends with an important piece of metalanguage by the speaker remarking on the journey the message has travelled: "The message has gone through all the various wards and has come finally to you," he says to the chief. Here once again, the chosen path of the message's transmission is ratified with a political statement.

The chief's acceptance message is characteristically brief, but not its animation by the òkyeame-in-chief. The akyeamehene greets in succession the various social and political units assembled and alerts the next-ranked òkyeame as the intended recipient of the message he reports. Being the initial reporter of that statement, the head òkyeame projects the entire course to be travelled by the chief's reply, naming the potential message recipients in descending order (beginning from the highest ranked). The message itself, spoken in three words by the chief, is considerably elaborated by the highest ranked òkyeame. He rationalizes the chief's acceptance of the drink, attributing to her words she has not stated. The second recipient of the chief's reply, on other hand, refrains from elaborate comment. He passes on the message to the people's orator (OKY 4) with a token animation formula.

Each of the speakers above guides the message received to its intended target in various modes of animation. Redundant as such relayed messages seem, though, the audience does not feel restless; neither do the intermediaries feel obliged to hurry the message along by restricting themselves to token animation formulae. The fact is that laid-down modes of transmission are not considered unnecessarily repetitive. For one thing, as seen from the text above, no rendition of the message is an exact repetition of the previous one. Each relayed message brings into sharper focus an aspect of the previous message, without undermining the logic. Indeed, the more the message is relayed, the greater the sense of urgency conveyed to the listeners.

The audience thus sits patiently through the relay process, listening for interesting strategies of animation and elaboration—modes of animation that reveal all the nuances of the message. But it is not the animation strategies only that the audience relish; they also enjoy the allied dramatization of the political process that goes with it, for the passage of messages from the base to the top, and vice versa, is a public reinforcement of the political order, an enactment of the power process.

The political convenience of this process of relay as a stalling strategy should not be overlooked either. The relatively slow passage of the message allows for critical reflection over any issues that may be at stake, and naturally makes possible the refinement of emotional or crude elements in speech that could otherwise threaten the stability of the forum. Indeed, the deployment of such a circuit of communication, like other surrogate-related strategies we have examined, considerably minimizes the potential risks in face-to-face communication.

8 / INTERPRETING THE CHIEF'S WORD

Awerewerewaa na ėnim anadwoboa kasa

(It's the cockroach that best understands the
language of the night beast)

THIS CHAPTER gives ample illustration of ways of interpreting the chief's words with reference to specific speech events. The aim is to examine the mutual affinities between the principal's delivery and the orator's interpretation, and discuss their artistic merits. This way, we are enabled in part to portray the Akan view of accuracy in artistic representation, which becomes particularly crucial in the interpretation of authoritative discourse. In other words, to what extent is the ȯkyeame's pledge to be true to the chief's word consummated on the scene of interaction? In what way are the integrity and authenticity of authoritative speech maintained in the process of relay? And in what proportions do fact and fantasy combine in an ȯkyeame's metadiscourse?

Role Dynamics

In addressing these issues, one does not only have to juxtapose source and interpretative texts. There is the need also to reiterate the thin line the ȯkyeame treads, as a political subordinate to his principal, but also as a counsellor who, in many cases, has greater political sophistication than his lord. This implies that his position as interpreter is not to be equated with that of an inert medium, a static conduit of authoritative dogma. Unlike the situation in puppeteering and ventriloquism, not only is the medium here endowed with an intellect, he also has political rights to edit and reinterpret authoritative discourse within the framework of official policy.

Looking closely at the dynamics of formal speech events, as we will in this chapter, we will be able to note that many of our earlier assumptions about participant roles in the animation process have been to an extent oversimplified. The drift of our discussion so far appears to convey the following impressions: 1) that the principal necessarily has limited rhetorical competence, 2) that the ȯkyeame is necessarily superior to the chief in the art of public speaking, 3) that the principal's source speech is clearly identifiable as source discourse, and not a response to or interpretation of the "animator's" speech.

The above impression, albeit simplistic, is not unintended. It was meant to initiate the reader into the basic tenets of Akan royal speech, without the burden of discerning the complex interplay and transformation of role boundaries. For in real-life situations, there is an element of fluidity in the positions represented.

Even though the oratorical competence of chiefs and akyeame is generally depicted as tilted in favor of the orator, this pattern is occasionally reversed, and a principal may equal or outstrip the oratory of his surrogate on certain occasions, or in general practice. In chapter 5, I illustrated the rhetorical assertiveness of a woman chief who often/not unseldom upstages her orator in public forums due to her overwhelming love of oratory.

Such occasional reversal of the norms indicate a degree of flexibility in the public conduct of formal events, allowing scope for creativity and dramatic surprise in formal discourse. To a large extent, it also paves the way for a rethinking of the position that a principal's speech in a formal setting can be easily marked as the source speech, and the ȯkyeame's necessarily as its animation. Within the continuum of complex public events of which a chief's and ȯkyeame's utterances may be part, it is sometimes problematic assigning roles of principal and animator.

As was noted earlier, the ȯkyeame in the midst of a complex event is capable of non-attributive discourse, and has political license to independently initiate a thought; this trend generated by a surrogate could set off a pattern of argumentation in the mind of his principal. If the principal articulates a viewpoint based on his orator's originality, whose is the source discourse here and whose the animation?

In brief, participant roles in such complex events are in constant flux, as long as each unit of conversation is cued by a previous utterance (see Grice 1971; also Yankah 1989: 120-121). Bakhtin articulates this view more precisely;

> Any speaker is himself a respondent to a greater or lesser degree. He is not, after all, the first speaker, the one who disturbs the eternal silence of the universe. And he presupposes not only the existence of the language system he is using, but also the existence of preceding utterances—his own and others'—with which his given utterance enters into one kind of relation or another (builds on them, polemicizes them, or simply presumes that they are already known to the listener). Any utterance is a link in a very complexly organized chain of other utterances. (1986:69)

This is one sense in which assigning unqualified roles of source speaker and respondent (or animator) to the chief and ȯkyeame respectively is problematic.

Having said that, one would still be able to discern certain divergent structures (linguistic and stylistic) between a principal's discourse and his animator's, so long as the two largely speak from different perspectives—the former projecting his own ego, and the latter minimizing or eliminating traces of ego involvement since he speaks for another.

This chapter is thus divided in three parts. The first is a summary of the salient deictic features that distinguish a principal's speech from an interpretation. The emphasis here will be on shifts in grammatical perspectives in the fulfillment of the two roles.

The second part illustrates two important modes of animation—verbatim and analytic—and the overlap between them, based on excerpts from formal events in different Akan localities. This will focus on the rhetorical continuities or transformations observed between a principal's performance and the ɔkyeame's metadiscourse. The third part further substantiates the various modes of animation, but this time dwells on the dynamics of animation within one unbroken discourse event—an entire arbitration proceeding. This would enable us to observe more closely the interplay of all the attributive modes of animation in one single formal event, as well as witness a dynamic enactment of the social norms of communication as well as their occasional reversal or transgression. In all the three parts, source discourses and their interpretations are juxtaposed, but it is in the third part that all the facets of formal discourse (journey through surrogates, grammar, style, rhetoric) come into play.

Pronoun Semantics and Rhetorical Strategy

From a grammatical perspective, three types of text may be distinguished in formal talk: a) text addressed to a chief (or principal) through an ɔkyeame; b) interpretation by an ɔkyeame; and c) text spoken by a chief (or principal). Even though the three texts may address the same theme, they may involve grammatical shifts in perspective to reflect distinctions between authorial and reported speech and between speech directed to an addressee and that routed through a spokesperson.

Specific marks of grammatical distinction would largely depend on context and subject matter, yet it is possible to make a few generalizations about pronoun shifts, since, for example, in an ɔkyeame's reported speech, referencing expressions in the original statement are changed to suit the orientation needs of the current speaker.

We begin with a few generalizations about the deictic orientation of words addressed to a chief through an ɔkyeame. Since the speaker here does not have direct access to the addressee, all references to him can only be marked by the third person pronoun, or terms of address encoding the addressee's social distinction. In such addresses, there is a marked absence of the second person pronoun, except in formulaic reference to the recipient of the message (ɔkyeame). The use of the third person in reference to an entity present on the scene of discourse deflects the directness of the message and grammatically marks the phenomenon of indirection. The absence of directness here overlaps with the situation in signifying among African Americans (Mitchell-Kernan 1986), or *sanza* among the Zande. Among the Akan, it overlaps with *akutia* (innuendo), except that by contrast with *akutia,* the use of a third person pronoun here in reference to an entity present does not index irony, parody, or ridicule, but is a politeness phenomenon.

Words spoken by a chief, on the other hand, have a wider scope of pronoun reference, even though his speech is similarly routed through a third person. The chief's higher social status and the power differential between him and his addressee allow him flexibility in pronoun reference, whether or not his addressee is on the scene of interaction (see also Brown and Gilman 1972). He may directly use the second person pronoun even as the speech is routed, or may doubly mark the indirection through a third person reference to his addressee. The chief's speech may also be less marked with terms of respect or other social deixis in reference to others.

A significant aspect of royal speech is also the privilege of using the first person pronoun, either singular or plural, in refering to himself or the general royal domain. Since this is authorial, and not reported discourse, a principal's speech may contain egocentric references. If the principal is a chief, responses to his speech by akyeame mark it out (see Section II below).

On the other hand, a royal orator's interpretation, which is normally unmarked by responses, may use the first person pronoun only in exceptional cases; for an òkyeame is a reporter, an interpreter. In his reporting, there is a deictic shift from his principal's first person perspective to third person (in reference to the principal).There is little or no evident ego involvement as long as the speech is attributive. In reference to an addressee, an òkyeame may use the second or third person, depending on whether or not the addressee has his own òkyeame.

The Impact of Style

The language of akyeame is replete with honorifics in reference to "authorized recipients" (Levinson 1986:91), apologies, politeness formulae, and softening mechanisms. It may also contain metaphors, proverbs, and other poetic devices, depending on the speaker's rhetorical competence, the nature of the source speech, and the type of speech event.

These rhetorical features may, in fact, be common in Akan oratory in general (whether delivered by a chief, commoner or òkyeame), but they tend to be particularly relished by akyeame, since embellishment of the source speech is their specialty. The fact is, the retelling of a source speech which has been heard by listeners must be justified by elaboration and embellishment, since the news value of the source speech has in all probability diminished.

It is with this sort of phenomenon in mind that Leech discusses the significance in conversation of the Interest Principle. According to this principle,

> . . . conversation which is interesting, in the sense of having unpredictability or news value, is preferred to conversation which is boring and predictable. One common way in which this principle manifests itself in our everyday linguistic experience is the temptation we feel, when retelling a personal anecdote, to embroider on the anecdote various kinds of elaboration and exaggeration. (Leech 1983:147)

Typical stylistic and grammatical shifts appertaining to various participant roles in formal speech events may be illustrated with the following excerpt from one such occasion, which took place in an Akan location. Here, at a fortieth-day festival (*Awukudae*), the people of the town were giving a formal welcome to the chief, who had hitherto been detained for interrogation by the military Government of the day. [1]

In this event, a subchief, speaking on behalf of his lineage, and the queenmother made a formal presentation to the chief through the latter's ɔkyeame. The subchief's speech, which lasted for less than a minute, was elaborated by the ɔkyeame, who spoke for over three minutes. Note the use of the third person pronoun (italicized) by the speaker in reference to the chief, and the shift in perspective in the ɔkyeame's representation (1982):

Subchief [addresses message to the chief's ɔkyeame]:

Nana Kyeame,
Megyina abusuafoɔ anan mu.
Ma ne nto Nana
Ene sɛ,
Nneɛma bɔne a ɛtoo no no   5
Onyankopɔn ne nsamanfoɔ adaworoma
Ɔkɔeɛ no bɔne biara anka no
Enna wɔasan de no abɛhyɛ yɛn nsa
Ɔbaeɛ no ɔbɛhyiaa bere bɔne
Ɔbaeɛ ara na ne nua panin nso da kɛtɛ so   10
Eno nti sɛ asɛm bi wɔ n'ano koraa a
Na ɔntumi nka papa
Nti gye sɛ bosuo bi agu so
Ennɛ, Nana atena ase a ɔredi Awukudae
Me ne Nana Hemmaa ne me mpanimfoɔ   15
Ne m'abusuafoɔ ne mmaa no nyinaa se
Onyame adom ɔde Nana aba abɛhyɛ yɛn nsa
Megyina wɔnom anan mu
Whisky akɔtowa
Odwan fufuo a ɔtua dua   20
Ɔrebɛdware ne kra
Yɛkuta sika sidi ahaasa
Ɔmfa ntɔ nkosua
Nka ɛsɛ sɛ yɛtɔ kosua
Na ɛha no yɛayɛ ara yɛannya bi   25
Nana mfa ntɔ nkosua
Nhyira ne ho
Asɛm a megyina ha ka ne no.

Subchief [addresses message to the chief's ɔkyeame]:

Nana Kyeame,

---

1. The location of this interaction has been deliberately omitted.

I stand on behalf of the lineage
Let it reach Nana, the Chief
That the mishap that befell *him*,
By the grace of God and the ancestors   5
When *he* went away
He met with no evil and
Has come back to our fold
On *his* return, though, *he* walked into misery
His elder brother, *Panin* X, was on the deathbed   10
Thus even if *his* lips were ready with words
He could not speak out
The blessings of dew had to be awaited to fall
Today, *Nana* has sat observing the Awukudae festival
I, together with the queenmother and my elders,   15
My lineage and all the women,
We say God's grace has brought *Nana*
Back into our fold
I stand on their behalf to present
One bottle of whisky,   20
A white sheep with a tail
Since he will go through soul cleansing rites,
We have in hand three hundred cedis cash
To be used to purchase eggs
These should have come together with the gift   25
But were hard to get
He should buy eggs and cleanse himself
That's the message I stand here to deliver.

In the interpretation by the ὀkyeame that follows, there is a slight ego involvement (use of the first person pronoun) on the ὀkyeame's part owing to the relevance of the chief's arrest to the entire township, including the ὀkyeame. There is also an initial indirect reference to the chief in the third person (lines 5-7), instead of second, due to the delicateness of the topic of political arrest. A direct reference to the chief as having been arrested would have posed a threat to the royal face. The third person pronoun, however, shifts to the more typical second person from line 7 onwards.

Chief's Ὀkyeame [turns to the chief sitting on his left]:

Nana mese wo ahenewa
Saa na Nana Adὀnten ka
Ὀse deė ėdi kan no
Nananom adaworoma, nsamanfoo adaworoma
Ėna seesei Nana abėka yėn nsa   5
Asėm a ėbaeė no, na obi nte ne nka

Yėse Aban se, ȯde ne nsa ato ne so
W'adaworoma, wonni hȯ no
Na awerėho aka yėn
Abusua ne oman no nyinaa   10
Afei yėgu mpaebȯ so, na yėsan yi mmusuo
Yėfrėė nsamanfoȯ no, sė w'asamanfoȯ no mmoa
Na bȯne biara anka wo
Na bėka yėn nsa
Ampa ara wobaeė no, wȯbėkyiaa abusua no nyinaa   15
Yėn nso yėmaa wo akwaaba
Saa berė no na owu ne yarebere nso akȯhyia
Na w'akonta da kėtė so
Na sė abusua no ka sė
Yėreboa Nana Adȯntenhene ne Nana Hemmaa   20
Ma yėayė biribi a ėnyė yie
Ena yėtwe too hȯ kakra
Ena yėhuu sė yėapam biribiara a ėyė fi
Nsamanfoȯ adaworoma, wobaeė yi
Eno ne tete hȯ no a   25
Nka nkosua yi yėabėhyehyė no prėte mu
Nkokȯ na ėgugu so
Ennė nso deė
Ade no nyinaa ayė hwehwė-pė
Etȯ da bi a wopė ade a wonnya   30
Nso wosuro ayėketewa a
Na yėpae wo ayamuonwono
Nti sė wȯn nso yė no sė
Yėnnyaa nkosua nkaa ho
Nti yėretwėn yėretwėn a   35
Na berė no retia wȯn
Nti Nana Adȯtenhene, Nana Hemmaa
Sėbe, adehyeė mpanimfoȯ no ne mmaa no
Yėse yėma wo odwan fufuo a ȯtua dua yi
Sika sidi ahaasa,   40
Nkosua no deė ne no
Whisky kakra ka odwan no ho
Gye na fa hyira wo kra
Na wo sunsum nsan mmra
Na amanneė a ȯde faa w'akyeame so ne no.   45

Chief's Ȯkyeame [turns to the chief sitting on his left]:

Nana, to you I say *ahenewa* [a term of respect].
So says Chief of the Advanced Guards
He says, first of all,

It's by God's grace and the ancestors'
That *Nana* has returned to our fold   5
When the event occurred, nobody heard from him
The government confined him . . . and put their hands on him
By your grace,
Grief overwhelmed us in *your* absence
The entire lineage and state together   10
But we kept praying, performing sacrifices
And invoking the spirit world
To help protect *you* from evil
That *you* might return safe and sound to our fold
On *your* return, *you* did come to greet the entire lineage   15
And we also bade *you* welcome
Those were not favorable times
Days of death met with days of ill health
It was a time that *your* brother-in-law was on the deathbed
It was thus decided by the lineage   20
That the times were not favorable for *them*
To help the Chief of the Advanced Guard
And the queenmother to make a presentation.
Thus action was withheld for a while
As of now, all matters of filth have been cleared   25
By the grace of the spirit world,
Your return should have been marked by *gift* trays
Filled to overflowing with eggs and chickens
Yet times are hard, and all items are scarce
Times there are when you do not get what you want   30
Yet it is said,
If you are afraid to do little favors
They accumulate and earn you a stingy reputation.
Thus, were *they* to decide
To wait endlessly   35
Till eggs became available
Time would not be on *their* side
Thus the Chief of the Advanced Guard and the queenmother
Together with, apologies, the royal family, and the women
They say they offer *you* a white sheep with a tail   40
Three hundred cedis cash, that's for the eggs
A big bottle of whisky to boot
Take these and cleanse *your* soul
To retrieve *your* spirit
That's the news *he* has relayed through your akyeame.   45

Besides the shift in personal perspective between the subchief's speech and its interpretation, we notice in the ókyeame's interpretation a conscious attempt to rationalize the presentation by elaborating on its themes. He refers to events missing in the first speaker's message: the chief's confinement, the misery that overwhelmed the town, their prayers to the spirits; and he rationalizes in greater detail the timing of the presentation. Whereas the ɔkyeame makes much the same references as the original speaker to the gifts, he embellishes his discourse with a proverb that justifies the unusual cash present. His speech is double the length of the original speaker's, and is undoubtedly richer in tropes.

That akyeame normally speak longer than their principal has also been observed among the Ewe of Ghana (who borrowed chieftaincy and related institutions from the Akan). Referring to interaction between the Anlo chief and his *tsiame,* Verdon states,

> He may indeed edit or embellish upon the chief's speech at his liking. Throughout Eweland, the linguist is in fact a public figure on his own right and he may play very important roles in public gatherings according to his oratorical skills. The chief may utter two sentences and the linguist takes fifteen minutes to repeat what the chief said (1983:62).

Verbatim/Analytic Animation

The ɔkyeame's analytic elaboration of the chief's or principal's message, together with the linguistic and stylistic shifts common in the ɔkyeame's interpretation, will be further illustrated in this section, where I discuss combinations of verbatim and analytic reporting by akyeame. For as earlier stated, the various ways of animating a principal's speech are not bounded. Not only can one trace the interplay of verbatim and analytic reporting in a single speech event (with several speakers), but an ɔkyeame's interpretation of a single message may contain both elements. He may repeat the exact words of a chief in one segment of the interpretation, and add his own words in other segments. I hasten to add, though, that verbatim reporting does not imply a wholesale adoption of the chief's personal perspective; the shift in grammatical perspective is inevitable since the ɔkyeame's rendition is invariably an indirect report.

At sittings of the Kumasi Traditional Council at the palace of the king of Ashanti, the king rarely makes a lengthy speech uninterrupted by reframings. After every two sentences or so the king pauses, and one of his akyeame amplifies his word to the audience. The king speaks softly, to the accompaniment of intermittent affirming responses from the chorus of akyeame, after which a senior ɔkyeame repeats his words louder to the wider audience who often do not hear what the chief has said. The chief's words and the ɔkyeame's often answer each other word for word, even though there are occasional stylistic variations between the two.

The occasion was a judicial sitting in 1988 by the Kumasi Traditional Council. A subchief, among others, had been charged with failure to attend the wake of one of the king's akyeame, who had died a few months before. This negligence on the part of the subchief had been greatly lamented by the jury, since the deceased was an important state dignitary. In the course of the deliberations, the Asantehene, Otumfuor Opoku Ware II, exploited the situation to convey his concern about the subchief's negligence. His words were relayed simultaneously to the wider audience. Once again note the shift in perspective between the two texts, and also the unique interspersing of the king's words with ratifying phrases (*sio*) by the six akyeame standing around the king. The animation itself was executed by one of the king's senior akyeame, Nana Amoateng (Kumasi 1988).

KING:
Deė ama m'ani abre saa ayie ho ne sė   sio
Owura no a ȯkȯ ne kra akyi no   sio
Wasom ahenfie ha mfeė aduasa-nkrȯn   sio

OKYEAME:
Otumfuo se deė ama n'ani abre saa nsėm yi ho ne sė,
Owura no a ȯkȯ ne kra akyi no,   5
Wasom ahenfie ha mfeė aduasa-nkrȯn.

KG:
Yėn nyinaa nim dwuma a wadi no ahenfie ha   sio

OKY:
Ȯse yėn nyinaa nim dwuma a wadi no ahenfie ha

KG:
Biribiara nni hȯ a nka yėde bėhyė no anuonyam   sio
Sė nka yėbėkȯ akȯsiri ne pė   sio   10
De agya no kwan   sio

OKY:
Ȯse biribiara nni hȯ a
Nka yėde bėhyė no anuonyam,
Sė nka yėbėkȯ akȯsiri ne pė,
De agya no kwan.   15

KG:
Ėno nti ne mekaa sė nka mpanimfoȯ nyinaa nkȯ   sio
Ma ėnyė fė   sio

OKY:
Ȯse ėno nti na ȯkaa sė nka mpanimfoȯ nyinaa nkȯ,
Ma ėnyė fė.

KG:
Mon nyinaa monim sė   sio   20

M'akyeame deè   sio
Menyè wòn ayie basabasa   sio

OKY:
Òse n'akyeame deè
Mo nyinaa monim sè ònyè wòn ayie basabasa   25

KG:
Ènam hia a èhia   sio
Ène aseda a èsè sè yède da no   sio
Nti na yekòòe   sio

OKY:
Òse ènam hia a èhia,
Ène aseda a èsè sè yède da no,   30
Nti na yèn nyinaa kòòe.

KG:
Mpanimfoò, mesrè mo   sio
Momfa eyi nyè adesua kèse   sio
Sè asèm bi ba saa a, momma yèn nyinaa nkò   sio
Na obi nnim òkyena asèm   sio 35

OKY:
Ose òsrè mo,
Mon nyinaa mfa eyi nyè adesua kèse.
Sè asèm bi ba saa a momma yèn nyinaa nkò,
Na obi nnim òkyena asèm.

KING:
I am serious about this funeral   *sio*
Because the gentleman
Who has returned to his soul's origins   *sio*
Served at this palace for thirty-nine years.   *sio*

OKYEAME:
Otumfuor says,   5
He is serious about these events
Because the gentleman
Who has returned to his soul's origins
Served at this palace for thirty-nine years.

KG:
The role he has played in this palace   10
Is known to you all   *sio*

OKY:
He says the role he has played in this palace
Is known to all

KG:
We would have done him no greater honor   *sio*
Than to observe his wake   *sio*   15
To bid him farewell   *sio*

OKY:
He says we would have done him no greater honor
Than to observe his wake
To bid him farewell

KG:
That's why I said   20
All elders should together   *sio*
Attend to make a good impression   *sio*

OKY:
He says that's why he said
All elders should together
Attend to make a good impression   25

KG:
You all know   *sio*
I don't observe the wake of my akyeame   *sio*
In a haphazard way   *sio*

OKY:
He says, for akyeame's wake
You all know he does not observe them   30
In a haphazard way

KG:
It's due to the importance of this   *sio*
And the need to thank him   *sio*
That we all went   *sio*

OKY:
He says it's due to the importance of this   35
And the need to thank him
That we all went

KG:

Elders, my pardon	*sio*
Learn a good lesson from this, all of you	*sio*
If any mishap occurs we must all attend	*sio* 40
For one knows not	
What misfortune the future brings	*sio*

OKY:

He says he begs you all, elders	
Learn a good lesson from this, all of you	
If any mishap occurs we must all attend	45
For one knows not	
What misfortune the future holds	

Except for a few lexical changes (as in line 1) and clause transpositions (as in lines 26–31), the òkyeame's animation is a precise replica of the chief's message, with all its stylistic contours. The difference between them is evidently that the òkyeame's renditions introduced by the reporting verb (*se,* 'to say') are the indirect counterpart of the chief's direct speech. There is subsequently a shift in the orientation of the discourse, the chief's authorial voice maintaining a first person (singular or plural) pronoun to depict his power and control over the interaction situation, and the interpretation rendering most of these in the third person, to create a distance between the primary and secondary speech situations. This way, the force of the chief's illocutions is stepped down. Significantly, some of the first person plural pronouns remain unshifted in the animation (as in lines 14–19, 31–37) because the òkyeame considers the inherent messages applicable to all, including him.

While the above example largely demonstrates verbatim animation of the principal's word including shifts in pronoun between direct and indirect speech forms, the following illustrates the flexibility privilege of the chief in his use of second/third person pronouns to refer to his addressee. In the text below (Kumasi, Manhyia Palace 1988), the chief straddles between directness and indirection. While he adheres to the protocol of formal communication and speaks to his addressee through the òkyeame, he takes liberties in directly referring to his addressee with a second person pronoun. The turn of the discourse demanded this; arguments were becoming heated, his addressee had provoked the assembly with unruly behavior, and had to bear the brunt of a direct rebuke. The rebuke, though, had to be routed through the spokesperson. But note here the òkyeame's own shift in the strategy of reporting, to meet the emotional turn the interaction had taken. He occasionally shifts from indirect speech to direct quotation of the principal. Here, the reporting verb is occasionally omitted, and the animator's personality almost merges with that of his principal; he speaks his words and replicates his emotions. Volosinov calls this form of representation *quasi-direct discourse* (1973:141).

KG:
Mon nyinaa ahu deė X ayė no ha　　　　　　　sio
Ėyė aniėmmȯwoho　　　　　　　　　　　　　　sio

OKY:
Ȯse mon nyinaa ahu deė X ayė no ha
Ėyė aniėmmȯwoho paa

KG:
Mo adaworoma　　　　　　　　　　　　　　　5
Nyė nnipa anim a　　　　　　　　　　　　　sio
Nka mėtea no paa　　　　　　　　　　　　　sio

OKY:
Ȯse mo adaworoma
Nka ȯbėtea no paa

KG:
Yėrekasa a, wogye akyinnye　　　　　　　　sio　10
Na woreyė deė ėmfata　　　　　　　　　　　sio

OKY:
Ȯse, yėrekasa a na wogye yėn akyinnye,
Na woreyė deė ėmfata
Asėm yi nso nyė asėm kėse

KG:
Wo na wo bo yė hyeė?　　　　　　　　　　　sio　15

OKY:
Wo na wo bo yė hyeė?

KG:
Wo bo yė hye a
Wo kyėn Baafoȯ?　　　　　　　　　　　　　sio

OKY:
Wo bo yė hye kyėn Baafoo?

KG:
Ėyė aniėmmȯwoho kėse　　　　　　　　　　　sio　20

OKY:
Ȯse ėyė aniėmmȯwoho kėse

KG:
Megyi di se wonnyė saa bio   sio

OKY:
Ȯnim sė wonnyė saa bio

KG:
Ėba saa bio a   sio
Akonnwa no me dea   25
Mėgye m'adeė   sio

OKY:
Ȯse ėba saa bio a
Akonnwa no ne dea
Ȯbėgye n'adeė.

KG:
You all have seen the conduct of X   *sio*
It is unruly behavior   *sio*

OKY:
He says you all have seen the conduct of X
It is truly unruly behavior

KG:
By your grace, [*referring to the assembly*]   5
I would have dealt him a severe punishment   *sio*
But I am restrained by faces here   *sio*

OKY:
He says by your grace
He would have dealt him a severe punishment

KG:
As we speak, you challenge us   *sio* 10
And you do unworthy things   *sio*

OKY:
He says, as we speak you challenge us
And you do unworthy things
Though it's a trivial problem

KG:
Do you claim to be bad-tempered?   *sio* 15

OKY:
Do you claim to be bad-tempered?

KG:
If you are bad-tempered
Do you surpass Baafuor?   *sio*

OKY:
If you are bad-tempered
Do you surpass Baafuor, Chief of Bantama?   20

KG:
It is utmost unruliness   *sio*

OKY:
He says it is utmost unruliness

KG:
I believe you will not repeat that   *sio*

OKY:
He knows you will not repeat that

KG:
If it happens again   *sio* 25
The stool is mine
I will take it back!   *sio*

OKY:
He says if it happens again
The stool is his
He will take it back!   30

The principal, in this segment of the discourse, begins with a third person pronom-
inal reference to the addressee in front of him (line 5), but shifts to a second person
(from line 10 onwards) to sharpen the impact of his rebuke. The spokesman, for his
part, follows the mood of the discourse. He adopts the conventional mode of reporting
at the beginning (using the reporting verb), but merges his role with the king's in
portions of the discourse where overt reporting would have been inappropriate (lines
15–20). In such segments, the ɔkyeame removes himself, grammatically, from the
intermediary position; he enacts the authorial voice, projecting the primary perspective from which the king speaks. No doubt the addresser's unruly behavior was
unprecedented and the king had every right to display his wrath, which the ɔkyeame
believed should not be stepped down with words in order to deter future miscreants.

The chief's speech, indeed, had been preceded by a brief autonomous oration by one of his senior orators, Ọkyeame Baafuor Akoto, who had counselled the congregation against such unruliness as was displayed by the elder. His speech was laced with lessons from history (Kumasi, Manhyia Palace 1988):

Tete no, woreba ahenfie a
Wonnim amane a wobėnya
Nti na yėreba ha a yėfura kuntunkuni no
Wo yere koraa wie aduane a
Wose twėn kọsi sė mėba
Nti nananom a moahyia ha
Yėtena na Otumfoọ tena ase
Na morekasa a, ėyė a mesrė mo
Momfa ahobrėaseė nkasa
Hwė, se wote wo fie a
Wo yere ne wo ba mpo wopė sė
Wọde ahobrėaseė kasa kyerė wo
Yėse sėbe aberaw,
'Wogye hempa ma wo wura di a
Wo nso wonya akoapa yọ'
Yėte ha yi yėn nyinaa yėnim yėn ho
Nso woyė biribi a ėnyė a,
Na ėwọ sė yėka kyerė wo.

In the olden days you could never tell
The legal charges that might be awaiting you at the palace
That's the reason those attending court
Came wrapped in mourning clothes
Even after your wife had cooked, you would say
"Wait till I return from court"
Thus, elders here assembled
When we meet here in Otumfuor's presence
Please speak with patience
Even while at home with your wives and children
You expect them to address you with courtesy
It is said, my apologies,
If you seek good kingship for your master
You reap good benefits as servant
As we sit here we all know one another
Yet we are liable to correct you
If you misbehave.

Coming as the above speech did before the chief's address, it could be said to have prompted the chief's, in which case labelling the chief's speech as "source" would be imprecise. Ọkyeame Akoto's autonomous address could be considered a source speech of sorts, while the chief's message, even though depicted as a source pure and simple, is only a source relative to Ȯkyeame Amoateng's "verbatim" relays. Relative to the entire formal interaction, the chief's speech could be arguably considered an animation.

While a greater part of the relayed statements above approximate "verbatim" reports by akyeame, there were certain segments of the interaction that exemplify analytic animation (editing the chief's words). For despite his concern about his unruliness, the king showed his mercy by pardoning the culprit.

In his words,

KG:
Kyere̊ X se̊ mede ne ho kye̊ no
Ma onnye̊ saa bio

Tell X he is pardoned
He should not do that again

These words, which he said in an undertone, were relayed by Ȯkyeame Akoto with a proverb elaboration. The ȯkyeame passed his relay through a chief to whose jurisdiction the culprit belonged:

OKY:
Nana X
Otumfoȯ se memma w'aso nte se̊
Anie̊mmȯwoho a Owura yi aye̊ yi
Nka e̊se̊ se̊ ȯtea no paa,
Ama obi anye̊ saa bio
Se̊be se̊be se̊be, Oburu
Se̊ wo ne wo mfe̊foȯ nam
Na ye̊redane mmoa a dane wo ho bi
Na ebia na ye̊rebe̊kye wo awe
Otumfoȯ se ȯde kye̊ wo.

OKY:
Nana X
Otumfuor bids that it reach yours ears
The misdemeanor by the elder
Should have been severely penalized to deter others
Apologies, apologies, apologies, *Oburu*
If you walk in step with your colleagues
And they transform into beasts
Do likewise
It may be a ploy to eat you up!
Otumfuor says you are forgiven.

In this relay, the ȯkyeame transforms the chief's brief words of pardon into an elaborate caution. Even though he routes the king's official pardon through another chief, he exploits the situation to display his proverbial art. The proverb he deploys appears momentarily out of context with the immediate discourse, since it is not preceded or followed by contextualization cues (see Yankah 1989, chapter 5). In truth, though, the proverb telescopes sentiments that had been expressed in the initial segment of the interaction—sentiments that strike to the very core of the issue at stake. The defendant, during the time of the wake, had been at an informal meeting with other elders. Those elders had wisely abandoned the meeting and attended the wake, knowing its political significance. The defendant should have followed suit, but had imprudently stayed out, not joining his colleagues. The consequence he faces, according to the ȯkyeame, is comparable to that of an imbecile, who failed to join his colleagues' magical transformation and became their victim. Prudence demands strategic adaptation where necessary, to keep from being destroyed, the orator cautions.

Significantly, the orator here overtly attributes his entire message to the king ("Otumfuor bids. . . . Otumfuor says"). "These are not my own words, they are the king's," he implies. Equally important is the ȯkyeame's overindulgence in apologies (sὲbe sὲbe sὲbe) prior to his words of wisdom. Moved by the maxim of politeness in discourse (discussed in Leech 1983: 131–151, Brown and Levinson 1979), the orator profusely apologizes to unratified participants in his message as a way of mitigating the intrinsic discourtesy of appearing to teach wisdom to elders. "Elders, the impending proverbial counsel is not directed at you," is the implication.

Dynamics of Interpreting

The last section of this chapter synthesizes the various strategies of "animating" the chief's word by illustrating them with one unbroken sequence of formal interaction. This example, which is taken from traditional court proceedings, enables us to bring together both formal and stylistic perspectives of speech within the royal domain, depicting the structure of formal speech interaction as well as the various ways in which the chief's words may be relayed.

The proceedings took place in the Bono town of Afrisipa (the Bono are Akan). The case under arbitration was one between the town and Opanin K.M., aged 50, and his colleague, K.D. The chief, a man of over 60, sat with his ȯkyeame, aged 45. In attendance were other elders and attendants. The total number present was about twenty.

It was a case in which K.M., who lives at the boundary point between Afrisipa and another village, had been summoned by the chief for refusing to take part in communal labor. K.M. apparently takes advantage of the neutral location of his hut and argues he is not part of the village of Afrisipa. Earlier in the year, K.M. lost his son, and was nearly refused burial in the village. The burial permit was granted on condition that KM appear later before the chief to settle the matter. In this episode,

KM argues his case in a fiery manner that agitates the chief and his elders. He is eventually asked to pacify the jury of elders with a drink.

Note, in this illustration, not just the various strategies of relaying the chief's words, but also the occasional abandonment of formal norms in portions of the interaction where tempers run high. The defendant and the chief occasionally bypass the intermediary and directly jibe at each other. As a rule, though, all the discourse participants route their messages through the ȯkyeame, who animates the discourse at his own discretion. Being the chief's representative, though, he displays greater bias towards the chief's words. In this illustration, the chief's speech is not accompanied by regular responses as in the previous example; the responses come at long intervals (Afrisipa, Brong Ahafo 1988).

CHIEF (CH):
Ȯkyeame, sė mahyia me mpanimfoȯ a
Asėntia a mepė sė wode to K.M. ne K.D. anim ne sė
Berė bi a atwam no
Asėm bi sii a mepė sė meka
Ma ėfiri hȯ   5

. . . .
Nti sė yėabėhyia ha a
Ȯkyeame, wo nsėmpa.

OKYEAME (OKY):
Yoo Ȯbarima M. sėdeė Nana seė ne no.

KM (defendant):
Seesei deė, menni asėm biara meka.

OKY:
Nana, sėdeė ȯseė ne no.

CH:
Ma no nte sė   10
Yėne wȯn nyinaa na ėbȯ akuraa pam
Nti yėnya akwasafo dwuma a
Ėsė se yėne no na ėyė
Ȯtee ne ho sė ȯrenyė
Ėduruu berė bi a n'ani beree wȯ kwan bi so no,   15
Ȯde ho asėm bėkyerėė yėn
Mpanimfoȯ no yėė sė nka yėmma no baabi koraa
Mma no nkora n'agyapadeė

. . . .
Ȯde kyėwpa baa sė
Akyire yi obėma yėaka asėm biara a ėwȯ hȯ   20

Ebesi nnė ȯmma mmėkaa ho hwee
Nti yėrebisa no dekode nti a
Yėakora n'gyapadeė ama no
Na ėbėsi nnė ȯmmėkaa ho hwee.

OKY:
Yoo KM wo nsėmpa.   25

KM:
Nsėmpa yė
Nana Kyeame, wobėtie ma ato Nana sė
Berė bi mofreė me
Na meyėė no sė seesei
Meyė ȯmandwuma wȯ Tanȯso   30
Na bere a yėyė Tanȯso dwuma no
Saa berė no ara na yėyė kurom ha deė
Sotorȯ mmienu nso yė anihanehane
Nti merentumi nyė ȯmandwuma wȯ ha
Na masan akȯyė bi nso wȯ Tanȯso   35
Mekaae no, ntease anyė n'adwuma
Nti meyii me ba abarimaa no sė
"Seesei mayė yarefoȯ
Wȯrekȯ ȯmandwuma a mentumi nkȯ bi
Nti gyina me gyinaberė
Na ȯmandwuma biara a yėbėyė no   40
Wakȯ bi"
Akȯdaa no nso annyi me amma
Nti berė biara a mobėkȯ ȯmandwuma kurom ha no
Sė akȯdaa no wȯ ha deė a ȯne mo na ėkȯ.

CH (vexed):
Ȯkyeame, bisa K.M. ma me sė   45
Wode asėm bi to wo panin anim
Na nteaseė anyė n'adwuma a
Na ėkyerė sėn?

OKY:
K.M. W'aso mu a.

KM:
Nteaseė a anyė n'adwuma ne sė   50
Mayė yarefoȯ
Na mede me ba abėsi m'anan
Na menka sėn bio?

CH:
Bisa no sė wayė ȯman no bȯne dada no
Nteaseė bėn na ėbaeė a   55
Yėmaa no kwan maa ȯde ne ba bėsii n'anan?

OKY:
K.M. deė, mpanimfoȯ no pė sė wȯkyerė ne sė
Nka berė a yėreyė adwuma wȯ ha saa no
Na nka wone wo kuromfoȯ nyinaa
Na nka moaba   60
Esiane sė ėha ne ėha nyinaa yė adekoro
Nti wo nso woyii wo ba yi
Woantumi ansȯ ne nsa ammėkyerė kȯmitiifoȯ
Anaasė mpanimfoȯ no sė
Ebia me nso Tanȯso adwuma no a meyė no nti   65
Mennya kwan nti ebia
Mede me ba rehyė m'anan
Nti sė wohu sė me ba no wȯ mu a
Na ėkyerė sė ėyė me a
Ėno koraa nka yėrente aseė   70
Ȯno wawie sukuu a ȯyė ȯmandwuma a ėyė yie
Na ėyė dėn na obi de ne nan kȯhyė obi nan
Ȯno nso yė ȯbarima a ȯtumi yė ȯmandwuma
Wo nso wose mayi me nan ahyė no
Ȯno nso nyi ne nan nhyė hwan?   75
Woka asėm a kyerė aseė yie.

KM:
Mese seesei yare a meyare a
Mese me ba no nhyė m'anan no
Ėno na monte aseė no?
Nti meyare no, memfa yareė no mmėyė adwuma?   80

OKY:
Daabi.

KM:
Na afei deėn?

OKY:
Ėno na merekyerė sė, mpanimfoȯ buu bė sė
Yėrekȯ sa koraa a yėsuae yi yarefoȯ yi bėtwani
Yadeė deė yėnka sė fa bėyė adwuma.   85
Nanso dada no a na yėreyė adwuma no nyinaa
Na wonnyare

Yadeė no, bėyė afeė baako ne fa na woyareė
Dada nyinaa wonyare
Na nyė dadaada asėm nso na yėreka 90
Ėno deė yėn a yėwȯ kurom ha koraa
Woyare a yėnka nkyerė wo sė fa bėyė adwuma.

AN ELDER:
Mommisa K.M. mma me sė
Mpanimfoȯ bėn na ȯde ne ba no bėhyeė wȯn nsa?

KM:
Me no mennim. 95
Meduru hȯ a wȯreyė adwuma no
Manhu panin biara.

OKY:
K.M., mepa wo kyėw woresėe yėn bere
Yėmfa no sė wonnim ȯpanin biara
Na wonnim ȯhene nso a ȯde kuro yi? 100
Anaa wonnim ne mpanimfoȯ a ȯne wȯn wȯ kurom ha?
Ebia nka wose: "Nana mebaeė a ėnyė bȯne
Seesei mayė yarefoȯ, mpanimfoȯ nso ėbu bė bi sė
Akwakora to sa a ėkȯ ȯbaabunu deė mu.
Nti mayė yarefoȯ a merentumi nyė adwuma 105
Nti me ba ni a mepė sė mede no bėhyė m'anan
Nti mpanimfoȯ merema mo aso ate."
Ėno na yėrehwehwė sė wobėka ho asėm
Nso wode renwonwae.

CH:
Yoo Nana Kyeame, hyia a yėhyiaa mpanimfoȯ ne K.M. yi 110
Mpanin se paapae-mu-ka ma ahomeka.
Deė mepė sė mesi no pi ne sė
Deė ėdi kan, ȯno ara ano mu asėm kyerė sė wayė bȯne
Meresi no pi aka akyerė no sė
Bȯne a ȯyė tiaa mpanimfoȯ no nti 115
Ȯnka bȯne no ho asėm
Na afei asėm a ėwȯ hȯ no yėnka nkyerė no
Sė ȯrekata so amuamua so deė a
Ȯremma koryė a mepė sė ėbėda yėn ntamu no mma
M'asėm a mepė sė meka ne no. 120

OKY:
Yoo, K.M., wo nsėmpa.

KM:
Edeėn bóne na mayė?

AN ELDER (advising another elder)
A.D., ma Agya Mensa nte aseė
Na asėm no ntwa tia mma yėn nyinaa.

KM:
Mpanimfoȯ, mokyerė sė medi fȯ manyė no yie
Nti deė mopė sė moka kyerė me no monka.   125

CH:
Nana Kyeame, ma me nua K.M. nte sė
Obi ntete nam porȯe nhyė obi ano
Obi kȯduru baabi na sėbe yėbėku no a
Na ėnam n'ano.

OKY:
Ȯse menka nkyerė wo sė
Asėm a yėreka no wonnyaa wo ho nteaseė   130
Nanso obi ntete nam porȯe nhyė obi ano
Nti woaka no saa a
Yėma wo kwan sė sȯre
Na yėne wo nni asėm biara bėka.
Meboa anaa, Ȯdekuro?   135

CH:
Ėno ara ne no.

OKY:
Me a anka wanka no saa anka
Saa na mėka no
Ėfiri sė asėm a yėne wo reka no
Nteaseė anyė adwuma   140
Nanso, sėbe,
Obi nka sė putuo nhye na yėnni dwo
Nso ėhye a yėdi dwo
Sė Nana aka no saa a
Me deė mene no yė adwene sė   145
Ėsė sė yema wo kwan na wokorȯ.

KM:
Nana Kyeame wȯ hȯ?

OKY:
Aane!

KM:
Deɛ Nana aka no merentumi nka sɛ
Waka saa na meretwi afa mpanimfoɔ no so akɔ
Ɛnyɛ buo, nti deɛ ɛwɔ hɔ ne sɛ
Mede dwanetoa bɛma me wɔfa ba, A.Y.

AY:
Nana Kyeame, wobɛtie
Ma Nananom ne mpanimfoɔ ate sɛ
K.M. se deɛ oyɛeɛ no, wanyɛ no yie
Wayɛ bɔne.

OKY:
Yoo mpanimfoɔ, sɛdeɛ A.Y. seɛ ne no
Ɔse K.M. de dwanetoa abɛsi ne so dendenden
Kyerɛ sɛ wayɛ bɔne.

CH:
Nana Kyeame, tie ma me nua no nte sɛ
Mpanimfoɔ na ɛkaa sɛ
Yɛpɛ a yɛbɛhu nti na yɛkyekyere boa a
Yɛde ano siata
Mpanimfoɔ no ara nso na wɔse
Tikorɔ nkɔ agyina.
Ɛno nti na yɛpaw ɔhene a
Yɛpaw ne mpanimfoɔ nso.
Nti sɛ mene me mpanimfoɔ ahyia na
Wɔde K.M. bɔne akyɛ no deɛ a
Merenntumi ntwe wɔn ano nnwɔ fam.
Na mmom, deɛ mepɛ sɛ meka kyerɛ yɛn nua no ne sɛ
Obiara yɛ bone ba yɛn anim ha a
Deɛ ɛsɛ sɛ yɛka kyerɛ no no yɛbɛka.
Mpanimfoɔ se akokɔ baatan nan tia ɔba
Na ɛnkum ɔba.
Sɛ me nua yi aba ha na yɛreka biribi akyerɛ no a
Ɔmma ɛnnyɛ no sɛ yɛpɛ no ɛkabɔ
Na mmon sɛ ɔbɔ ka biara a
Na ɔno ara na wayɛ
Ɛfiri sɛ wasɛe yɛn berɛ.
Na anka asɛm no yɛ tiatiaa bi
Ɛnyɛ sɛ yɛtan no, na mmom
Nokorɛ da hɔ na woka a ɛnyɛ mfomsoɔ

150

155

160

165

170

175

180

Tėkyerėmadė ma abaa tó,
Sėdeė mpanimfoó buu bė no   185
Woama yėaseė berė nti meresi no pi sė
Mėma me mpanimfoó agye no nsa
Na afei yėagye no ato mu.

OKY:
A.Y. mpanimfoó se wo dwanetoa no wóaso mu.

CHIEF:
Ọkyeame, if I have met my elders today,
The small matter I would like to put across
To K.M. and K.D. is as follows:
Some time ago, there was an incident
Which I now want to dispose of.   5

[Speaker goes into a long narration of the incident]
. . . .
If we are here today
The matter is for your consideration.

ỌKYEAME:
Gentleman K.M., so says the chief.

KM (defendant):
Kyeame, as of now, I have nothing to say.

OKY:
Nana, so he says.   10

CH:
Let him hear
That we of this village work together
So we are supposed to do communal labor together
Yet he declines to join us at work
Some time ago when his eyes were flaming in some ways   15
He sought our help
In our rage, the elders even decided
We should refuse him space to secure his property.
. . . .
He then pleaded and promised coming later
To settle the matter.   20
Until now, he never showed up.
So we ask him today,

Why after we allowed him to secure his property
He never showed up to settle the matter.

OKY:
Yes, K.M., the matter is for your consideration.   25

KM:
It is, indeed.
Nana Kyeame, listen so Nana might hear
That you summoned me some time ago
And I explained that owing to the communal labor
I do at Tanoso (the next village)   30
I cannot join in the work here
Because the work schedules coincide.
Two successive slaps cause dizziness
So I cannot do communal work here
And do the same at Tanoso.   35
When I said that,
Understanding did not prevail
[Among the elders]
So I told my [surviving] son,
"I am now a sick man
I cannot do communal labor   40
So stand in my stead
And join in all communal labor."
My son did not disappoint me
Any time you do communal labor in this town
He works with you if he is around.   45

. . . .

CH [vexed]:
Okyeame, ask K.M. on my behalf
To explain what he means by his words,
"Understanding did not prevail"
When he put the matter before the elders.

OKY:
K.M., [it was said] for your hearing.   50

KM:
By "understanding did not prevail"
I only mean I am a sick person
And I have been sending my son as substitute;
What else should I say?

CH:
Ask him, having already offended the village,   55
Was there any agreement between us
Permitting him to use his son as substitute?

OKY:
K.M., what the elders mean is,
Having seen us do communal labor
You and your townsmen should all have come over   60
For this town and that are both the same
But when you sent your son
You could not hold his hand
And introduce him to the committee, saying,
"Due to my work in Tanoso, the other village   65
I have no time
Thus my son is my proxy. . . .
If you see my son, it's me."
Even so, that would still be unacceptable
For your son himself has completed school   70
And is legally liable to communal work
How then does one plant his feet on the other?
He is a man in his own right
Liable to communal work
Having planted your feet on his   75
On whom should he also plant his feet?
Make yourself clear when stating a case.

KM:
I say I am ill
I have asked my son to be my substitute;
Is that what you don't understand?   80
Do you expect me to work while indisposed?

OKY:
No.

KM:
But what?

OKY:
What I mean is, the elders have said
Even in times of war, we swear   85
To exempt the indisposed
And swear to exempt the wine tapper
We are not forcing you to work with ill health.

You were not ill during the previous years
Your illness started only a year and half ago   90
Before then you were healthy
It's the past days we speak of
Men in this town who are truly ill
Are not forced to work.

ELDER:
Ask K.M. on my behalf   95
To which elders did he introduce his son?

KM:
I don't know
I did not see any elder working
When I reported

OKY:
K.M., please
You're wasting our time   100
Let's assume you don't know any elder
Do you not also know the chief of this town?
You could have excused yourself with the words:
"Nana, I came with no bad news
I am now indisposed and the elders have said,   105
When the old man's buttocks shrink
They find their way into his son's
This is my son, he will be my proxy"
That's what we expect of you
But you deviate from the telling.   110

CH:
Nana Kyeame, at this meeting between K.M. and elders,
The elders have said
Plain words bring about relief.

[Speaker continues with a long narration of how he once prevented
another man from burying his kinsman on the village soil because he
was a regular absentee from communal work]
. . . .
The point I wish to stress is,
First, he has himself admitted guilt   115
I am candidly saying he offended the elders
It is this offense he should address
So we can tell him our mind
If he seeks to conceal the matter

The harmony I seek will elude us   120
That's what I seek to tell him.

OKY:
It's for your consideration.

KM:
What is my offense?

AN ELDER [addressing another elder]:
A.D., advise K.M. to cooperate
For the matter to end for us all   125

KM:
Elders, if you mean I am in violation of the law
Tell me what you wish.

CH:
Nana Kyeame,
Let it be understood by my sibling, K.M.
That no one forces rotten meat into another's mouth   130
If one is killed in a strange land
It's from his spoken words.
[Vexed, the chief invites the defendant to walk out if he so
wishes]

OKY:
He says to tell you
You don't seem to appreciate his viewpoint
Yet no one forces rotten meat into another's mouth   135
Thus, if that's the stand you take
We permit you to rise and leave
For we have no case with you
[Turning to the chief]:
Isn't that right, Chief?

CH:
That's right.   140

OKY:
If the chief had not spoken thus
That would have been my own stand
For you have already accused us of lacking understanding
Yet, my apologies,
Nobody prays that the yam barn be destroyed by fire   145

So we could eat roasted yam
Yet if fire happens to destroy the barn
We eat the yam
If that is Nana's word
I agree with him   150
You ought to be allowed to leave

KM:
Is Ọkyeame alert?

OKY:
Yes, I am.

KM:
I cannot take advantage of Nana's words and take leave
In an open show of contempt for the elders   155
It's not a sign of respect
Thus, I seek the intervention of A.Y.

AY:
Nana Kyeame,
You will listen
So the chief and his elders might hear   160
K.M. says he has erred in his conduct.

OKY:
Elders, so says A.Y.
He says K.M. has sought his intervention in earnest
And that he is at fault.

CH:
Nana Kyeame,   165
Listen so it reach my sibling, K.M.
The elders say
It's for the sake of quick retrieval
That we tie a firm knot around a headload
The elders have also said   170
One head does not stand in council
That's why a chief's election
Is followed by the election of his councillors
Thus if my elders say they have pardoned K.M.
I cannot thrust their lips to the floor   175
What I seek to tell our sibling
Is that we shall not spare words on offenders
The elders say the mother hen steps on its young one

Not to kill it
If my sibling has been summoned here   180
And we rebuke him, he should not think
It's from an anxiety to inflict a fine
Yet if he is fined, it's his own fault
For he has wasted our time
The matter should have been a trivial one   185
It's not that we hate him
But truth-telling is no offense
It's the sweet tongue
That disarms the aggressor
He has wasted our time   190
So I will, frankly, ask the elders
To demand a drink from him
Before we accept him into our fold

OKY:
A.Y., the elders say your intervention has been accepted.

(The interaction ends when the defendant pays the drink fine.)

Analysis: Form

The most active participants in the discourse here are the defendant (K.M.), the chief (CH), and the chief's òkyeame. Even though the òkyeame is mainly an interpreter here, his executive role as counsellor asserts itself occasionally. At these times he becomes an active participant and is capable not only of critical analysis, but also of independent statements.

The most remarkable aspect of the discourse here is evidently its distinctiveness as a formal interaction. The metalinguistic indicators here are numerous, and the character of the interaction as socially mediated by an intermediary is evident. The two major participants (the chief and the defendant) route their speech through the intermediary (OKY), who passes it on to the intended addressee.

The chief's initial speech is structured around such formulae as *ma no nte sè* . . . (let him hear that . . .); *bisa K.M. ma me sè* . . . (ask K.M. on my behalf . . .); *tie ma ènto me nua* (listen so my sibling may hear); *ma me nua no nte sè* (let it be understood by my sibling). The defendant's speeches are similarly characterized, except that they display striking omissions of speech routing formulae in very significant portions of the discourse. He complies with the norms of addressing the òkyeame in his first and second speeches (lines 9 and 26), and omits it thereafter, until late in the discourse when peace is in sight (line 153).

The apparent violation of the norms of communication here may be explained by the very nature of the interaction at hand, and the inevitable potential for transgression it carries. For as is evident, the defendant is enraged throughout almost the entire interaction. This indeed appears to be a good test of the pragmatic efficacy of formal communication. Are the norms of routing messages through a third party conducive to tense formal interaction? If so, what are the alternatives available to an irate speaker challenging authority? Does one intending an instant rebuttal comply with the norms of formal communication, by channelling his message?

Indeed, the very nature of tense discourse enables participants to convey attitudes not neccessarily by the content of their message, but by the very mode of transmission they elect. Here the antagonistic nature of the interaction rules out strict conformity with communicative norms; for to channel one's message through a third person may send wrong signals of a peaceful intent.

In the case on hand, the speaker violates the norms of formal communication as a strategy to convey his resentment with authority. His violation *marks* his protest. Significantly, the defendant's violation of protocol begins at a portion of the discourse where he has been challenged by the chief to explain an apparently discourteous statement he had made. In his previous speech, he had implicitly abused the intelligence of the elders, saying that *nteaseè anyè n'adwuma* ("understanding did not prevail," line 37) when he asked them to exempt him from communal labor. Even though the chief elects to route his vexed reply through the spokesman (line 46), the defendant's explanation of the apparent insult ignores the intermediary (line 50), thereby conveying his fury. The strategic avoidance of routing formulae continues until harmony is reached (line 153), when the defendant at last routes his plea, *Ökyeame wò ho?* (Is Ökyeame alert?).

Avoiding the speech-routing formulae, however, does not imply the defendant also violated the norms of visual or kinesic avoidance. While he avoided the linguistic formula, he maintained a neutral gaze and posture: he never brought his body or gaze in direct confrontation with the chief's.

Significant also is the orientation of pronouns used. The chief maintains a first person (singular or plural) perspective throughout his speeches, thereby indicating the direct relevance of his ego to the course of events. Examples include *mepè sè meka ma èfiri hò* (I wish to discuss to dipose of it, line 5), *m'asèm a mepè sè mesi no pi ne sè* (the point I wish to stress is . . . , line 114). Similarly, he uses the third person in reference to the defendant throughout. This grammatical perspective (together with the chief's consistent routing of his messages) helps to distance the defendant (his addressee) from the immediate sphere of interaction and allows the chief to maintain a consistent posture of tact and diplomacy throughout the proceedings. This posture agrees with the content of his rhetoric (see below).

The deictic perspective of the ökyeame in the discourse is equally important. While he maintains the perspective of an interpeter, he occasionally interjects his ego either to clarify the chief's viewpoint or to directly caution or challenge the defendant. In lines 58–77, he directly challenges the defendant, using a first person plural pronoun (line 100), to emphasize a trend of thinking he has contributed; even so, he is careful not to project his personality above the realm he represents. He thus avoids the first person, except in reference to his role as interpreter, and in allusion to his agreement with the chief (line 150).

Analysis: Animation

Certainly the most interesting aspect of the above interaction is the conflation of the òkyeame's role as royal advisor and analytic interpreter, as well as prosecutor. In combining these roles, he does not limit his speech entirely to a superstructure molded on, and artistically replicating, his master's message; he occasionally initiates thought through elaboration of the chief's discourse. This becomes clear in the discussion of the animation strategies below.

The modes of interpretation here are significant for three reasons. First, a secondary social intermediary (different from the òkyeame) emerges in the middle of the interaction; secondly, the òkyeame interprets for both parties (both the chief and the defendant); and finally, the òkyeame's principal (the chief) is himself a master of ornate speech, and displays his fondness for metaphorical language.

By the emergence of an ad hoc social intermediary in the interaction, I refer to the elder whose intervention is sought by the defendant prior to the latter's admission of guilt (line 157). The significance of this type of intermediary within the judicial setting has already been discussed (chapter 4). The judicial system leaves room for a guilty defendant to plead for leniency through a process known as *dwanetoa* (plea for intervention). The functionary here receives the defendant's plea, *medwane toa A.Y.* ("I seek the intervention of A.Y.," line 157), and analytically transmits it in the words *K.M. se deè òyèe no wanyè no yie* ("K.M. says he has erred in his conduct," line 161). This reported plea goes through another reporting phase, since the whole reported message has to be routed through the òkyeame to reach the chief and the elders. The wording by the òkyeame of this double relay demonstrates the three phases through which the message has passed.

The greater part of the animation, however, exists between the òkyeame and the two principal participants: the chief and the defendant. It is clear from the òkyeame's mode of interpretation, though, that he is not interested in according the two speakers equal rhetorical attention. While he merely passes on the defendant's words with token relay formulae ("so he says . . ."), he invests the interpretation of the chief's words with such elaboration and poetic metaphor as it can carry. The ornate speech of his patron, though, does not lend itself to easy embellishment by the òkyeame, and at certain points, the principal's speech is the more foregrounded. I shall examine the animation process from the beginning of the interaction.

The chief's initial narration of the day's agenda receives only token formulaic attention from the òkyeame, since it is a long narration. The trend continues through the chief's detailed report on the defendant's clash with the elders in the past. Note the euphemistic reference by the chief to the burial of the defendant's son. Verbal courtesy not permitting overt reference to burial of corpses, the chief uses the euphemism *kora n'agyapadeè* ("secure his property," line 18), a sign of his good linguistic breeding. His speech is matched by the defendant, who defends his position with a proverb that ratifies his inability to commit himself to labor on two locations: "Two successive slaps cause dizziness," he argues (line 33).

The first major elaboration of the chief's rhetoric by his orator comes when the chief interrogates the defendant about the propriety of using his son as substitute labor. The chief's few words are given depth by the orator, who argues (line 58 onwards) that the defendant's son cannot be a reasonable substitute, since the latter is himself legally liable to communal work. He challenges the wisdom of delegating this responsibility, since, among other things, it creates problems of accountability. This ornamentation of the chief's discourse introduces new elements. Significantly, the ókyeame prefaces his animation with a phrase that underlines its interpretive intent, *Deè mpanimfoò pè sè wòkyere ne sè* . . . ("What the elders mean is . . . ," line 58). This elaborate animation leads to a brief dialog between the ókyeame and the defendant, in which the ókyeame proverbially concedes that exemptions are inevitable in genuine cases. In wartime, for example, the sick and the wine tapper are excluded from conscription (the latter because he has to supply the warriors with palm wine). "Yours, however, is not a genuine case," the orator implies. It is to be noted that this speech by the ókyeame has no textual frame of reference from his patron. It was solely contrived and executed by the surrogate to meet the exigencies of court prosecution.

From this point, another elder injects a question to the defendant, whose reply begets another autonomous statement from the ókyeame (line 95 and following). Without reference to any source discourse, the ókyeame constructs a hypothetical alternative which the defendant could have earlier deployed to lessen his guilt: he could have passed through the proper channels in arranging for a proxy. There would have been nothing wrong in using a son as substitute, implies the orator; but this point is effectively driven home by a proverb that implies that father and son complement each other's efforts (line 105).

The orator returns to his role as interpreter after his patron has used a proverb underscoring the power of indiscreet speech to subvert order. It is obvious to all present that the defendant's imprudent choice of words could worsen his plight, and the chief nails home a timely proverbial reminder as a caution: "No one forces rotten meat into another's mouth" (line 130). This aphorism implies that the defendant is the cause of his own downfall. The chief's explanation makes it clear that choice of words can make or break a situation, and that the defendant has clearly chosen the latter. At this point, the chief ironically gives the angry defendant leave to quit the premises if he so wishes.

The ókyeame's animation of the chief's speech quotes the chief's proverb verbatim and relays his sarcastic permission. In the next breath, the ókyeame enlarges on his previous interpretation, saying the chief's sarcastic instruction was timely; for it was a course of action he was going to propose himself. This signals the ókyeame's prerogative to initiate new trends of argumentation during the debate (see chapter 9), without reference to his master's word. He then goes on to elaborate in proverbial terms the position his patron has taken. The defendant is to blame for his own plight, he argues; and as much as one does not pray for another's guilt, one does not protest if such guilt comes naturally, for it enables a fine to be assessed without effort. The proverb he invokes to capture this sentiment is refreshing (line 145): when the barn is naturally destroyed by fire, one is not to be blamed for eating the yam accidentally cooked.

This piece of autonomous rhetoric by the orator leads to a dramatic turn of events. Caught between walking away from the court premises and staying to face the music, the defendant admits his guilt and seeks the intervention of a respectable elder. Leniency is requested, and the defendant is ordered to pay a drink fine, with which he willingly complies.

In the chief's closing remarks, he once again produces a display of ornate speech which his orator, unable to match, passes on with a token relay formula. In this speech the chief, in proverbial language, rationalizes his agreement with the jury's pardon, alluding to the democratic principles that bind his political machinery: *Ti korò nkò agyina* ("One head does not stand in council," line 171). In the latter part of his speech, the chief turns once more to a proverb which alludes metaphorically to the ability of the spoken word to dissipate conflict—a rhetorical resource the defendant had woefully failed to exploit. Such an elegant display of oratory leaves no room for embellished animation. The òkyeame, sensing this, leaves it intact, and directs his attention to the fine assessed.

As one òkyeame put it: "When the chief's word lands on the right path, I don't add to it."

9 / WITHOUT HIS PATRON'S VOICE

IN THE PREVIOUS chapter, we discussed the interplay between the oratory of the royal spokesperson and that of his patron, pointing out their symbiotic stylistic and rhetorical features. Even so, it was stressed that the ɔkyeame has political authority to assert his own rhetoric on behalf of the royal domain, public speech that *substitutes* for, rather than *supplements,* the chief's word. In our discussion of the analytic mode of reporting by the ɔkyeame, we noticed the occasional liberties he takes in initiating trends of thought and argumentation that are capable of cueing his principal's rhetoric. Such illustrations themselves point to the continuity rather than the discreteness of the substitutive and supplementative categories of animation. Besides this, formal interactions leave room for autonomous or substitutive rhetoric by the orator—speech that is not basically metalinguistic, or interpretive of a patron's.

Indeed, akyeame are more often heard than their patron, since their voice is the more indispensable in a royal speech act (as was discussed in chapter 7). They are very active in court, where they may prosecute a case or advise the court on history and customary law. Akyeame may also counsel a newly installed chief or enact a libation prayer. Akyeame may carry out an entire prosecution or cross-examination without a word from the chief; they may interrogate litigants and witnesses, and may directly debate a disputed point on the basis of past experience and customary lore. During judgment, they voice their opinion on the verdict before the chief, even though the latter's word is final. It is the akyeame, indeed, that often sustain the rhetoric in a court of law and set the mood for final judgment by the jury of elders presided by the chief. A greater part of akyeame's contribution during prosecution is not structurally linked to a patron's; it is independent. Akyeame become the source or principal of that discourse, and at the same time the voice box that sounds it.

The implication is that their autonomous speech is not necessarily restrained from ego involvement, even though it still belongs politically to a subordinate frame. Indeed, in spite of its autonomy, the akyeame's contribution is still made on behalf of the royal realm, to which it may make occasional references. Source statements by akyeame may be either in the form of dialogues or extended monologues. It is often in extended statements that orators indulge in refined court speech, replete with metaphors, proverbs, euphemisms, and deferential politeness formulae. During cross-examination of litigants, by contrast, akyeame are more interested in fact than ornamentation.

Below is part of an ɔkyeame's questioning of a plaintiff, who has reported the infringement of his farm land by its former owner. The family of the plaintiff had purchased land from a man long ago. Later, the original owner attempted to reclaim the land, arguing that the original agreement entitled him to. Deliberations on the case by the Kumasi Traditional Council included the following cross-examination by one of the Ashanti king's akyeame, Ọkyeame Banahene (Kumasi, Manhyia Palace 1988):

> OKY: Was there agreement that you wouldn't plow the land, nor plant cocoa, coffee, palm trees? PL: Yes, it was agreed we wouldn't plant those on the soil. OKY: Don't you know he arranged that because he might need his land in future? PL: No, he had handed the land over. OKY: Was it given to you as gift? PL: The takeover had been accomplished. Libation had been poured on it. OKY: Is it virgin forest or cocoa farm you contest? Is it shrubs you speak of or is it land? PL: Shrubs. OKY: Are you aware a landowner has the right to reclaim his land anytime he wishes? PL: Yes, but even so, land on which libation has been poured cannot be reclaimed without reference to the elders. OKY: What is the prevailing agreement? PL: None, except that those to whom the land had been leased should contribute to defray his debt. Everybody contributed. After that we made a written agreement that we wouldn't interfere with each other's farm land. OKY: Were you the first to clear the forest? PL: It's my grandfather that cleared the entire forest. OKY: Your grandfather? PL: Yes, my grandfather. OKY: Is it the shrubs on which libation was poured? PL: It's my grandfather that cleared the entire forest; he is no more. OKY: Is it the forest on which libation was poured? PL: It is shrubs; it's turned into shrubs. OKY: Does that mean it was once weeded? PL: My forefathers have weeded it over and over again.

This dialogue demonstrates the rigor that characterizes the ọkyeame's prosecuting duties. Without prompting by a patron, he presses the plaintiff on the exact status of the land and on how much "sweat equity" the plaintiff's family has put into it. Fairness in the chief's verdict often depends on the rigorousness of the prosecution, which the ọkyeame executes relying entirely on his own experience and knowledge.

In voicing his judgment on a case, the ọkyeame may offer historical hindsight and invite the jury to examine the issue from a broader perspective. In the following case, Ọkyeame Baafuor Akoto of the Ashanti state invites the jury to increase the defendant's penalty, since the offense he has committed does not befit an elder who once held a chiefhood. It was a case in which the defendant had been accused of illegally plowing a piece of land belonging to the plaintiff. The latter, claiming ownership of the land, had challenged the defendant with the great oath of Ashanti. On hearing the oath, Ashanti law would have required the defendant to stay off the land, or contest the claim with a counter oath. He had used none of these alternatives, but had encouraged his spouse to plow the land.

After judgment had been given, Ọkyeame Akoto, in an after-thought, gave a brief oration that worsened the accused's plight (Kumasi, Manhyia Palace 1984):

Nananom adaworoma, na wodi Yọkọhene
Wo ara wonim sẹ woyẹ panin
Sẹbe mpanimfoọ aka asẹm bi sẹ

Kwaeanoma na ėnnim se ėmo yė aduane
Na ėnyė serė-mu-anoma
Sė obi na ȯnnim a
Na ėnyė ȯpanin sė wo.

I remember you were once a subchief
By the grace of the ancestors,
You were once Yokohene of —
You yourself know you are an elder
Apologies, the elders have said,
It is the forest bird,
And not the bird of the grassland
That does not know rice is edible
If one should be ignorant of tradition
It should not be an elder like you.

We notice in this speech the speaker's reliance on his own perspective and experience to project his own view of the case. The oration here has none of the indexical marks of a report; it could as easily have been a principal's, since it highlights a
first person pronoun in the first line. The speaker, however, still maintains politeness formulae in recognition of the formality of the forum. He uses a deference
formula, *Nananom adaworoma* (By the grace of the ancestors) to acknowledge the
benevolence of ancestral spirits in the defendant's past position as chief, and he
frames the proverb he uses to denote his courtesy to the forum. The apologetic
preface he employs seeks to narrow the range of the proverb's target; it is directed
exclusively at the defendant, and not meant to impugn the sophistication of the
elders present.

Akyeame may also take advantage of a judicial forum to articulate the existing
customary law upon which their verdicts are based. In the following example,
Ȯkyeame Banahene (of Ashanti) at a judicial sitting of the Kumasi Traditional
Council, sheds light on customary law. The defendant had failed to present drinks
to the chief of his village, on the death of the former's sister, with the excuse that he
is politically superior to that village chief. After judgment had been given against
the defendant, the ȯkyeame volunteered information to the court on Ashanti custom
(Kumasi 1988):

Adeė a ėyė amanneė a yėsuro paa
Ėne, sėbe akudȯntȯ sunsum ho adwuma
Asieė, tete hȯ no
Sėbe, oburu, sė obi tȯ hȯ sei tim
Ėyė anȯpa a na yėabua so   5
Sė abusuafoȯ nkasa nkyereė onipa no
Nyii no adwareė a
Yėnto tuo, yėnsu

Ėno ėyė akyiwadeė a ėda hȯ a
Ėyė Asante amanneė   10
Ėnna yėtena ma adeė kye nso a
Mpanimfoȯ,
Ȯdekuro de nsa kȯbȯ Asaase Yaa amanneė
Bȯ nsamanfoȯ amanneė sė asėm a aba nie o
Aduru sė yėgya no kwan   15
Yėte man mu ha yi
Ėsoro ne asaase na yėsom

. . . .

Ansa na wode sȯsȯ bėbȯ fam no
Na wonim sė owura a ėsė sė
Woka kyerė no ma ȯyė saa adeė no   20
Ėsė sė wokȯbȯ no amanneė
Wode nsa kȯma no ma ȯde akȯbȯ mpaeė
Ansa na wode sȯsȯ abȯ fa mu
Na sė woamfa nsa ankȯma no ammȯ mpaeė deė a
Na ėkyerė sė woato amanneė, akudȯntȯ . . .   25

One thing we highly revere in customary practice,
My apologies, *akudȯntȯ*,
Are rituals for spirits, rites of burial
In the olden days, apologies *oburu*,
As soon as someone fell, we covered him up   5
If it was morning.
If lineage members did not speak to the person
And remove him from the bath house
There were no gunshots, no tears
It is a big taboo in Ashanti custom.   10
If one waits till the next day,
The elders and the chief, with drink in hand
Tell the news to Asaase Yaa, Earth Goddess
They tell the news to ancestral spirits
Saying such and such has happened, alas!   15
It's then time for bidding farewell
In this state we live,
It's the sky and earth we worship

. . . .

Before you strike the earth with the hoe
You should inform the elder in charge of the rites   20
You should tell the news to him
Give him drink to say the prayer
Before you strike the earth with the hoe
If you do not give him drink to say a prayer,
You have violated the law, *akudȯntȯ*.   25

In the above speech, the delicate subject matter of death, coupled with the formality of the forum, compel the speaker to indulge heavily in euphemism and politeness phrases. He intersperses his address with apologies and polite addressives (*oburu, akudȯntȯ*) to reduce any incidental offense that may be conveyed by his apparent vulgarity. This is done to doubly assure that he does not offend the decency of the forum by overt references to death. Significantly, the lexical forms for which he apologizes are themselves euphemisms. The speaker makes no overt reference to death, corpse, grave digging, and burial. He uses euphemisms: *to* (fall) instead of *wu* (die); *nipa* (person) instead of *funu* (corpse); *fa sȯsȯ bȯ fam* (strike the earth with the hoe) instead of *bȯ nna* (dig grave); and *gya kwan* (bid farewell), instead of *sie* (bury).

The use of euphemism is, certainly, another dimension of indirection. Like the strategy of avoiding direct confrontation with royalty, euphemisms are used to ensure that the private sphere of participants in formal discourse is not unduly violated. Thus as the ȯkyeame educates on customary law, his speech is still bound by the norms of formal communication.

Like the above example, the following speech by Ȯkyeame Baafuor Akoto relies extensively on the speaker's experience in history and customary lore (Kumasi 1988). Ȯkyeame Akoto directly advises a new chief of Chiraa (in the Bono region) and the general public on chiefly comportment and good service prior to the chief's pledge of allegiance to the king of Ashanti. His speech is not introduced by a reporting phrase. Even so, he feels obliged to validate his word of advice by attributing one statement to his patron (line 50). The fact is that functionally, the autonomy of the ȯkyeame's speech here is only by comparison with other modes of animation where he responds to the chief's word. Note the politeness formulae, metaphor, proverbial language, and greater intrusion here of the ȯkyeame's ego.

The use of the present tense in the first 12 lines of the passage is also worth noting. Of the two chiefs referred to, one (Nsumankwaahene) is alive, and the other (the former chief of Chiraa) is dead. Since the two are linked in the argument, the speaker considers it safer to use the present tense: after all, the dead are of current relevance to the living. The closing part of the address is directed at the king, whom the ȯkyeame formally requests to release the stool to the new chief.

Mo mu pii wȯ hȯ a
Monnim Kyeraa akonnwa yi diberė wȯ fie ha
Mo nyinaa mo ani tua Nsumankwaahene, ȯba a
Ne ntoma da n'asene mu
Nkyeraahene, ne ntoma da n'asene mu   5
Dwuma a wȯbėyė ama Otumfoȯ no
Yėnnom sei yėnntumi nnyė
Ȯye ahenkwaa paa ara wȯ Kumase fie ha
Yėn a sėbe yėte Kumase ha mpo
Deė ȯyė no yėnnuru ho   10
Mowȯ Bono nohoaa yi, Megye di sė
Nka mohoahoa mo ho

Akyire yi na yėtete nsėm
Sė mote ȯman no fimfini ntira o
Mote hȯ yi,   15
Nka ȯhene aso ne mo aso
N'ani ne mo ani
N'ano ne mo ano
Biribi ara a mote anaa mobėhu no
Na nka moama Nsumankwaahene ate   20
Na Otumfoȯ ate
Ėfiri sė mote dȯm mfinimfini
Nti mesrė Nana a ȯrebėdi adeė yi
Sė sėbe, wosom sompa a
Na yepagya wo   25
Nyė sė wote hȯ ara a
Na yėapagya wo
Ebia mo ani da so sė
Aman a Otumfoȯ ayė won amanhene no
Nka mofata   30
Ampa nka mofata
Nanso yėhwė wo nsomee mu a
Yėmfa mma mo?
Yėnsina sika kȯkȯȯ nhyė akokȯhwedeė nan
Na ȯmfa ntu nkȯ?   35
Yėnyė no saa
Nti Nana a woaba
Mesrė wo sompa
Na sė wosom sompa a na yėma wo so
Nana wȯ hȯ yi, ȯntan obi na ȯnnȯ obi   40
Na wo a ȯhwė a wofata
Na wosom no, na wo kuro rekȯ so no
Na wapagya wo
Nti deė mesrė mo ne sė
Obi nnim ahentirim yi deė   45
Wo a wobėdi hene no
Som sompa
Wo mmaa ne mmarima mmoa wo na ėnko so
Na Otumfoȯ se ȯte saa na ȯreka asėm bi akyerė wo a
Na ȯnim sė ȯde ma wo a   50
Wobėtumi ayė deė ėfata
Nti morekȯ yi, mesrė mo
Monnyė wentwiwentwi
Onipa biara wohwė adeė na
Woanhwė no yie a   55
W'ani ka hȯ
Wohwė ha kakra na woakȯhwė ha kakra

Ebeye den na woahu
Wohwe faako a na wohu adee wo mu
Nti dee mereka akyere mo ne se 60
Nana adaworoma
Oma akyeame de ahennwa yi ma wo a
Hwe sompa
Opanin a mehunu se ote adwa yi so no
Na ote Kumase ha 65
Nkyeraa mpo dee, na oko ho nkakrankakra
Nti mesre wo, worebedi adee yi
Tena ha na w'ani mmra ha
W'ani ba ha, na woduru nohoaa a
Na obiara suro wo 70

Mese wo oburu
Nananom se, w'adaworoma
Se one ne mpanimfoo ne ne manfoo nyinaa aba se
Enne, worebesre onana tuo ama no a,
W'adaworoma, wontan no 75
Wo nana ne no
Nti fa ma no, oburu

OKY:
Most of you here know nothing
Regarding the importance to this state
Of the Chiraa stool
While here, you often see the Asumankwaahene
His cloth firm around his loin 5
The [late] chief of Chiraa
His cloth firm around his loin
The service they render to Otumfuor
Cannot be matched by us
He is authentically a courtier in Kumasi here
My apologies, 10
Even those of us in Kumasi here
Cannot surpass his services
You people from the Bono area, I believe,
Are proud to be part of us
In the past rumors were rife [about you] 15
Is it because you sit in the middle of the state?
Normally, the king's ears
Should have been your ears
His eyes your eyes
His lips your lips 20
Whatever you hear or see

Should have been passed on to the Nsumankwaahene
That he'd tell Otumfuor
For you sit in the midst of multitudes
Thus I plead of the new chief   25
If, my apologies, you are of good service
You will be elevated
One is not elevated for nothing done
You, in all likelihood, expect Otumfuor
To raise your chiefship to a paramountcy   30
As has been done for others
Truly you would have deserved it
But does the quality of your service merit a raise?
Should we tie a string of gold nuggets
Around the leg of the wood hen   35
That it may fly to the woods?
That's not the practice
Thus, incoming chief
I request good service of you
It's good service that brings about promotion   40
Nana the King loves none and hates none
He elevates him who serves well
And whose township progresses
What I request of you is that
Since the contents of a chief's head   45
Are known to none
Be a good servant
With the help of your women and your men
Otumfuor says if he is convinced you are of good service   50
Then he will be self-assured telling you good news
As you go now, I urge you not to create conflict
Any person with vision
Who does not look well sees nothing
If you disperse your looks here and there
How well can you see?
You command clear vision   55
If you focus on a single spot
All I say is if by Nana's grace
He permits the akyeame to give you the stool
Be of good service
The past occupant of this stool   60
He lived in Kumasi here
And went to Chiraa from time to time
So I request of you
As you inherit the stool there
Stay here and consult frequently

It's through frequent trips here   65
That your subjects will hold you in awe
[Turning to the king]
I tell you, Oburu, the elders say
By your grace,
If his councillors and citizens are here today
To request on his behalf the gun of his ancestors   70
By your grace, he is not your adversary
He is your grandchild
Give it to him, oburu

Ọkyeame Akoto's speech here depicts experience and knowledge of Ashanti history. Having been ọkyeame for more than 50 years, he volunteers advice to the newly installed chief, a man in his thirties. The words spoken here do not interpret prior words spoken by his patron. The situation indeed allows the speaker greater scope to display his knowledge and creativity, since he is not operating within a textual frame of reference.

Even though he speaks on behalf of his patron, he feels free to personalize the opinion he projects, in phrases like *megye di sè* ("I believe," line 11), *mesrè wo sompa* ("I request of you good service," line 38), *Deè mereka ara ne sè* . . . ("All I say is . . . ," line 57). It is true that he overtly attributes one statement to the king: "Otumfuor says if he is convinced you are of good service," (line 50), and makes allusions to his perspective in 13-25. More important, the entire speech is made with the aim of soliciting loyalty to the king. Nonetheless, most parts of the speech have the structural trappings of a principal's.

Also significant are the politeness phrases and apologies used by the orator to mitigate possible offense in his use of words. Making reference to the unsurpassed services of the previous chief of Chiraa, the speaker, in line 10, prefaces his remark with an apology, lest his words are interpreted as trivializing the services of other courtiers. Similarly, note the frequent use of performative phrases of politeness, *mesrè sè* . . . to overtly mitigate any appearance of discourtesy to the addressee.

The orator's message here partly touches on delicate matters, for there was a historical controversy of divided allegiance in the area where the new chief belongs. But the issue is tactfully managed. He only glancingly alludes to the new chief's pride in associating with Ashanti (line 13), but stresses the loyalty of the previous chief. This stress on loyalty has historical echoes and reaches a climax in the orator's use of a proverb (lines 34-36) that depicts the political inexpedience of rewarding a disloyal subject. Such a reward would be as injudicious as decorating an alien bird with a nugget of gold, according to the ọkyeame. This proverb is followed by an extended metaphor that portrays the negative effect of unstable vision. It is a concentrated gaze that yields clarity; in the future, implies the speaker, the new chief should not be lured into unfocused attention.

In the latter part of the speech, Ọkyeame Akoto directs his speech to his patron, formally inviting him to symbolically release the reins of power to the new chief. Here once again, deference formulae intersperse his speech. The politeness forms,

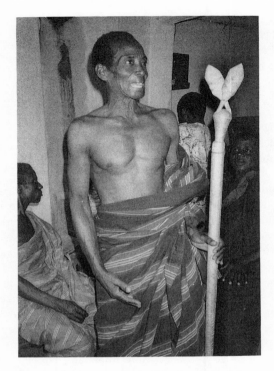

9.1. An ɔkyeame at the height of a public debate, with a staff depicting two identical leaves: "The genuine and the false cola leaves are discerned by the wise child." Agona Nsaba, 1988.

Wo adaworoma (By your grace) and the term of address *oburu,* reduce any impression of imposing on the king. Also noteworthy is the symbol denoting the transfer of royal power: *tuo* the ancestral gun.

Libation

The one single genre in which akyeame virtually hold a performance monopoly is *mpae,* libation prayer. Even though chiefs and other elders may say formal prayers when the need arises, the delivery of *mpae* (or *apae*) on public occasions among the Akan is generally held to be the duty of the ɔkyeame.

It is true that the ɔkyeame is held to be acting on the chief's behalf. As the political and religious head of his people, the chief constitutes the link between the human and ancestral worlds. Thus it is he who has to invoke the help of the spirit world through libation prayers on festival days and in times of crisis. However, this

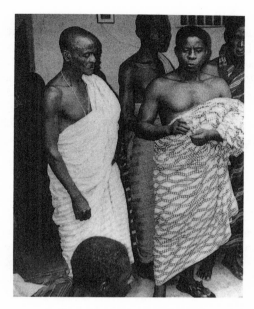

9.2. An ɔkyeame pouring libation. Agona Nsaba, 1988.

royal duty, like other religious ones, is delegated to the ɔkyeame, who is a specialist in prayer.

Mpae-yi, prayer delivery, involves a highly structured recital accompanied by drops of gin (or wine) for the spirits. But the recital is not a commonplace one. It requires mastery of lineage history and genealogy, familiarity with the pantheon of benevolent gods, and a good memory for the formal appellations of the various entities named in the prayer. Beyond this, a good officiant has to be fluent enough to move the audience with a continuous flow of stylized speech and metaphor.

Two types of audience from asymetrical realms need to be distinguished here. The first is the primary but unseen audience of deities and spirits for whom the prayer is meant; these are the forces of beneficence.

There is also the secondary audience, those physically present on the scene of discourse—the potential beneficiaries of the prayer. Both audiences exert some influence on the mode of performance and rhetoric employed (see Ben Amos 1972; Yankah: 1985b). In recognition of the power differential between the performer and the spirit world, a libation performance requires kinesic self-humbling on the officiant's part. He bares his shoulders and feet to signal his humility, and speaks with a tone of politeness.

But the performance is not necessarily a single-voiced one. Libation prayers offer a unique opportunity for words spoken by the ɔkyeame to be affirmed by a responder. In this case, the ȯkyeame's normal role as responder for a patron is delegated; he generates the source discourse and allows an ad hoc "interpreter" to ratify his message. Here, the normal recipient of formal speech becomes the source (of a sort), even though the entire performance is on behalf of another principal. Response in libation prayer is an intrinsic part of performance; for besides responding, it is the assistant's duty also to hold the drink bottle and replenish the officiant's glass as it progressively empties in the course of the prayer.

The rigid structure of *mpae* is notable. Even though the officiant is allowed an unlimited scope of creativity in his diction, he sticks to the following sequence in the organization of his message.

a) Invocation
b) Message
c) Solicitation
d) Curse

During the invocation, the officiant invokes the forces of beneficence, observing the Akan religious hierarchy where God is the supreme being, followed by Mother Earth, the pantheon of lesser gods, and the ancestors. The message segment of libation often highlights the occasion and the purpose of the prayer. This is followed by solicitation, in which the speaker solicits support for the spiritual, moral, and material well-being of the lineage or society. Officiants here often exploit the occasion to make oblique references to delicate political problems for which the society needs help or counseling. In a few cases, a chief's misdemeanor will receive indirect mention, in the hope that wiser counsel from the spirit world may prevail on him. The concluding segment of *mpae* is often reserved for the pronouncement of a curse on the forces of evil.

The libation prayer in the final analysis is a poetic enactment: a unique interplay of worship and verbal wit. We find below a vivid libation enactment by Ȯkyeame Yaw Kwakye, orator of the paramount chief of Kwahu, on the occasion of an Akwasidae festival at Abene, May 1988. Responses have been included here. The delivery was extremely fast and fluent, and the prayer was highly acclaimed by the audience for its flow, historical allusions, and metaphorical phrasing (Kwahu Abene 1988).

Libation by Kwahu Kyeame (Ȯkyeame Yaw Kwakye)

Onyankopȯn Twediampȯn, nsa	sio
Asaase Yaa, nsa	sio
Tena ne Biretufoȯ nsamanfoȯ, nsa o	
Obunyame Yirententu, nsa o	
Werȧkyekye Asamoamono, nsa	
Okwawu Mampong Agyei, nsa o	ampa
Subiri Amponkye, nsa	
Akasu, nsa	
Agoso, nsa	
Adanhemaa Koduedu, nsa	ampa 10

Asuo Kwasi Kotobrigya, nsa   sio
Awomfra Bediako, nsa
Awonso Abena, bėgye nsa nom   sio
Okwawu Asuo Afram, nsa o   ampa
Mintiminim Akwasi bėgye nsa nom o   sio
Ohene nana Fofie Agyeman
Okótóbuo a ósi Afram agya   sio
Gye nsa nom, Opeafo
Okwawu Buruku, ani a ėho miae   20
Gye nsa nom, ópeafo   ampa
Ėnyė bóne
Nana Agyepon, nsa o   ampa
Nana Agyepon, nsa   ampa
Nana Agyepon, nsa   ampa
Obarima na yėbó no din   sio
Woyė biribi na anyė yie a
Wowu a yemmó wo din   sio
Kwabena Fori nsa o   sio 30
Kwabena Fori nsa
Osaman foforó na ógye adeė
Kóma ósaman dada   sio
Ėnnė yi woawu
Na sėbe wode abusua agya hó   sio
Ėnnė nso, abusua abėhyia ha
Kuronti ne Akwamu,
Okwaw Akuamoa   sio
Wiė, ntama a ėfata ban
Bėfata onipa   ampa 40
Opanin Atta, wo nso soa wo nua tuo ė   ampa
Ansana wobėfa tuo
Na yėn so yėbėgye wo so nsa no
Na gye yėde biribi ama Nananom nsamanfoó   ampa
Tena ne Biretufo nsamanfoó
Nana Agyepon, nsa   wie
Woabėgye nsa yi
Yėbėsrė nkwa   wie
Asrė nkwahosan   wie
Na yėasrė nyinkyėre   wie 50
Ne anomaa bedeė amanyó   ampa
Adwumayie, abusuadó   wie
Na Opanin Atta rebėsó saa abusua yi mu yi
Mma ėnnye sė órebu mum fó   wie
Wobu mum fó de a
Na anyė yie   sio
Onyankopón Twediampon

Asaase Yaa
Obaa bayifoȯ
Anaa barima abȯnsam   60
A ȯse merekȯtena Opanin Atta ho
Na mayi no hinohino   ampa
Adedie yi a orebėdie yi
Kampėsė wanhunu di
Na wonim sė onipa busufoȯ ne no   sio
Nso obi nkȯhyirahyira ne busufoȯ
Obusufoȯ deė yėnyi nkȯ akyiri
Yėn a yėahyia mu ha nyinaa
Yėn bosom ne yėn nkwa so   ampa

God, the dependable, drinks   sio
Asaase Yaa, Earth Goddess, drinks   sio
Spirits of Tena and Biretuo clans, drinks alas!
Spirits of the Oyoko clan, drinks alas!
Obunyame Yirententu, the tall, drinks alas!
Asamoamono, the comforter, drinks
Mampong Agyei of Kwahu, drinks   *ampa*
Subiri, the river god, drinks
Subiri Amponkye, drinks
Akasu, drinks   10
Agoso, drinks
Koduedu, the building queen, drinks   *ampa*
Kwasi Kotobrigya, the resilient river god, drinks   *sio*
Bediako, the procreator, drinks
Awonso Abena, come and receive drinks   *sio*
The Afram river of Kwahu, drinks   *ampa*
Mintiminim Akwasi, drinks alas!   *sio*
Fofie Agyeman, grandchild of the chief
The crab trap sitting on the banks of Afram river   *sio*
Receive drinks, Opeafo   20
Buruku of Kwahu,   *sio*
Eye muscles taut with stress   *sio*
Receive drinks, Opeafo   *ampa*
It's no bad news
Nana Agyepon, drinks alas!   *ampa*
Nana Agyepon, drinks   *ampa*
Nana Agyepon, drinks   *ampa*
It's the man of valor on whom one calls   *sio*
If you do not lead a worthy life
Your name is not invoked in death   *sio* 30
Kwabena Fori, drinks alas!   *sio*
Kwabena Fori, drinks

It's the newly departed spirit
That takes messages to those gone before   *sio*
Today, you have died and, my apologies,
Left the lineage behind
Today, the lineage has assembled too   *sio*
Kurontire and Akwamu divisions, yes!
Okwaw Akuamoa,   *sio*
Yes, the cloth that befits the wall   40
Will also befit a human!   *sio*
Atta, the Elder,
It's your turn to hold the gun of your departed brother   *ampa*
Before you pick up the gun
And we demand drink from you
We should serve first the ancestral spirits   *ampa*
Spirits of Tena and Biretuo clans,
Nana Agyepon, drinks   *wie*
As you receive drinks,
We seek life and prosperity,   *wie 50*
We seek long life
And the statecraft of the female bird   *ampa*
Business prosperity, love within the lineage   *wie*
This lineage to be ruled by Opanin Atta
Let him not pronounce guilt on the speechless   *wie*
If the speechless person is pronounced guilty,
It's a vain verdict   *sio*
God, the dependable
Asaase Yaa, the earth goddess
The witch or wizard   60
That seeks to sit beside Opanin Atta
And frustrate him   *ampa*
Wishing he prove inadequate in his reign
Then you know s/he is a devil   *ampa*
Yet no one pronounces blessings on the devil   *sio*
Drive the evil one far beyond
To our health, those here assembled   *ampa*
To the health of our gods and our souls!
Mo ne kasa (Well spoken)!

In this prayer, we notice the ɔkyeame in an autonomous performance, one in which there is no metaphrasis. Here, not only does the orator fully assert his uniqueness as a public speaker; he also acquires the speaking status of principal, having delegated his answering role to another assistant. Aside from recalling the royal mode of speaking, the pattern of performance here is parallel to the dialogic modes of formal speaking, storytelling, sermon, and prayer in parts of Africa, black America, and South America (discussed in chapter 2). The pres-

ence of a responder in this genre is an integral part of the structure of performance.

The responder in this prayer maintains a response consistency almost throughout
the performance. His answering varies from *ampa* (it's true), to *sio* and *wie* (both
meaning 'yes') at the end of pauses. The final congratulatory phrase, *Mo ne kasa*
(Well spoken), was uttered in unison with the congregation, which numbered 50 or
more. It was a sign of collective appreciation for a prayer well executed.

In the invocation segment of the prayer, the speaker names God, Mother Earth,
and an array of deities and ancestors. These are the targets of the communicative
act, the principal benefactors of man. Each invocation is followed by a drink offer
marked by a drop of liquor. The linguistic realizations of the invitation to drink
vary from the full illocutionary forms, *Bẹgye nsa nom* (Come and receive drinks)
and *gye nsa nom* (Receive drinks), where the invitation is directly expressed, to
truncated, indirect illocutions in which reference is only made to the item offered,
nsa (drinks). The latter pattern is the most regular in this prayer. In this case, the
illocutionary predicate (request form) is omitted, partly to reduce the literal force of
the invocation, and partly as a stylistic variant. In other cases, polite addressives
like *òpeafo* (line 20) have been suffixed to the explicit formula to emphasize the
speaker's courtesy to the sublime forces.

Even though the main targets of the prayer are supernatural forces, the speaker
demonstrates the relevance of the potential beneficiaries of the prayer. From lines
40 to 44, he briefly addresses an important personage in the human gathering, a
newly appointed lineage head, about to be added to the pool of elders. But the
address here is not as focused as the dialogue with the spirit world. When the
officiant directs his address at the newly installed functionary, it is ostensibly to
emphasize the latter's secondary significance in the interaction. "Before you pick
up the gun, we should serve first the ancestral spirits," he says (line 44). Thereafter,
however, he realigns the focus of his prayer.

Significantly, the human focus of this brief address is himself not an ordinary
social entity. Since he is on his way to occupy the seat of the ancestors, the officiant
sees him as the converging point of the two audiences of his message: the human
and spirit worlds.

The effectiveness of this prayer lies in its eloquent mode of delivery as well as its
allusive language and evocative content. The officiant lists the significant spirits in
order of significance, beginning with God, whom the Akan believe is the ultimate
supreme force, and Mother Earth on which God has displayed His wonders. Names
of the river gods and ancestors are occasionally accompanied by their notable deeds
or appellations. Fofie, grandsire of the chief, is remembered for his daily trap-
setting for edible prey, Buruku for his endurance, the ability to withstand stress.
Invoking a recently deceased personage, the speaker exploits the opportunity to
make a socio-religious statement explaining the Akan method of message communication to the ancestral world: new spirits send messages to older ancestors (line
33/34). In this way the speaker emphasizes the continued interaction between the
human and ancestral worlds, fostered by prayer and constant journeys. Lest the
audience forget the essence of invocation, the officiant makes a passing meta-

statement, an educative allusion to the criterion for ancestorship. Prayer invocation is aimed at forebears who led worthy lives; social misfits pass into oblivion (line 29/30) (see Opoku 1978:36). Such meta-statements are evidently made to inspire exemplary behavior among the human audience.

The very long invocation segment (lines 1-32) sees over twenty entities invoked, each name modified by a notable trait, comment or message from the officiant. In line 36, the speaker briefly states his mission, namely to mark the transfer of political power to a new lineage head. Then comes the solicitation for long life, prosperity, and intralineage love. For the new lineage head, the ɔkyeame solicits the fair judgment and devoted statesmanship typical of female leadership (line 52). The final 10 lines or so constitute the curse on negative forces and agents of chaos. May the society be rid of these, the ɔkyeame prays.

It is, perhaps, the unusual terseness of the ɔkyeame's discourse achieved through allusion and metaphor, that stands out in the prayer. Such important occasions as the Akwasidae festival provide akyeame the greatest opportunity to display their knowledge and linguistic skills before a very large audience of chiefs, subchiefs, public functionaries, elders, and the general public. The speaker of the above prayer, Ɔkyeame Yaw Kwakye, lives up to this expectation. Besides his precision in recalling the spirits and deities, he embellishes his invocation with high-sounding, evocative appellations that foreground numerous archaisms. Imposing names like *Mintiminim, Kɔtɔbrigya, Yirententu* are appropriate here for the aura of mystery they convey about the relevant entities, but they also raise the discourse to a lofty realm due to their evocative, majestic flavor (see Yankah 1983).

Important here are also the metaphorical and proverbial allusions. Reference to the political transfer of power is appropriately prefaced with a proverb portraying the new head as worthy of the honor. The two images deployed in reference to the new head and his predecessor, however, obliquely cast the newly enthroned in a better light (The cloth that befits the wall/ Will also befit a human), yet does not make explicit comment on the predecessor (line 40). The judicious handling of such a delicate topic is carried over in the next few words, where the ɔkyeame prays for fairness on the part of the new chief. Note his obliqueness in cautioning against the abuse of power—here, the restriction of free speech, "Let him not pronounce guilt on the speechless/ If the speechless person is pronounced guilty, it's a vain verdict" (lines 54-56).

Such delicate advice to new political heads in public forums is often expected of akyeame. What is important is the tact with which sensitive topics are handled. In such public interactions where face and dignity are at stake, experienced orators resort to veiled utterances to mitigate the hazards of the spoken word.

It is often in asserting himself as an independent thinker and speaker that the ɔkyeame displays his unique trait as a man (or woman) of experience. It is his personal knowledge of traditional lore that informs his cross-examination of witnesses in court; it is his unlimited experience that enriches his advice to newly installed chiefs; and if his mastery over the art of libation is unquestionable, this stems from his familiarity with lineage history and chronologies, as well as his deep understanding of traditional religion.

9.3. An ọkyeame relaying a message.
Agona Nsaba, 1988.

Speeches made without reference to a patron's discourse are often the best index of the spokesman's rhetorical competence. In the absence of a rhetorical frame of reference, the orator is liberated from the constraints imposed by another's words, and exercises greater discretion and ingenuity in self-expression. The liberties exercised by the ọkyeame in the above situations, however, bring with them greater responsibilities, for just as he takes the sole credit for any display of professional competence, the ọkyeame is unconditionally liable for any flaws incidental to his autonomous rhetoric. Very common flaws include anomalies in genealogies and the omission of significant entities in a libation prayer. These may attract a warning or penalty (see chapter 6), as might other flaws in the general conduct of the ọkyeame's duties. The rationale is that whether or not his speech is an elaboration on another's, the ọkyeame acts on behalf of a realm that must not be defiled. Hence, though speaking in the absence of his master's word may enhance the ọkyeame's social, political and artistic prestige, it may also be the quickest route to self-ruin, since any misconduct in autonomous oration does not have the benefit of extenuating circumstances.

EPILOGUE
The King's Exit

PROCEEDINGS HAVE COME to an end, and the King gets ready to leave the public event. One of the praise singers jumps into the arena wearing a very stern look. He holds a sword in one hand, and has half covered his lips with the other. The praise singer points the sword at the king, and directs the following verse at him:

There he is!
There he is!
Who is the king, alas!
Who is the king, alas!
I refer to Opoku Ware, alas!
The leopard to whom the bare floor is a taboo!
The leopard upon which leans the weight of the palm tree!
The leopard restless until game is hunted!
The agile leopard that springs for wild game!
Okwaaten Amaniampon, the provocateur, that never recoils
It is you, Opoku Ware!

Among the Denkyira-Akan, the chief's rise to leave would be preceded by a fitting exit praise:

Warrior Chief!
Warrior Chief!
The majestic bird, when ready to fly
It stirs itself
Its colourful plumes vibrate with life

The herald yells, "The king rises! the king rises!" and the entire assembly in anticipation deferentially rises as the king is literally lifted to his feet by his courtiers. The talking drums throb in the background,

Step slowly and gently
Lest you fall
Step slowly and gently
Lest you stumble
The valiant one steps slowly and gently
The valiant one steps slowly and gently.

Majestically, the king departs from the meeting surrounded by a horde of staff-
bearing akyeame, councillors, courtiers, and attendants.

It is such public enactments, preceding and following the rhetoric of mediation in
public forums, that complete the cycle of power enactment. They mark the center
of power, and lend mystery to the aura of kingship. Yet the construction of power
discussed here has inherent paradoxes in the realm of formal communication, since
the latter is overtly structured to lend greater visibility to the royal orator and relative obscurity to the principal himself. On the other hand, the enactment of power
here does not thrive on visibility as such. Power here derives from the converse: the
control of access and visibility, since these have crucial implications for the maintenance of face.

When the Akan say, "It's a taboo for the royal orator to be chief," they do not
only refer to a ritual prohibition cultivated to curb overambition; they also refer to
the unique aesthetics of royal power enactment, which is incompatible with the
orator's high-visibility profile.

The mode of royal oratory depicted here, where the principal's speech is animated by a series of orators, would also appear to be imbued with a considerable
degree of redundancy (arising from the repetitions) which would reduce the aesthetic value of formal speeches. Paradoxically, though, it is this very recursive
frame which enhances the beauty of formal talk. Each version of a message relayed
may convey a linguistic, poetic or thematic nuance missing from the others, such
that the subtle inflections within a single viewpoint eventually get spelled out
through a collective effort. Besides this, there is a built-in aesthetic within any
mode of communication that consciously avoids directness and promotes suspense.
As the same message moves from one phase to another, action or reaction is
momentarily frozen in a stylized state of suspension.

It would be puzzling if this mode of formal communication remained exclusively
within the royal sphere. Granted that royalty is the ultimate incarnation of political
power, and could adopt various strategies to reflect royal ego, the fact remains that
it is not the only embodiment of power. Subordinate levels of power exist, and can
also be constructed and maintained using the same symbolic methods as the highest
levels of the prevailing socio-political hierarchy, even though not with the same
level of ceremonial intensity.

Outside the socio-political structure, the mode of royal oratory discussed here
has had a trickle-down effect; it permeates all formal encounters involving face-to-
face communication. As was mentioned above, indirection is a pervasive aesthetic
in this part of the world. And while it is true that formal speech outside the hierarchy cannot hope to replicate the degree to which it has been embellished in the
royal realm with a panoply of insignia and appurtenances that transforms the composite end product into a unique whole, yet fragments of this totality may be
enacted at other levels. For outside the royal realm, mediated oratory permeates all
modes of formal talk in Ghana and in several other parts of Africa as well. In these
cases, an ad hoc intermediary may be appointed on the spur of the moment to
represent a party or dignitary, or these may bring designated orators well known in
the community to relay their speech in style.

While such orators may attract the label akyeame, that designation can only be said to be temporary, since these functionaries do not wield the executive power often symbolized by the staff. Indeed, the royal orators themselves normally do not perform in such forums.

The permeation of formal speech in general with mediated/surrogate oratory, means that the analyses in this book, for the most part restricted to the royal domain, have not benefited from the wealth of oratory and ornate diction spontaneously deployed by skillful speakers in other formal domains.

One such domain is that of formal bride-price negotiation, where orators representing various parties transform the ritual into a competitive dialogue, and positions are negotiated with a combination of wit, drama and grandiloquence.

The opportunities this provides for the study of power construction, negotiation, and maintenance in everyday life are unlimited; for in real life, power is not static. It is equipment for living.

GLOSSARY OF AKAN WORDS

aberewa   old woman
aberewa nana   grandchild of old woman; eloquent child, wise person
abusua   lineage group(s), clan(s)
abusuafie   lineage house, where lineage assembles
abusuapanin   lineage head
adehye kasa   royal speech
adenkum   women's song group
adinkra   type of funeral cloth
adwabo ase, badwam   public place, assembly
ahenfie   chief's palace
akonnwa tuntum, pundwa   blackened stool, ancestral stool
akutia   insinuation
akyeamehene   head of orators, orator-in-chief
akyeamepoma   spokesman's staff
amánneè   custom, ritual
amànneè   telling of mission
ammódin   unspeakable word
amoase   women's cloth worn between the thighs
ananse   spider, folk hero
anibóne   evil eye
anóna   name of lineage group
apae   praise appellation
asénni   judicial hearing
asésédwa   kind of stool
awaregyae   divorce
awaregye   official marriage request
badwam   public
boseabó   loan request
Daasebrè   The Magnanimous (chief's title), one deserving endless thanks
dampan   empty parlor
dawurobófo   public announcer, gong beater
dwamu kasa   oratory, public speaking
dwanetoa   plea for intervention
èbè   proverb
kaka   whitlow disease
kasakoa   figurative language, metaphor
kente   silk/cotton cloth woven on loom
kye dadua   arrest, take prisoner
mmaafi   lineage house for women
mmo ne kasa   well spoken
mmobome   women's song sung for warriors
mpae   libation prayer
mpanin kasa   speech of elders
ngyesoó   response formula, phrase
nkómmó, nkòmmóbó   conversation
nkonnwafieso   sacred stool room

nnwonkoró   women's song group
nsedie   type of oath
nsekuo   gossip
nsóso   completive phrase, formula
nsuae   oath swearing
ntahera   horns
ntam   unmentionable historical incident
òbosom   deity; abosom, pl.
òbosom kyeame   spokesman, interpreter of priest
òbrafo   praise singer, executioner; abrafo, pl.
obuo kasa   polite speech
òdekuro   chief of town, village
òhemmaa   queenmother
òhene   chief, king
òkamafo   advocate, one who speaks on another's behalf
òkòmfo   priest, priestess
òkra   soul
òkyeame,   spokesperson, orator; akyeame, pl.
òkyerèma   talking drummer
òman   state
òman kyeame   state orator, spokesman
òmanpam   monitor lizard
Onyame   God the Almighty
Otumfoò   Custodian of Power, All-Powerful: title of King of Ashanti
panin   elder
prae   broom
sèbe   apologies
suman   charm
tete kasa   speech of ancient times
waduro   mortar
wòmma   pestle

BIBLIOGRAPHY

Abrahams, Roger. 1986. "Ordinary and Extraordinary Experience." In *The Anthropology of Experience*. Ed. Victor Turner and Edward Bruner. Chicago: University of Illinois Press. pp. 44–72.

Addi, Lydia. 1988. "The Language of Linguists' Staffs." Unpublished manuscript.

Adjayi, Joseph. 1984. *Diplomacy and Diplomats in Nineteenth-Century Asante*. New York: University Press of America.

Agovi, J. K. 1973. "Preliminary Observations on the Modern Short Story and the African Folktale Tradition." *Research Review* (Legon, Institute of African Studies, University of Ghana) 9, pp. 123–29.

Alagoa, E. J. 1977. "The Niger Delta States and Their Neighbors." In *The History of West Africa 1*. Ed. J. F. Adjayi and Michael Crowder. New York: Columbia University Press, pp. 331–72.

Albert, Ethel. 1964. "Rhetoric, Logic, and Poetics in Burundi: Cultural Patterning of Speech Behavior." *American Anthropology* 66.6. Reprinted in *Directions in Sociolinguistics*. Ed. John Gumperz and Dell Hymes. New York: Holt, Rinehart and Winston, 1972, pp. 35–71.

Amankwaa, Adu. 1988. "Proverb Variants in Akan." B.A. Long Essay. University of Ghana.

Amory, Deborah P. 1985. "The Kanga Cloth and Swahili Society." M.A. Thesis. Yale University.

Anyidoho, Kofi. 1983. "Oral Poetics and Traditions of Verbal Art in Africa." Diss. University of Texas, Austin.

Anyidoho, Kofi., ed. 1983. *Cross Rhythms* (Papers in African Folklore). Bloomington, Indiana: Trickster Press.

Appiah, Michael A. 1979. "Okyeame: An Integrative Model of Communication Behavior." Diss. University of New York at Buffalo.

Argyle, W. J. 1966. *The Fon of Dahomey*. Oxford: Clarendon Press.

Arhin, Kwame. 1983. "Political and Military Roles of Akan Women." In *Female and Male in West Africa*. Ed. Christine Oppong. Boston: Allen & Unwin. pp. 98–106.

Assimeng, J. M. 1976. *Traditional Life, Culture and Literature in Ghana*. New York: Conch Magazine.

Austin, J. L. 1962. *How to Do Things with Words*. Cambridge: Harvard University Press.

Babalola, S. A. 1966. *The Content and Form of Yoruba Ijala*. Oxford: Clarendon Press.

Bakhtin, M. M. 1981. *The Dialogic Imagination*. Ed. Michael Holquist. Austin: University of Texas Press.

———. 1986. "The Problem of Speech Genres." In his *Speech Genres and Other Essays*. Trans. Vern McGee. Austin: University of Texas Press.

Bateson, Gregory. 1955. "A Theory of Play and Fantasy." In *Steps to an Ecology of Mind*. New York: Ballantine.

Bauman, Richard. 1977. *Verbal Art as Performance*. Rowley: Newbury House.

———. 1983. "The Field Study of Folklore in Context." In *Handbook of American Folklore*. Ed. Richard Dorson. Bloomington: Indiana University Press. pp. 362–68.

———. 1983. *Let Your Words Be Few: Symbolism of Speaking and Silence among Seventeenth-Century Quakers*. Cambridge: Cambridge University Press.

Bauman, Richard, and Joel Sherzer, eds. 1974. *Explorations in the Ethnography of Speaking*. Cambridge: Cambridge University Press.

Ben-Amos, Dan. 1972. "The Elusive Audience of Benin Narrators." *Journal of Folklore Institute* 2, pp. 177–84.

Bisilliat, Jeanne. 1983. "The Feminine Sphere in the Institutions of the Songhay and Zarma." In *Female and Male in West Africa*. Ed. Christine Oppong. pp. 98–106.

Bloch, Maurice, ed. 1975. *Political Language and Oratory in Traditional Societies*. New York: Academic Press.

Bravmann, Rene. 1972. "The Diffusion of Ashanti Political Art." In *African Art and Leadership*. Ed. Douglas Fraser and Herbert Cole. pp. 153–71.

Brenneis, Donald L., and Fred Myers, eds. 1984. *Dangerous Words: Language and Politics in the Pacific*. New York: New York University Press.

Brown, Penelope, and Stephen Levinson. 1978. "Universals of Language Usage: Politeness Phenomena." In *Questions and Politeness*. Ed. Esther Goody. Cambridge: Cambridge University Press.

Brown, R., and A. Gilman. "The Pronouns of Power and Solidarity." In *Language and Social Context*. Ed. P. Giglioli. pp. 252–82.

Burton, Richard. 1966. *Mission to Gelele*. New York: Praeger.

Busia, K. A. 1951. *The Position of the Chief in Modern Political Systems of Ashanti*. London: Oxford University Press.

Cole, Herbert. 1972. "Ibo Art and Leadership." In *African Art and Leadership*. Ed. Douglas Fraser and Herbert Cole. Madison: University of Wisconsin Press.

Cole, Herbert, and Duran Ross. 1977. *The Arts of Ghana*. Los Angeles: Museum of Cultural History, University of California.

Cole, Peter, and Jerry Morgan, eds. 1971. *Syntax and Semantics 3*. New York: Academic Press.

Combellach, Frederick M. 1947. "Speakers and Scepters in Homer." *Classical Journal* 43/44, pp. 209–17.

Dorson, Richard, ed. 1983. *Handbook of American Folklore*. Bloomington: Indiana University Press.

Duranti, Alessandro. 1983. "Samoan Speech Making across Social Events: One Genre in and out of a Fono." *Language in Society* 12, pp. 1–22.

———. 1988. "Intentions, Language and Social Action in a Samoan Context." *Journal of Pragmatics* 12. pp. 13–33.

Ellis, A. B. 1969. *A History of the Gold Coast of West Africa*. New York: Negro University Press. Originally printed in 1893.

Evans-Pritchard, E. 1956. "Sanza: A Characteristic Feature of Zande Language and Thought." *Bulletin of the School of Oriental and African Studies* 18.

Farb, Peter. 1977. *Word Play*. Stoughton: Coronet.

Fernandez, J. W. 1986. *Persuasions and Performances: The Play of Tropes in Culture*. Bloomington: Indiana University Press.

Ferry, Marie Paul. 1976. "Pourquoi Conter." *Psychopathologie Africaine* 12, pp. 219–44.

Finnegan, Ruth. 1967. *Limba Stories and Storytelling*. Oxford: Clarendon Press.

———. 1970. *Oral Literature in Africa*. Oxford: Oxford University Press.

Firth, Raymond. 1975. "Speechmaking in Tikopia." In *Traditional Language and Oratory in Traditional Societies*. New York: Academic Press. pp. 29–40.

Fox, James. 1974. "Our Ancestors Spoke in Pairs: Rotinese Views of Language, Dialect and Code." In *Explorations in the Ethnography of Speaking*. Ed. Richard Bauman and Joel Sherzer. pp. 65–85.

Freeman, R. A. 1958. "Journey to Ashantee, 1888." In *Pageant of Ghana*. Ed. Freda Wolfson. London: Oxford University Press.

Fynn, J. K. 1971. *Asante and Its Neighbors 1700-1807*. Evanston: Northwestern University Press.

Galli, Silvano. 1983. "Storytelling among the Anyi Bona." In *Cross Rhythms*. Ed. Kofi Anyidoho et al. pp. 13–42.

Geertz, Clifford. 1983. "Centers, Kings and Charisma: Reflections on the Symbolics of Power." In his *Local Knowledge: Further Essays in Interpretive Anthropology*. pp. 121–46.

————. 1983. *Local Knowledge: Further Essays in Interpretive Anthropology*. New York: Basic Books.

Giglioli, Pier Paolo, ed. 1972. *Language and Social Context*. Harmondsworth: Penguin.

Gladwin, Thomas, and William Sturtevant, eds. 1962. *Anthropology and Human Behavior*. Washington: Anthropological Society of Washington.

Goffman, Ervin. 1963. *Behavior in Public Places*. New York: Free Press.

————. 1967. *Interaction Ritual*. New York: Pantheon.

————. 1969. *Strategic Interaction*. Philadelphia: University of Pennsylvania Press.

————. 1974. *Frame Analysis: An Essay in the Organization of Experience*. New York: Harper Colophon.

Goodwin, Charles. 1981. *Conversational Organization: Interactions between Speakers and Hearers*. New York: Academic Press.

Goody, Esther, ed. 1978. *Questions and Politeness*. Cambridge: Cambridge University Press.

Grice, H. P. 1971. "Logic and Conversation." In *Syntax and Semantics 3*. Ed. Peter Cole and Jerry Morgan. pp. 41–58.

Gumperz, John, and Dell Hymes, eds. 1972. *Directions in Sociolinguistics*. Oxford: Blackwell.

Hanks, William. 1991. "Interactive Structure of Indexical Reference." Unpublished manuscript.

————. 1991. "Metalanguage and Pragmatics of Deixis." Unpublished manuscript.

Hayakawa, S. I. 1978. *Language in Thought and Action*. New York: Harcourt Brace & World.

Hayford, Caseley. 1903. *Gold Coast Native Institutions*. London: Frank Cass.

Herskovits, Melville J., and Frances Herskovits. 1936. *Surinam Folklore*. New York: Columbia University Press.

Himmelheber, Hans. 1972. "Gold-Plated Objects of Baulé Notables." In *African Art and Leadership*. Ed. Douglas Fraser and Herbert Cole. Madison: University of Wisconsin Press. pp. 185–208.

Hobart, Mark. 1975. "Orators and Patrons: Two Types of Political Leader in Balinese Village Society." In *Political Language and Oratory in Traditional Society*. Ed. Maurice Bloch. pp. 65–92.

Hymes, Dell. 1962. "The Ethnography of Speaking." In *Anthropology and Human Behavior*. Ed. Thomas Gladwin and William Sturtevant. pp. 15–53.

————. 1972. "Models of the Interaction of Language and Social Life." In *Directions in Sociolinguistics*. Ed. John Gumperz and Dell Hymes. pp. 35–71.

Jakobson, Roman. 1960. "Linguistics and Poetics." In *Style in Language*. Ed. Thomas Sebeok. pp. 350–77.

Johnson, John. 1986. *The Epic of Son-Jara*. Bloomington: Indiana University Press.

Johnson, M. *Salaga Papers I*. Institute of African Studies, University of Ghana, n.d.

Jones-Jackson, Patricia. 1987. *When Roots Die: Endangered Traditions on the Sea Islands*. Athens: University of Georgia Press.

Keenan, Elinor. 1973. "A Sliding Sense of Obligatoriness: The Polystructure of Malagasy Oratory." *Language in Society* 2. pp. 222–40.

————. 1974. "Norm Makers and Breakers: Uses of Speech by Men and Women in Malagasy Community." In *Explorations in the Ethnography of Speaking*. Ed. Bauman and Sherzer. pp. 125–43.

Leech, Geoffrey. 1983. *The Principles of Pragmatics*. New York: Longman.

Levinson, Stephen. 1983. *Pragmatics*. Cambridge: Cambridge University Press.

Malinowski, Bronislaw. 1926. *Myth in Primitive Psychology*. New York: Norton.

————. 1935. *Coral Gardens and Their Magic: A Study of the Methods of Tilling the Soil and of Agricultural Rites in the Trobriand Islands*. New York: American Book Company.

Marcus, George. 1984. "Three Perspectives on Role Distance in Conversation between

Tongan Nobles and Their People." In *Dangerous Words: Language and Politics in the Pacific*. Ed. Don Brenneis and Fred Myers.

Mensah, Owusu. 1977. "Prince Owusu Ansah and Asante-British Diplomacy 1841-1884." Diss. University of Wisconsin.

Mensah-Brown, A. K. 1976. "The Nature of Akan Native Law: A Critical Analysis." In *Traditional Life, Culture and Literature in Ghana*. Ed. J. M. Assimeng. New York: Conch Magazine. pp. 137–64.

Mitchell-Kernan, Claudia. 1972. "Signifying and Marking: Two Afro-American Speech Acts." In *Directions in Sociolinguistics*. Ed. John Gumperz and Dell Hymes. pp. 161–79.

Moerman, Michael. 1988. *Talking Culture: Ethnography and Conversational Analysis*. Philadelphia: University of Pennsylvania Press.

Nketia, J. H. K. 1971. "The Linguistic Aspect of Style in African Languages." *Current Trends in Linguistics* 7. pp. 733–57.

Okonjo, Kamene. 1983. "Sex Roles in Nigerian Politics." In *Female and Male in West Africa*. Ed. Christine Oppong. pp. 210–22.

Ong. Walter. 1982. *Orality and Literacy*. New York: Methuen.

———. 1987. "Literacy and Orality in Our Times." In *Oral and Traditional Literatures*. Ed. Norman Simms. pp. 8–21.

Opoku, K. A. 1975. *Speak to the Winds*. New York: Lothrop, Lee and Shephard.

———. 1978. *West African Traditional Religion*. Jurong: F. E. P. International.

Oppong, Christine. 1983. *Female and Male in West Africa*. Boston: Allen & Unwin.

Ottenberg, Simon. 1983. "Artistic Roles in a Limba Chiefdom." In *Female and Male in West Africa*. Ed. Christine Oppong. pp. 76–90.

Owomoyela, Oyekan. 1985. "Proverbs: Exploration of an African Philosophy of Social Communication." *Ba Shiru* 12, pp. 3–16.

Paine, Robert, ed. 1981. *Politically Speaking: Cross-Cultural Studies of Rhetoric*. Philadelphia: Institute for the Study of Human Issues.

———. 1981. "Introduction." In *Politically Speaking: Cross-Cultural Studies of Rhetoric*. Ed. Robert Paine. pp. 1–5.

Park, R. E., and W. Burgess, eds. 1969. *Introduction to the Science of Sociology*. Chicago: University of Chicago Press.

Penfield, Joyce, ed. 1987. *Women and Language in Transition*. New York: State University of New York Press.

Proschan, Frank. 1983. "The Semiotic Study of Puppets, Masks and Performing Objects." *Semiotica* 47, pp. 3–44.

Rattray, R. S. 1923. *Ashanti*. Oxford: Clarendon Press.

———. 1927. *Religion and Art in Ashanti*. Oxford: Clarendon Press.

———. 1932. *Tribes of the Ashanti Hinterland*. Oxford: Clarendon Press.

Reade, W. 1874. *The Story of the Ashantee Campaign*. London.

Rosaldo, Michelle. 1973. "I Have Nothing to Hide: The Language of Illongot Oratory." *Language in Society* 2, pp. 193–223.

Ross, Duran. 1982. "The Verbal Art of the Akan Linguist Staffs." *African Arts* 16:1, pp. 56–67.

Saah, Kofi, 1986. "Language Use and Attitudes in Ghana." *Anthropological Linguistics* 28. pp. 367–77.

Salmond, Anne. 1975. "Mana Makes the Man: A Look at Maori Oratory and Politics." In *Political Language and Oratory in Traditional Societies*. Ed. Maurice Bloch, pp. 45–64.

de Saussure, Ferdinand. 1977. *Course in General Linguistics*. New York: McGraw-Hill.

Schollon, Ron, and Suzanne Schollon. 1981. *Narrative, Literacy and Face in Interethnic Communication*. Norwood, NJ: Ablex.

Sebeok, Thomas, ed. 1960. *Style in Language*. Cambridge, MA: MIT Press.

Sherzer, Joel. 1974. "Namakke, Sumakke, Koirmakke: Three Types of Speech Event." In

Explorations in the Ethnography of Speaking. Ed. Richard Bauman and Joel Sherzer. pp. 263–82.

Simmel, George. 1969. "Sociology of the Senses: Visual Interaction." In *Introduction to the Science of Sociology.* Ed. R. E. Park and W. Burgess. pp. 356–61.

Simms, Norman, ed. 1987. *Oral and Traditional Literatures.* Hamilton, New Zealand: Outrigger Press.

Smith, Robert. 1976. *Warfare and Diplomacy in Pre-Colonial West Africa.* London: Methuen.

Spencer, Ann. 1982. *In Praise of Heroes: Contemporary African Commemorative Cloth.* Newark: Newark Museum.

Staniland, Martin. 1975. *The Lions of Dagbon: Political Change in Northern Ghana.* Cambridge: Cambridge University Press.

Tait, David, and P. D. Strevens. 1955. "History and Social Organisation." In *Transactions of the Gold Coast and Togoland Historical Society* 1:5.

Talbot, P. A. 1926. *The Peoples of Southern Nigeria.* London: Frank Cass.

Tarr, Delbert Howard, Jr. 1979. "Indirection and Ambiguity as a Mode of Communication in West Africa: A Descriptive Survey." Diss. University of Minnesota.

Thompson, Robert. 1972. "The Sign of the Divine King: Yoruba Bead-Embroidered Crowns with Veil and Bird Decoration." In *African Art and Leadership.* Ed. Fraser and Cole. pp. 227–60.

Urban, Gregg. 1986. "Ceremonial Dialogues in South America." *American Anthropology* 8.2, pp. 370–86.

Vansina, Jan. 1972. "Ndop: Royal Statues among the Kuba." In *African Art and Leadership.* Ed. Fraser and Cole. pp. 79–97.

Verdon, Michael. 1983. *The Abutia Ewe of West Africa.* New York: Mouton.

Ward, W. E. F. 1958. *A History of Ghana.* New York: Praeger.

Weiner, Annette. 1984. "From Words to Objects to Magic: Hard Words and the Boundaries of Social Interaction." In *Dangerous Words: Language and Politics in the Pacific.* Ed. Brenneis and Myers. pp. 162–91.

Whiteley, W. H. 1964. *A Selection of African Prose I.* Oxford: Clarendon Press.

Wilks, Ivor. 1975. *Asante in the Nineteenth Century.* Cambridge: Cambridge University Press.

Wolfson, Freda, ed. 1958. *Pageant of Ghana.* London: Oxford University Press.

Yankah, Kwesi. 1983. "To Praise or Not to Praise the King: The Akan *Apae* in the Context of Referential Poetry." *Research in African Literatures* 14:3, pp. 382–400.

———. 1985a. "The Making and Breaking of Kwame Nkrumah: The Role of Oral Poetry." *Journal of African Studies* 12:2, pp. 86–92.

———. 1985b. "Risks in Verbal Art Performance." *Journal of Folklore Research* 22:2/3, pp. 133–53.

———. 1989a. *The Proverb in the Context of Akan Rhetoric: A Theory of Proverb Praxis.* New York: Peter Lang.

———. 1989b. "Proverbs: The Aesthetics of Traditional Communication." *Research in African Literatures* 20:3, pp. 325–346.

INDEX

KWESI YANKAH is Associate Professor in the Linguistics Department at the University of Ghana, Legon, and is author of *The Proverb in the Context of Akan Rhetoric*.